Transforming Your Business with AWS®

Transforming Your Business with AWS®

Getting the Most Out of Using AWS to Modernize and Innovate Your Digital Services

Philippe Abdoulaye

WILEY

I dedicate this book to two exceptional women: my mother, Mrs. Julienne Roger, and my aunt, Mrs. Simone Massard. I will always remember you for your care, humanity, and incredible support. My eternal gratitude.

A special dedication to my wife, Michelle Agarande, and my son, Samuel Abdoulaye-Agarande, for their patience and incredible support.

And a special thanks to my father, Mr. Georges Mocktar Abdoulaye, for his inspiring and exemplary career.

About the Author

Philippe Abdoulaye is a technology executive specializing in digital transformation and cloud migration with a focus on Amazon Web Services (AWS). He is ranked in the Top 20 global cloud thought leaders and influencers, and he is an official Amazon-rewarded AWS Hero. In his current role, Philippe advises IT executives about digital transformation and AWS cloud migration strategies, enterprise cloud architecture design and implementation, as well as the implementation of DevOps as the foundation of digital products and services development platforms. He's written seven books on cloud computing, DevOps, and digital transformation.

With the expansion of the digital economy, it's increasingly obvious that IT executives need coaching in critical areas such as business models digitization and digital products and services development platform implementations consistent with DevOps principles. Philippe is the author of numerous industry publications and delivers workshops worldwide on digital transformation and cloud migration.

Philippe's experience has been extremely diverse, but he has long focused on business and IT transformation using cloud solutions to equip businesses with the agility, operational efficiency, and rapid time-to-market that they need to meet the challenges of the growing digital economy. Philippe has a masters in computer science from ESI SUPINFO Paris, France. He can be found online at www.itaasnow.com and www.jsfood.org.

About the Technical Editor

Joe McKendrick is an author, independent researcher, and speaker exploring innovation, information technology trends, and markets. He is a contributor to Forbes, as well as CNET's ZDNet "Service Oriented" site. Joe is co-author, along with 16 industry leaders and thinkers, of the SOA Manifesto, which outlines the values and guiding principles of service orientation. He speaks frequently on cloud, data, and enterprise computing topics at industry events and webcasts. Much of his research work is done in conjunction with Forbes Insights and Information Today, Inc., covering topics such as cloud computing, digital transformation, enterprise mobility, and big data analytics.

In a previous life, Joe served as communications and research manager of the Administrative Management Society (AMS), an international professional association dedicated to advancing knowledge within the IT and business management fields. Joe is a graduate of Temple University.

Acknowledgments

I would personally like to thank Ross Barich, principal developer community manager at Amazon Web Services, for the extraordinary work that he's done promoting the AWS Heroes Program. I would also like to thank Claude Barrail and Michel Gaillard of Orange, the French multinational telecommunication corporation, for the invaluable business transformation project management, enterprise architecture, and customer relationship management (CRM) lessons learned.

Although this list could be infinite, I would like to thank my brother, Georges Abdoulaye—a passionate software engineer—for the long hours spent debating the value of object-oriented approaches and the invaluable benefits of AWS.

I would also like to thank Harvard University's Michael E. Porter, Robert S. Kaplan, and David P. Norton, as well as the Massachusetts Institute of Technology's (MIT) late Michael Hammer, for their work around business transformation including the competitive five forces model, the value chain, the strategy map, and the business revolution theories. This book, like many others, is a demonstration that, years ago, you laid the foundation for engineering business frameworks, which today we might call the business transformation discipline. Likewise, this list is not exhaustive, but for the sake of brevity, I would like to offer an extended thank you to the many great people I have worked with and have had the honor to lead in this organization. I can't thank all of you enough.

I would like to additionally extend my thanks to the amazing team at Wiley. First and foremost, Kenyon Brown, for having trusted this book project and sharing in my excitement. Thanks for allowing me to do this. I would like to extend a debt of gratitude to my project editor, Gary Schwartz, who helped me create this book every step of the way. Your help, insight, and assistance are very much appreciated, and I can't thank you enough for your efforts on making this a great book. And I would like to thank Joe McKendrick, my technical editor, for pointing out things that made this book even better. I felt like we have been working together for so many years. Thank you!

Lastly, I would like to thank my family for their support while writing this book. I'd like to believe that I am present in their lives at all times, but when it comes to work and then doing a book project in the evenings and weekends, sometimes that takes some extra time away from "fun," so thank you.

— Philippe Abdoulaye

Contents at a Glance

Contents

Introduction

The origins of this book can be traced back to March 2019, after four conference presentations I gave in France at the Econocom DevOps Summit. All participants—from 15 prestigious international companies representing the energy, aviation, aerospace, defense, and banking industries—agreed that the ongoing wave of IT infrastructure migrations to cloud computing was only the preparatory phase for a more strategic milestone: equipping businesses with the digital products and services development platform that they need to compete.

As one who was consulting and writing on both cloud computing and digital transformation, my objective over the most recent three-year period has been to raise awareness about the key role that digital products and services will play in business competitiveness and on the importance of properly transforming a business into a high-quality digital products and services development organization.

This book explains how businesses can take advantage of the rich set of Amazon Web Services (AWS) services and features to transform themselves into world-class digital products and services development organizations. It's written for CEOs, CIOs, CTOs, and enterprise architects seeking an actionable vision, best practices, and solutions to digital transformation. Above all, this book seeks to guide the implementation of world-class digital products and services development platforms.

While there are numerous digital transformation books on the market, I've found that none of them addresses this topic comprehensively. In this book, you will learn about the fundamentals of world-class digital products and services development organizations, how they build on AWS to deliver high-quality digital products and services, and how to take advantage of AWS cloud services to implement such organizations.

Throughout the 16 chapters of the book, you will learn about the strategic perspectives and approaches for taking advantage of critical AWS capabilities such as the following:

- DevOps acting as the framework for the digital products and services development organization's value chain.

- Integration of various AWS Application Deployment Services into a technology platform supporting the organization's digital products and services development strategy.

- Containers, container management solutions, and microservices as the foundation of the architecture of the organization's digital products and services development platform.

- Enterprise architecture design patterns for the cloud used as the means to abstract technical complexity and provide AWS executive insights.

- Agile organizational principles, processes, and tools as the foundation of digital products and services development effort.

This book will contribute to standardizing sound digital transformation practices that not only stress infrastructure implementation but also profitable digital products and services development. *Transforming Your Business with AWS: Getting the Most Out of Using AWS Cloud to Modernize and Innovate Your Digital Products and Services* examines AWS, its services, and its features from the executive standpoint to provide the big picture needed to develop informed digital strategy and implement world-class digital products and services development platforms.

Early in this book project, I spent time identifying and understanding the issues that make digitalization efforts so challenging. The findings included a lot of improvisation resulting from the lack of proven engineering practices in areas like artificial intelligence (AI), big data analytics, Internet of Things (IoT); confusion between software development for business applications and software development for digital products and services; mismatch between AWS operational benefits and the organization of the product development effort; design approach ignoring the importance of usability; and many more. I concluded that a *Universal AWS Cloud Architecture* was needed to take digital transformation practices using AWS to the next level.

The book consists of 16 chapters grouped into three parts:

Part I: Understanding the Digital Transformation Challenges includes Chapters 1–4. It discusses the disruptive impacts of the growing digital economy on industries, and by extension on business competitiveness, and it explains why world-class digital products and services development platforms based on AWS are the essential competitive advantage.

Part II: Digitizing the Business Model Using AWS covers Chapters 5–9. It shows how via a variety of infrastructure as a service (IaaS) solutions, AWS helps to meet the digital transformation challenges discussed in Part I. Through a case study of a fictitious company, J&S Food, which is the backbone of this book, it illustrates comprehensively, step-by-step, the business model digitalization process.

Part III: Developing World-Class Digital Products and Services Using AWS spans Chapters 10–16. It addresses the other key aspects of the digital transformation project: the development of the business's digital products and services using AWS. Through the case of a smart shopping bag digital product, it illustrates how the Unified Modelling Language (UML) methodology is leveraged to specify and design not only digital products and services but also microservices architecture. It comprehensively explains the digital products and services implementation process consistent with DevOps principles using AWS services as varied as Amplify, Containers, Lambda, and Modern Application Development.

By providing AWS insights for executives, the material contained in this book will greatly help CIOs, CTOs, and enterprise architects not only perform rapid, easy, and successful digital transformations but also how AWS features and services are pivotal to any business transformation initiative.

Reader Support for This Book

If you believe you've found a mistake in this book, please bring it to our attention. At John Wiley & Sons, we understand how important it is to provide our customers with accurate content, but even with our best efforts an error may occur.

To submit your possible errata, please email it to our Customer Service Team at wileysupport@wiley.com with the subject line "Possible Book Errata Submission" and book title.

I

Understanding the Digital Transformation Challenges

Companies that successfully complete their digital transformation have all adopted a holistic approach that considers cloud computing, agile operational models, and digital products and services as the epicenter of their business model. These companies are correct because ongoing digital disruptions are changing industry structures and by extension the way that companies do business.

Part I, consisting of Chapters 1–4, highlights the changes introduced by the growing digital economy and its impact on businesses, but above all, it shows why it is urgent for companies to transform as a whole the four pillars of their business model: technology, people, processes, and organizational structure.

Chapter 1, "The Digital Economy's Challenges, Opportunities, and Relevance of AWS," addresses the digital economy's challenges and opportunities with which businesses have increasingly had to deal with, and it introduces the concept of AWS universal architecture to highlight the operational and technological features that make AWS the essential competitive advantage.

Chapter 2, "What Is a Digital Product?" and Chapter 3, "Digital Product and Service Development Challenges," discuss the second key part of the digital transformation initiative: digital products and services and the development approach. These chapters elaborate on the digital products and services building blocks, the overall ecosystem, and the underlying AWS technology stack.

In Chapter 3, a framework for evaluating digital products and services development platforms is presented, which aids in improving quality, efficiency, and time to market.

Chapter 4, "Industrializing Digital Product and Service Development," discusses how companies can leverage DevOps, AWS architectural design patterns, and agile and object-oriented methodologies to industrialize their digital products and services development process.

The Digital Economy's Challenges, Opportunities, and Relevance of AWS

Digital transformation isn't a technology makeover. It's a business revolution.

—Kaan Turnali

It's a fact that the expansion of the digital economy is accelerating, it's affecting industries and businesses worldwide and confirming its disruptive nature.

Businesses will have to adapt to the changes and requirements of their competitive environment.

Although the habit in IT is to overlook business considerations in favor of rapid technology implementation, the fact is, if you don't understand how the digital economy impacts your company, chances are that you will miss out on the benefits of going digital and fail.

This disruptive digital economy affects your industry and by extension your company's business and operational models; without a 360-degree view into how far your work organization, processes, and underpinning IT have been made irrelevant, the only thing you'll get is a technology platform disconnected from your businesses' priorities.

Make no mistake, without a big picture mindset that highlights not only the challenges but also the business opportunities that you can take advantage of using cloud-based solutions such as Amazon Web Services (AWS), there is no way that your company can survive the economic crisis.

This chapter discusses the expanding digital economy's challenges and opportunities, as well as its impact on the business and IT; it highlights the benefits that businesses can derive from cloud-based solutions, including AWS, to build successful digital products and services development organizations.

Understanding the Digital Economy's Impacts

We're in the midst of a pandemic that's confirming four trends that industry experts have been observing in connection with the digital economy. Businesses will deal directly with their industry's disruption, and tackling issues head-on including work from home, ecommerce, data science, and innovation are among the competitive advantages they will need to survive and thrive. These trends are the new business normals. Let's discuss them now.

Surviving Disruptions Are Your Business's Primary Challenge

The first new normal is the notion that the conditions for frequent industry disruptions are here to stay. The reason is that the world is in the midst of a wave of innovation that's expected to last for decades. This will lead to repeated disruptions forcing businesses to adapt. That's what is meant by digital disruption and that the COVID-19 crisis should be understood as an industry disrupter.

As you can see in Figure 1.1, there's a correlation between the pandemic and ongoing job destruction. In 2020, in the United States and France, unemployment hit a yearly total of 8.9 percent, in Italy 11 percent, and in Brazil 13.4 percent. As you probably have realized, surviving industry disruptions will be part of your business challenges over the next three to five years.

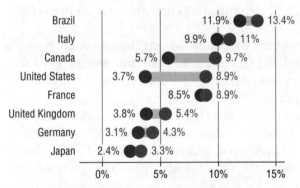

Figure 1.1: COVID-19 impact on unemployment
Source: International Monetary Fund (IMF)

Understanding the Digital Economy's Opportunities

The second new normal is the emergence of work from home, ebusiness, data science, and innovation as the digital economy's opportunity enablers. A quick look at the handful of companies doing well in this crisis shows that in addition to competitive pricing, superior customer experience, and short time to market, they rely on these four pillars.

As to *work from home* and the related collaborative technologies, you must keep in mind that these are the competitive assets that your business needs to retain staff and preserve production capacity.

With regard to *ebusiness*, consider that having such an infrastructure is another asset; it allows the business not only to adapt to the emerging digital economy but also to compensate the activities destroyed by the economic crisis.

Data science capabilities relate to utilizing and analyzing data to inform or enhance the company's processes, decision-making, and even revenue model.

Innovation is the ability of your organization to take advantage of technology, including AWS, to develop highly profitable digital services that guarantee superior customer experience, differentiate your company, and help it reap profits.

Work from home, ebusiness, data science, and innovation will be discussed throughout this book. For now, what you need to remember is that they're the foundation of the digital transformation strategies that will help your organization succeed in the highly competitive environments that are taking place around the globe.

The next section elaborates on the theme that technology, particularly AWS, provides the levers that businesses need to survive and succeed in this disruptive digital economy.

Surviving the Disruptions: The AWS Solutions

Last but not least of these new normals is the emergence of leading cloud solutions including Microsoft Azure, Google Cloud, and, specifically, AWS, the topic of this book. They're the hub of successful digital business models and are essential for implementing the competitive advantages discussed previously.

The AWS Universal Architecture: Simplifying AWS Understanding

The AWS Universal Architecture is a logical cloud architecture model whose objective is to facilitate AWS learning and understanding.

AWS HERO AWARD

The AWS Universal Architecture is an achievement of this book's author who earned the AWS Hero 2020 award for the best contributions to AWS practices.

As illustrated in Figure 1.2, the AWS Universal Architecture conceives AWS through four components including infrastructure as a service (IaaS), platform as a service (PaaS), innovation as a service, and AWS integration. Each building block supports specific cloud functions; IaaS provides virtual infrastructure resources over the internet while PaaS provides complete application development platforms. Building blocks are composed of what is referred in this book as *AWS extended services*. Extended services are aggregations of formal AWS services that perform specific functions such as computing, networking, security, or storage.

- AWS IaaS
- AWS PaaS
- Innovation as a service (INNaaS)
- AWS integration

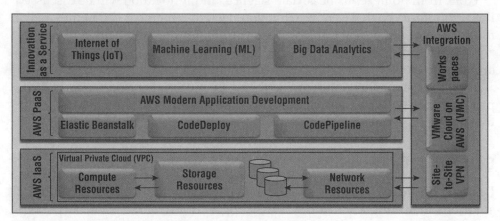

Figure 1.2: Overview of the AWS Universal Architecture

These features effectively enable the work from home, ebusiness, data science, and innovation capabilities. Here is what you need to know about the AWS Universal Architecture fundamentals.

Navigating AWS IaaS Building Block

Think of the *AWS IaaS* building block as the representation of your organization's virtual datacenter; it acts as the virtualized facility that hosts and provides three categories over the Internet of AWS virtual infrastructure resources including compute, network, and storage.

AWS Compute Resources

The objective of the AWS compute resources is to host and run applications efficiently that support your business activities including customer use of digital services. Examples include Elastic Compute Cloud, Elastic Load Balancing, and Containers. Let's briefly discuss them.

Amazon Elastic Compute Cloud (EC2) by analogy acts as a virtual server in the AWS environment to provide secure, resizable computing capacity. Its primary goal is to host and run applications supporting the business activities including customer use of digital services. EC2 has the same features as physical servers including CPU, memory size, internal storage, and network interface. *Amazon Machine Image (AMI)*, which defines the EC2's software configuration, and the *instance type*, which describes its computing power configuration, are what should matter to you. The instance type provides eight families of computing power configurations, each of which are comprised of combinations of CPU, memory, storage, and networking capacities. Examples of EC2 benefits are as follows:

- Contribution to your organization's competitive pricing resulting from the cost saved due to EC2's affordability

- Superior customer experience with your organization's digital service resulting from robust networking and security due to the EC2 location in *Amazon Virtual Private Cloud (VPC)*

- 99.99% availability of your organization's digital services

- Wide array of computing capacity and software configurations

AWS Elastic Load Balancing (ELB) deserves the same attention; it's the load balancing service for AWS deployments. Its purpose is to ensure superior customer experience with applications and digital services by increasing their availability and fault tolerance. In addition, it builds on health check mechanisms to monitor the health of your computing resources and sends requests only to the healthy ones.

ELB distributes incoming application or network traffic across the AWS resources involved in providing optimized and secure computing capacity such as EC2 instances and containers.

ELB scales your load balancer as traffic to your application evolves. Accordingly, it adds and removes compute resources as your needs change. Examples of ELB benefits include the following:

- High availability of your organization's digital services due to ELB's native awareness of failures that allows it to add capacity automatically

- Robust monitoring capacity through its ability to monitor application health and performance

- Robust security features including integrated certificate management, user authentication, and SSL/TLS decryption
- Integration with other AWS services including EC2, ECS/EKS, and CloudFormation

Amazon containers merit your attention as well. They provide a standard way to package your developer's application code, configurations, and dependencies into a single and easy-to-manage object.

AWS containers are lightweight, and by providing a portable software environment to run and scale applications easily from one computing environment to another, they not only make the developer's job easy but they also shrink the application deployment process and speed your organization's time to market.

With its *Amazon Elastic Container Service (ECS)* or *Amazon Elastic Kubernetes Services (EKS)*, AWS offers a wide range of services for storing, running, and managing containers. Examples of benefits include the following:

- Highly portable applications resulting from the fact that they can be deployed to a wide array of operating systems and hardware platforms
- IT operations efficiency resulting from the fact that containers allow applications to be deployed, patched, and scaled more rapidly
- Containers support Agile and DevOps efforts to accelerate development, test, and production cycles

AWS Network Resources

The objective of networking resources is to route traffic effectively back and forth between the Internet and your AWS cloud. Examples of resources include Amazon VPC, *Internet Gateway (IGW)*, and subnets. The following are the key things to know about them.

Amazon VPC is a virtual network dedicated to your company's AWS account and supports traffic generated by AWS resources. Its primary purpose is to ensure privacy and security and, more importantly, prevent loss of proprietary data. Some of its benefits include the following:

- VPC provides advanced security features including *subnets*, *route tables (RTs)*, *network access control list (network ACL)*, and *security groups (SG)* to secure traffic within your cloud.
- VPC acts as a virtual facility that hosts the infrastructure resources of your AWS cloud.

IGW is also a VPC component that allows communication between VPC and the Internet. Without it, the virtual resources within your AWS cloud cannot be accessed from the Internet.

Subnets are VPC components used either to allow communication with the Internet or to prevent it. Subnetting is its main benefit. It allows virtual network segmentation into public subnets permitting access from the Internet and private subnets preventing it.

AWS Storage Resources

The primary goal of virtual storage resources is to store data safely and effectively manage it. Examples include Simple Storage Service, Elastic Block Store, and Redshift. Let's discuss them briefly here.

Simple Storage Service (S3) is an AWS service that provides object storage through a web interface. It stores objects in resources known as *buckets*. Additional S3 use cases include the following:

- Storage for Internet or cloud applications
- Backup and recovery, which creates and stores copies of data used to protect organizations against data loss
- Disaster recovery, which allows organizations to regain access to their IT infrastructure after events like natural disaster
- Data lakes for analytics purpose
- Archiving for long-term storage of end-of-lifecycle object

Elastic Block Store (EBS) volumes are another AWS storage solution. They're attached to EC2 instances to provide raw block-level storage and to support uses like formatting devices with a filesystem, snapshotting, and cloning. EBS benefits include the following:

- Data and application replication to prevent loss
- Data persistence achieved through its off-instance storage nature where EBS can persist even if the instance is stopped and restarted
- Snapshots, which are the ability for EBS to create backups of any EBS volume and write a copy of the data in S3 buckets

Amazon Redshift is a fully managed data warehouse service in the AWS cloud. It's a system used for reporting and data analysis. Consider it a core component of your organization's data science capability. It is a collection of resources called *nodes*, which are either computing resources or datastores holding the data to query. Nodes are organized into groups called *clusters*. Redshift is utilized through client connections with varied applications including business intelligence (BI) reporting, SQL query, and analytics tools. It optimizes storage and query performance through a combination of mechanisms including massively parallel processing (MPP), columnar data storage, and data compression.

Understanding Essential AWS PaaS Tools

You can think of the *AWS PaaS building block* as a collection of software deployment platform options that you can use to implement digital products and services. However, from the enterprise architecture perspective, the PaaS layer is a representation of your organization's application or digital service development and deployment platform. Examples of software deployment platform options include Elastic Beanstalk, CodeDeploy, and CodePipeline. The following sections tell what you need to know about them.

AWS Elastic Beanstalk

Elastic Beanstalk is a service that simplifies the deployment and management of applications that your developer uploads to your AWS cloud. The process is as simple as this: the developer uploads and deploys the application, and Elastic Beanstalk automatically provisions and configures the desired computing environment including the EC2 instance and the required security, load balancing, autoscaling, and health monitoring mechanisms. Examples of benefits include the following:

- Greater focus on application deployment instead of worrying about the underlying resources
- Ability to deploy applications in a variety of programming languages including Java, Python, Ruby, Node.js, and PHP
- Selection of the most appropriate EC2 instance types required by your applications
- Ability to adjust the overall computing environment configuration

Elastic Beanstalk is combined with AWS CodePipeline to implement DevOps in AWS computing environments.

AWS CodeDeploy

CodeDeploy is a service used to automate code deployment to EC2 instances as well as additional AWS services such as AWS Fargate, AWS Lambda, and on-premises servers. It scales with the cloud infrastructure to allow application deployments to thousands of instances. Additional benefits include the following:

- Allows deployments of both traditional applications on servers and serverless-based applications
- Full automation of application deployments across development, test, and production environments
- Enables tracking deployment status through the CodeDeploy console

CodeDeploy is combined with AWS CodePipeline to implement DevOps in AWS computing environments.

AWS CodePipeline

CodePipeline is a service used to automate your software deployment process based on DevOps principles. It provides your developers with a graphic user interface to model the configuration of the workflow supporting the organization's continuous delivery approach. Additional benefits include the following:

- Enhances developer's productivity and accelerates time to market through automation, which removes the complexity and overhead in building applications

- Cost savings resulting from the use of more efficient application development and deployment tools

- Integration with not only other AWS resources but also with existing IT infrastructure and tools

Understanding Innovation with AWS: Machine Learning, Internet of Things, and Elastic MapReduce

Over the next three to five years, innovation should be viewed as the ability to improve the customer's experience continuously with a digital service and product using technology. From that perspective, the innovation as a service building block represents the set of AWS technologies supporting digital service and product innovation. Examples of such technologies include AWS Machine Learning, AWS Internet of Things, and Amazon Elastic MapReduce. Let's briefly discuss them.

AWS Machine Learning

AWS Machine Learning (ML) is a product that allows developers to discover patterns in data through algorithms, construct mathematical models based on these patterns, and then create predictive applications. Primary use cases include the following:

- **Image recognition**: This is used to perform machine-based visual tasks, such as labeling image contents with meta tags.

- **Speech recognition**: This allows users to interact with their mobile devices through speech.

- **Product recommendation**: This seeks to predict and show the services that a customer is likely to purchase.

- **Fraud detection**: This analyzes millions of transactions to detect fraudulent behavior.

AWS Internet of Things

AWS Internet of Things (IoT) is a platform that collects and analyzes data from Internet-connected devices and sensors and connects that data to AWS cloud applications. Examples of IoT-supported innovative products and services include the following:

- Smart watches, fitness trackers, and wearables developed by companies such as Apple, Fitbit, and Misfit

- Home connections to the Internet enabling your household electronics to perform varied voice-activated functions

- Machine-to-machine (M2M) connected devices that allow two machines to communicate without human intervention

Amazon Elastic MapReduce

As a reminder, big data is large and complex dataset collections supplied from varied new data sources. The data is so voluminous that traditional data processing techniques are ineffective.

Amazon Elastic MapReduce (EMR) is Amazon's big data solution. It's based on Apache Hadoop's MapReduce algorithm, and like Redshift, it relies on an architecture structured around cluster and nodes implemented as instances running Apache Hadoop's MapReduce algorithm.

The Hadoop MapReduce algorithm processes data in two phases: Map and Reduce. *Map* tasks deal with splitting and mapping input data in parallel to create smaller chunks, while *Reduce* tasks are about shuffling, reducing, and aggregating data.

Amazon EMR is primarily used for processing and analyzing significant amounts of data. Additional uses include the following:

- Processing data for analytics goals including finding meaning in data and using derived knowledge to inform decisions

- Mining data for business intelligence goals including transformation of data into actionable business insights

- Transformation and movement of data into and out of other AWS data stores and databases

- Support for real-time data streaming

Understanding the AWS Integration Building Block

The integration of public clouds with entities such as your organization's on-premises infrastructure and your business partner's infrastructure, along with the need to implement hybrid cloud and multicloud platforms, is an increasing priority. This is the goal of the *AWS integration building block*.

AWS offers varied solutions to address cloud integration issues. Examples of AWS integration services include AWS Site-to-Site VPN and VMware Cloud on AWS. Let's briefly discuss them now.

Site-to-Site VPN

AWS Site-to-Site VPN is a service that enables access to your organization's on-premises infrastructure or remote network from your VPC.

As illustrated in Figure 1.3, an AWS site-to-site connection involves three components on both sides of the connection including: a virtual private gateway on Amazon's side, a customer gateway on your remote network's side, and two encrypted VPN endpoints, also known as *encrypted tunnels*.

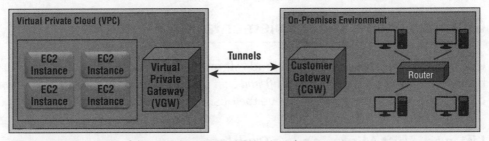

Figure 1.3: Overview of the AWS Site-to-Site VPN principles

Hybrid Cloud with VMware Cloud on AWS

VMware Cloud on AWS (VMC) is a hybrid cloud service whose core principle is to run a VMware software-defined data center (SDDC) in the AWS public cloud. This joint initiative between VMware and Amazon seeks to enable the combination of a wide variety of VMware tools with the flexibility and simplicity of the AWS cloud.

As illustrated in Figure 1.4, AWS provides an elastic bare-metal infrastructure on top of which VMware implements its SDDC platform. You should view VMware SDDC as a datacenter with no physical intervention; all components including compute, storage, and network are virtualized, and their management including provisioning, load balancing, backup and restore, and disaster recovery are entirely automated by software.

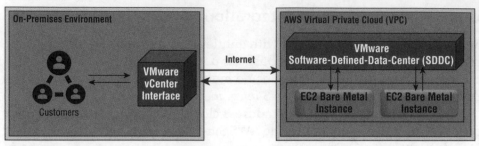

Figure 1.4: Principles of VMware Cloud on AWS

Most VMC-based use cases are derived from the organization's need to extend their datacenter to the AWS cloud and take advantage of its flexibility. They include the following:

- Easy configuration of on-premises compute, storage, and network infrastructure without knowing SDDC tools
- Easy configuration of load balancing mechanisms resulting from the use of AWS Elastic Load Balancing

Changes in the AWS Implementation Paradigm

Contrary to widespread opinion, cloud migration projects fail far more than it is believed. The reason is that today's *lift-and-shift* paradigm is booming. The majority of companies still struggle to achieve the business benefits that they expect.

Lift-and-Shift Migration Is a Problem

Lift-and-shift is about migrating applications to the cloud with minimal or no changes at all. Cloud infrastructures, including AWS, are considered freight depots where applications are stored hoping that the promised benefits happen instantaneously and miraculously. The problem with lift-and-shift as it is currently applied is that it's based on a combination of failure factors incompatible with the digital transformation stakes. Let's examine the flaws of the lift-and-shift paradigm migration mentality.

Failure Factors Making Lift-and-Shift Irrelevant

Cloud migrations fail for a variety of reasons, but most cloud computing thought leaders and influencers agree on the following reasons:

- Migrating without a business purpose
- Lack of cloud migration strategy

- Mimicking on-premises environment
- Migration at once
- Rushed migration

As suggested, *migrating without a business purpose* is the IT-centric practice in which applications are migrated to AWS without a specific business objective. Absence or inadequate cloud strategy alignment with the business goals results in sophisticated cloud platforms that, unfortunately, don't bring in the expected business benefits.

Lack of cloud migration strategy is a practice based on improvisation in which applications are migrated regardless of unknowns, uncertainties, and risks. Overlooking the development of cloud adoption business cases including feasibility, risk analysis, return on investment (ROI), and migration roadmap results in unstable and failed cloud platforms.

Mimicking on-premises environment is a practice wrongly based on the belief that replicating on-premises IT in the cloud guarantees the same levels of security, reliability, and performance. Not using reliable architecture frameworks doubled with improvised architecture design based on erroneous assumptions results once again in unstable and failed cloud platforms.

Migration at once is the irresponsible belief that a workload can be migrated all at once instead of moving it a little bit at a time. Lack of hindsight and experience results in unstable and failed platforms.

Rushed migration is another irresponsible practice in which haste is confused with speed. As with the previous failure factor, lack of hindsight and experience results in unstable and failed platforms.

Understanding the Benefits of Enterprise Architecture for AWS

The five cloud migration failure factors show that using AWS as a business opportunity demands a new migration paradigm tailored to deliver business value.

Enterprise Architecture (EA) for AWS is a cloud migration approach inspired from traditional EA principles. It seeks to help businesses use their AWS cloud platform as business value enablers. Just as traditional EA promulgates rules like "Group individual applications into independent business domains" as the means to avoid application overload, benefit fast response time, and offer superior customer experience, EA for AWS recommends AWS migration and architecture practices that enable business opportunities.

Examples of such AWS migration and architecture basic practices include the following:

- Structure your VPC around public subnets holding applications with Internet direct access.

- Use private subnets holding databases to prevent direct access from the Internet as the means to implement your organization's virtual datacenter.

Key Takeaways

Surviving in a pandemic-driven economy or succeeding in the growing digital business environment is not about hastily migrating your IT to the cloud and hoping that miracles happen.

The prerequisites for successful migration to the cloud are three-fold. They include first, understanding how your business, operational, and revenue models along with IT tools have been irrelevant. Second, rethinking your business, operational, and revenue models. And third, understand how technology, including AWS, can help.

You learned that in addition to competitive pricing, superior customer experience, and short time to market, there are new business normals including work from home, ebusiness, data science, and innovation. You also learned that technology was essential to meet these new normals and to help your business survive the pandemic crisis and even prosper.

Finally, you were provided with an overview of the AWS Universal Architecture and learned about its four building blocks of IaaS, PaaS, Innovation as a Service, and AWS integration and how they provide the foundation for building a world-class digital service development organization.

In the next chapter, we'll clarify the notion of digital product and service, and the impacts on today's digital product and service development.

References

1   Philippe Abdoulaye, "How to Thrive in the COVID-19 Recession by Going Digital," *Data Driven Investor*. (November 13, 2020) `https://www.datadriveninvestor.com/2020/11/13/how-to-thrive-in-the-covid-19-recession-by-going-digital-using-scenario/`

2   Kaan Turnali, "Digital Transformation Is Not a Technology Makeover. It's a Business Revolution" *Forbes*. (June 11, 2017) `https://www.forbes.com/sites/sap/2017/06/11/digital-transformation-is-not-a-technology-makeover-its-a-business-revolution/?sh=3a2f3c7bec52`

3   Amazon Web Services, "What is AWS?" *AWS*. (January 01, 2021) `https://aws.amazon.com/what-is-aws/`

What Is a Digital Product?

We've moved from digital product and infrastructure to digital distribution and web strategy to now more holistic transformations that clearly are based on mobile, social media, digitization, and the power of analytics and we think it's really a new era requiring new strategies!

—Saul Berman

The key role that innovation and ecommerce are playing in the expanding digital economy was discussed in Chapter 1, "The Digital Economy's Challenges, Opportunities, and Relevance of AWS." These factors are positioning digital products and services at the epicenter of the global competition.

Digital products and services are becoming an essential revenue stream for all businesses. Consequently, it's important for CIOs and technology leaders to understand them, not only from their usage perspective but also from the technology standpoint including their nature, ecosystem, and infrastructure.

This chapter clarifies the importance of digital products and services in the global competition, as well as the differences between both concepts. Next, it discusses their technological anatomy.

Finally, it elaborates on how innovation and ecommerce impact today's digital products and services development approaches in terms of concerns, focus, and priorities.

Differences Between Digital Products and Digital Services

Digital products and services are often confused. They're fundamentally different, and they can't be used interchangeably. The following sections discuss their differences.

Digital Service Delivers Information

A *digital service* refers to the electronic delivery of information including data and content. It's one that a company uses to market its staff's time, effort, knowledge, and skills. Examples of digital services include online teaching, online sport coaching, online medical consultation, and online consulting.

What's important to know at this point is that, like digital products, digital services are accessible through mobile devices including smartphones, tablets, game consoles, and laptops, as well as traditional desktop PCs.

Digital Product Exists in Intangible Formats

As to *digital products*, keep in mind that they refer to any product that exists in an intangible format. They're accessible by electronic mobile devices like smartphones, tablets, game consoles, and laptops, as well as traditional desktop PCs. Nevertheless, narrowing digital products just to smart mobile devices providing access to the Internet would be simplistic, as its anatomy makes it clear in the next section.

A digital product is one that a company delivers and sells repeatedly without having to reproduce the effort and time consumed to develop it. Examples of digital products include online course videos, e-books, video games, and streaming music.

Anatomy of the Digital Product

CIOs and technology leaders don't always pay attention to the detailed technological and technical aspects of digital products and services. They focus on the immediate business benefits. The following section offers a simplified perspective of the technology stack underlying digital products and services.

The Digital Product's Technology Stack

Digital products are based on a complex technology stack that deserves your attention. Figure 2.1 gives an overview of the technologies involved, and it suggests how complex their implementation is from human, operational, and technological perspectives.

Digital products combine three main building blocks, including the following:

- The 4G/5G services that build on 4G/5G networks to deliver capacities like voice, video, and wireless Internet

- The cloud infrastructure, AWS in Figure 2.1, which provides innovation capabilities
- Smart mobile devices, which enable access to digital products and services via the Internet

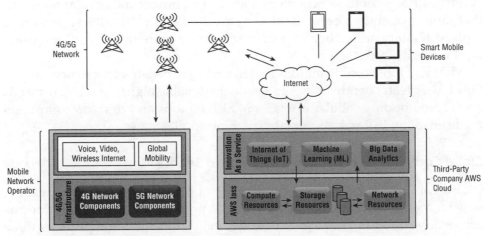

Figure 2.1: The digital product anatomy

Let's take a closer look at these components including their purpose, functions, and technologies.

The 4G/5G Services

Understand the 4G/5G layer as the set of broadband mobile networks whose role it is to connect smart mobile devices to the Internet and enable applications such as mobile web access, IP telephony, gaming services, high-definition mobile television, and video conferencing.

"G" stands for generation, and it relates to the changes taking place from one generation to another on technical issues, as varied as greater frequency bands, wider channel frequency bandwidth, and higher data transfer capacity. Keep in mind that 4G and 5G network services offer similar benefits and applications. The main differences are the greater speeds, increased bandwidth, and reduced latency that 5G offers over 4G.

The 4G Mobile Network Services

4G systems comply with the requirements of the International Mobile Telecommunications-Advanced (IMT) for mobile phone and Internet access service. The IMT-Advanced standard suggests that 4G systems are expected to deliver extensive all-Internet protocols–based mobile broadband solutions to laptops, smartphones, and tablets. Services such as broadband Internet access,

Voice over IP (VoIP), gaming, mobile TV, and streamed multimedia should be provided to users.

The 5G Mobile Network Added Value

5G is the fifth-generation technology standard for broadband cellular networks that mobile operators began deploying worldwide in 2019. It's supposed to replace 4G networks. They're predicted to have more than 1.7 billion users worldwide by 2025.

What you must bear in mind is that the primary benefit of these networks is they have greater bandwidth. As a result, they enable higher download speeds and serve not only cellular phones but also laptops and desktop computers while enabling IoT and machine-to-machine applications.

Cloud Computing Services: Innovation as a Service

Cloud computing plays an increasingly important role in digital product development. In addition to making digital product development platforms competitive by cutting IT costs and accelerating IT operations, it provides three services for supporting your organization's innovation strategy, including IoT, machine learning, and big data.

Learning About AWS IoT Added Value

As defined in Chapter 1, *IoT* is a platform that collects and analyzes data from Internet-connected devices and sensors and links that data to your AWS cloud applications. Figure 2.2 illustrates how it works and how it makes your organization's digital products innovative.

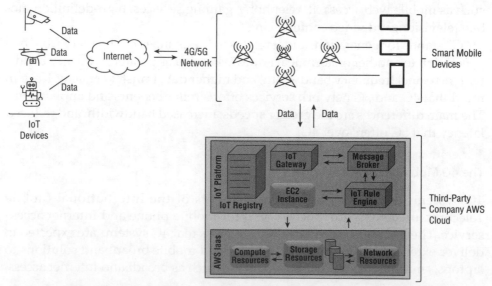

Figure 2.2: The AWS IoT ecosystem supporting organization's innovative digital products

Figure 2.2 shows that the AWS IoT ecosystem is complex. It involves four fundamental elements that enable your organization's innovation capacities:

- The IoT devices, also known as *things*
- The IoT platform hosted in your AWS cloud
- The 4G/5G networks
- The smart mobile devices

IoT devices are any electronic devices equipped with sensors, actuators, and specific software to give your organization's digital products the innovative features consumers expect to make their lives easier and safer.

Sensors collect data from the relevant environment and send it via the Internet to other "things" or applications in yours or in a third-party's AWS cloud. Upon receipt of data, actuators change or manipulate a specific aspect of the applicable environment.

The AWS IoT platform consists of the combination of AWS resources that coordinate and support the connected devices across the Internet. These resources include the following:

- An IoT gateway that acts as a network gateway between the Internet and the platform
- A message broker that dispatches connected device messages to an IoT rules engine
- The IoT rules engine whose role is to run the business logic associated with your organization's digital products

As you can imagine, keeping such a complex platform in an optimal secure and working condition isn't simple. Through its IoT Device Management console, AWS brings added value. It makes it easy to register, organize, monitor, and accelerate IoT device deployments securely. The impact on your organization's time to market is significant.

Additional tools include the IoT command-line interface (CLI), which is a tool for managing the IoT platform and services, and the IoT software development kit (SDK), which provides open source libraries and development guides needed to build innovative IoT software.

Understanding AWS Machine Learning Added Value

Machine learning (ML), as defined in the previous chapter, refers to a solution that allows your data scientists and developers to discover business solution patterns in data through algorithms, construct mathematical models based on these business solution patterns, and then create predictive applications.

Another significant added value that AWS provides is its powerful tools for developing ML applications. These tools make ML model development easy and fast, significantly impacting your organization's data science practice and time to market.

As illustrated in Figure 2.3, deployment of AWS's ML development tools results in comprehensive operational environments for machine learning. *Amazon SageMaker* is a fully managed service that provides developers and data scientists with the ability to build, train, and deploy high-quality ML models quickly. It organizes this process in three phases including generate data, train models, and deploy models.

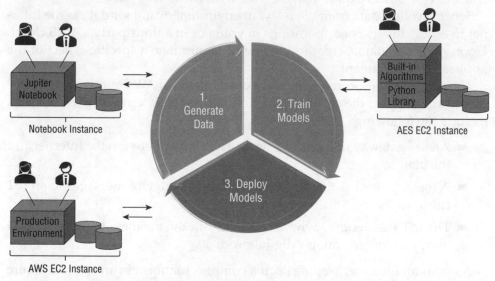

Figure 2.3: Amazon SageMaker complete operational environment

In the *Generate Data phase*, your organization's data scientists and developers seek to produce the sample data needed to train the ML model. After creating the model, they choose among the built-in algorithms in SageMaker the one likely to deliver the expected inferences and apply it to the model. They rely on a Jupyter Notebook instance to explore and preprocess the sample data needed to train the model.

As to the *Train Models phase*, your data scientists and developers seek to train and evaluate the ML model. They use AWS compute resources to train the model and determine the accuracy of the predictions or inferences.

In the *Deploy Models phase*, your data scientists and developers seek to integrate the evaluated model with their application and deploy it. With SageMaker, they have the option to deploy the model and use it independently from the application.

Understanding Amazon Elastic MapReduce Added Value

Big data refers to large and complex dataset collections supplied from varied new data sources. What AWS brings to your organization is the complete toolset needed for big data processing and analysis. *Elastic MapReduce (EMR)* is one of them. Let's see how EMR impacts your organization's data science practice and time to market.

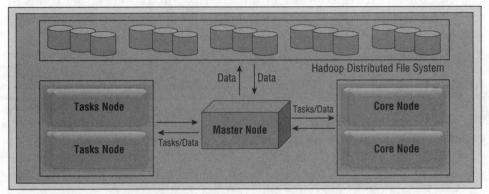

Figure 2.4: Overview of AWS EMR

EMR is a cluster platform running big data frameworks like Apache Hadoop and Apache Spark. Using parallel computing mechanisms, these frameworks accelerate and simplify data processing for analytical and business intelligence purposes.

EMR's basic component is the *cluster*, which is a collection of EC2 instances known as *nodes*. Each node plays a role characterized by one of the three types: Master, Core, and Task.

The Master node manages the cluster and runs Apache Hadoop and Apache Spark framework software to coordinate the distribution of data and tasks among nodes, track the status of tasks, and monitor the health of the cluster.

The *Core node* runs Apache Hadoop and Apache Spark framework software to perform tasks and store data in the *Hadoop Distributed File System (HDFS)*, a data store component that provides data awareness features between the master node and cluster nodes.

The *Task node* runs the Hadoop framework and Apache Hive and Apache Spark software to perform tasks without storing data in the Hadoop Distributed File System.

Smart Mobile Devices

Smart mobile devices are at the heart of people's lives. They're used for relaying and accessing information as well as for digital services. What's not often stressed is that smart mobile devices are the epicenter of your organization's digital product development strategy, so adequate infrastructure and platforms are needed.

AWS Device Farm is an application testing service that lets your developers improve the quality of your organization's web and mobile applications by testing them across a wide range of desktop browsers and real mobile devices without having to provision and manage any testing infrastructure.

Impacts on Digital Product and Service Development

The accelerated adoption of digital products and services, amplified by the COVID-19 crisis, has created two factors that will change the approach to digital products and services development. These factors will force digital products and services development organizations to innovate, develop, and deploy products and services more quickly while still ensuring quality. The factors include the growing complexity of the underlying technology and the fact that innovation alone might no longer be enough to make products and services profitable. Let's discuss these factors now.

The Growing Complexity of the Technological Stack

For almost 30 years, digital products have been following an evolutionary trajectory with four major changes in digital consumption habits driven by technology breakthroughs. As Figure 2.5 illustrates, from 1992 to 1994, the rise of the early business-to-consumer (B2C) websites and the emergence of Amazon encouraged and accelerated the use of online sales and purchases from personal computers. These services were the first generation of digital services to make your life easier.

From 2002 to 2008, by providing Internet connections delivered over mobile networks through smartphones, the rise of 3G network services accelerated the adoption of streaming radio and television content. 3G network services helped to establish smart mobile devices as the chief component of digital products.

Since 2009, 4G network services and the more recent deployment of 5G networks have been accelerating the use of smart mobile devices to access services as varied as surfing the web, checking emails, listening to music, watching TV, and video conferencing. They also enable IoT, ML, and big data applications.

As you know, companies and their product developers have been using technology innovation as the catalyst for digital product demand and consumption. That's about to change.

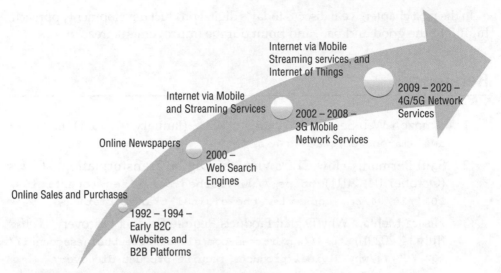

Figure 2.5: Digital product evolutionary trajectory

Technology Innovation Alone Isn't Enough Anymore

The story told by the digital product evolutionary trajectory is that innovation alone isn't enough anymore to guarantee benefits for society. What is happening today is that the ongoing digital disruption, amplified by the COVID-19 economic crisis, is driving unemployment, generating bankruptcies, and forcing households to spend differently. Thus, digital products and services development approaches must shift the focus from product and technology matters to consumer and customer experience concerns and priorities.

Key Takeaways

Digital products are complex from a technology perspective. This makes their development and deployment challenging.

In this chapter, you learned that due to the disruptive impacts of the digital economy's expansion, amplified by the COVID-19 crisis, digital products and services are becoming the hub of digital business.

You also learned that digital products and services are built on complex technology stacks that require adequate product development platforms involving 4G/5G network services, innovative technologies based on cloud computing, and smart mobile devices.

You got an overview of the added value AWS brings in innovation areas that are likely to provide a superior customer experience including Internet of Things, machine learning, and big data.

In the next chapter, we'll discuss today's digital product development approach, highlight the good and bad, and point out the improvement areas.

References

1   Amazon Web Services, "What is AWS?" (January 01, 2021). `https://aws.amazon.com/what-is-aws/`

2   Saul Berman, "How CEOs View the Digital Transformation," *Forbes* (October 04, 2011). `https://www.forbes.com/sites/robertreiss/2011/10/04/how-ceos-view-the-digital-transformation/`.

3   Nisarg Mehta, "Why Digital Products Require Product Discovery," *Forbes* (July 14, 2020). `https://www.forbes.com/sites/forbesbusinesscouncil/2020/07/14/why-digital-products-require-product-discovery`

CHAPTER 3

Digital Product and Service Development Challenges

All the businesses from the beginning of history have struggled with product development (assuming there is a market, doing the market testing and so on). But now they start with customer development. Get the customer who says, "Yes. I want that. I need it. I want to use it. I'll pay for it." And then you go back and work with your engineers. It is changing the world!

—**Brian Tracy**

In Chapter 1, "The Digital Economy's Challenges, Opportunities, and Relevance of AWS," we established that ecommerce and innovation are among the new normals in business. This is reflected in the increasing demand for digital products and services.

What's happening today is that digital consumption is accelerating, and the mobile devices are increasingly considered the product that makes life easier.

The impact on today's digital product and service development is not insignificant; it is moving the primary concern from technology and product considerations, as is unfortunately still the case in many companies, to consumer concerns. Digital product and service developers now make the customer their starting point.

To survive and thrive in the disruptive digital economy, your organization needs comprehensive digital product and service development approaches that not only leverage technology to innovate but that also build on customer concerns to receive the digital products and services that they expect. That's the safest way to make your digital product and service development platform profitable.

This chapter formally defines digital product and service development, evaluates the current digital product and service development approach including its strengths and weaknesses, and then elaborates on the areas of improvement needed to align this approach to the requirements of the digital economy.

What Is Digital Product and Service Development?

Let's make it clear, contrary to what you may have heard, there is no digital product and service development standard; practices vary from industry to industry and according to company cultures. Moreover, there's an angelic vision of the current approach, which reputedly would build on the practices introduced by agile methodologies to optimize the way that we work including collaboration, organizational synergy, focus on end-user satisfaction, and process automation. The reality is different.

After defining today's digital product and service development approach including its processes, practices, methodologies, and tools, this section discusses how most IT organizations run it on a daily basis. The section then highlights the differences versus current application development. Unlike digital product and service development, application development isn't involved in the various intricacies of the business—its operations, market, and profit.

Digital Product and Service Development Defined

Digital product and service development refers to the set of staff and skills, processes and practices, tools, and infrastructure mobilized to deliver a digital product or service in a specific operational and organizational context.

The key piece of information to bear in mind is that staff and skills represent the experts mobilized and their knowledge and competencies. Processes and practices, as the name suggests, cover specific processes, practices, and methodologies needed to achieve successful product and service development. Tools and infrastructure are the various technologies supporting the digital product's processes, practices, and methodologies.

Although rarely considered, operational and organizational context is central to any digital transformation. It relates to your work organization, and it is the belief that the way your product and service development tasks are distributed among your staff and the ways in which your teams are coordinated have an impact on your product and service development performance.

How Is Digital Product and Service Development Performed?

Since agile approaches became popular in IT, roughly between 2012 and 2015, hybrid product and service development approaches emerged not only as the software development norm but also as the digital product and service development standard. It's structured around a software development lifecycle (SDLC) implemented as an *agile stage-gate process* (see Figure 3.1), which mixes the best of both paradigms to orchestrate the development effort.

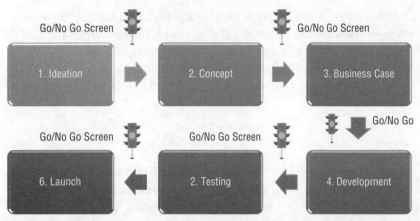

Figure 3.1: The agile stage-gate SDLC supporting today's digital product development effort

On a wider basis, the agile approach to software development emphasizes organizations focusing on incremental and continual delivery, transversal collaboration, continual learning and improvement, and process automation.

In addition to a *validation gate*, each phase involves specific staff and skills, processes and methodologies, and tools and infrastructure. The step names may vary according to the organization, but the purposes are the same.

Ideation

Triggered either formally three to four times a year or informally when possible, *ideation* is the process of generating problem-solving ideas. It's run as workshops involving your product owners, product and software developers, and architects who generate ideas and filter them to select the most innovative and practical ones likely to inspire new digital products and services or new features for existing digital products and services.

Ideation techniques with which you should be familiar include brainstorming, prototyping, and worst possible ideas. Let's discuss them individually.

Brainstorming   In *brainstorming*, a group of your company's experts, including data scientists, product owner, product and software developers, and architects, are expected to provide solution ideas aimed at solving clearly defined business and product design problems. Sessions are structured around answers to questions like, "What business or design problem do we have?" and "What are the best ideas to fix it?"

Prototyping   With *prototyping*, working samples of software supporting the digital product under development are created to allow your data scientists, product owner, product and software developers, and architects to evaluate specific features by trying them and providing immediate feedback.

Worst Possible Ideas   *Worst possible ideas* is the ideation technique where your data scientists, product owner, product and software developers, and architects are involved via brainstorming sessions to generate business or product design problem solutions and then use their creativity to challenge assumptions to eliminate the worst solutions and select the most promising solution.

Concept

The *concept phase* is performed once the best solution ideas have been selected. Its purpose is to inform your product development team about the product owner's expectations and draw from them the technological and technical implications of the solution in terms of relevant smart mobile devices, cloud computing services, and innovation technologies.

Workshops involving software developers, product developers, and architects are held using facilitation tools like use case diagrams and agile user stories, which help to identify the digital product's potential users, clarify features, define functions, and recognize customer experience elements.

What's validated in the go/no go screening process, implemented as a pre-product validation meeting, primarily includes the scope of the product to develop in terms of functions, features, and technologies. Your organization's customer profile, also known as *customer persona*, includes customer expectations, demographic details, interests, and behavioral traits.

Business Case

The *business case phase* is triggered when the digital product's scope is validated and its technical feasibility is established. The goal is to develop the business case that justifies your organization's investments; evaluates the benefit, cost, and risk of alternative options; and provides arguments in favor of the preferred solution.

The product owner and development teams are involved in the business case phase. The product owner provides the business and financial inputs while product developers, software developers, and architects provide the technological ones.

Tools like return on investment (ROI), total cost of ownership (TCO), and risk analysis are used to get executive buy-in. The business case is validated in the go/no go screening process, implemented as a product governance review involving relevant sales, marketing, product development, and IT executives.

Development

Brought about after the business case approval, the *development phase* consists of iterations that span product technical detailed design, development of the software that supports the product's functions, software code testing, and integration testing involving the product's entire ecosystem.

Your development teams, architects, and product owner are the main stakeholders, and agile methodologies are leveraged to manage the development effort. Approaches similar to object-oriented design are used to plan the software architecture underpinning the digital product, while integrated development environments (IDEs) are used to develop the software and perform unit and functional tests.

Testing

The *testing phase* is triggered once the software supporting the digital product has passed the OAT and UAT screening gate. The goal is to make sure that the digital product, through a series of tests known as OAT and UAT, meets the criteria for going to market.

OAT, which covers security, fault tolerance, automation, and performance, involves your product developers, software developers, and architects, while UAT, which involves getting the digital product tested from a functional standpoint, includes a panel of business users and sometimes actual customers.

The OAT and UAT test reports are approved in the go/no go screening process implemented as a product validation review involving sales, marketing, product development, and IT executives who decide when to go to market.

Launch

The final stage of the current digital product development approach, the *launch phase*, also known as the *go-to-market phase*, is triggered after the OAT and UAT approval. It involves taking the new digital product or the new features of existing digital products to market, which includes deploying the digital product software to a production environment, and it entails activities critical to achieving commercial success like digital partnerships, social media marketing, online sales, and customer support.

Digital Product and Service Development Approach Evaluation

The next sections in this chapter address how to use a tool that will be part of all of your digital business activities, from business digital transformation to implementing digital product and service development platforms and managing digital product and service development on a daily basis. The tool is the *assessment matrix* for digital product and service development platforms.

Using the assessment matrix to evaluate the current digital product and service development approach will familiarize you with issues including digital operational and organizational models, digital technology stack, and industry digital disruption challenges, opportunities, and requirements. They'll become part of your standard jargon.

Understanding the Digital Product and Service Development Assessment Framework

The assessment matrix for a digital product and service development platform is based on the proven belief that the more you understand your environment's challenges, opportunities, and requirements, the better you will adjust your digital product and service development strategy and capabilities, and the greater your performance.

Let's discuss the framework, its underlying principles, its major concepts, and how you can take advantage of it to make your digital product and service development platform profitable.

Assessment Framework Overview

The assessment matrix provides IT executives with a comprehensive framework that helps them capture and analyze the business context, identify the required performance levers, and derive from both the appropriate digital transformation solution (also known as *requirements*) from the human, operational, organizational, and technological perspectives (see Figure 3.2).

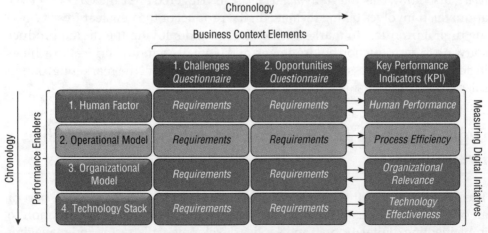

Figure 3.2: The assessment matrix for digital product development platforms

The assessment matrix rationale builds on three pillars: the Context Elements, the Performance Enablers, and the Requirements.

The Context Elements

The framework recommends starting your digital transformation effort with a complete analysis of the business context including the challenges that your organization faces and the opportunities of which it needs to take advantage.

The purpose of the *Context Elements* pillar is to provide you with questionnaires (or help you build questionnaires) that allow the identification of the business context's challenges, opportunities, and the related requirements.

Examples of questions for the challenge element would include:

"How does digital economy affect your business?"

"What are the requirements needed to meet these challenges?"

Likewise, examples of questions for the opportunities element include:

"What opportunities does the digital economy context offer?"

"What are the requirements needed to take advantage of these opportunities?"

The Performance Enablers

The *performance enablers* represent the human, operational, organizational, and technological resources your organization must mobilize to meet the requirements of the context challenges and opportunities.

The *human factor enabler* relates to the personnel profiles that your organization needs to meet the requirements associated with the challenges and opportunities. Examples of challenge statements would include "Understanding digital business customer persona expectations are challenging, and implementing big data is helpful." The related challenge requirements would be personnel profiles like, "Data scientist with three years of AWS experience and hands-on SageMaker and Python practice."

As to the *operational enabler*, also known as the *operational model*, what you must know is that it relates to the product and service development lifecycle (PSDLC) that your organization relies on to deliver digital products and services. It underpins your digital product and service development platform and combines a stage-gate process along with the personnel profiles, practices, methodologies, and tools associated with each stage.

Note that today's digital product and service development lifecycle is nothing other than the software development lifecycle augmented with business, market, and consumer concerns.

Scrum agile and software prototyping principles apply to digital product and service development. Therefore, they're valid examples of operational models.

The *organizational enabler*, also known as the *organizational model*, refers to the organizational structure in which your digital product and service development platform is immersed. You should understand it as the way that digital product and service development activities are performed, distributed, coordinated, and supervised across your organization.

Examples of organizational models include the project matrix, Agile organization model, and Project Management Office (PMO) model.

A *project matrix* is a cross-functional structure in which contributing resources are provided by your organization's functional areas. The specific project matrix that works within organizations consists of two chains of command: one along the functional lines and the other along project, product, or client lines.

The *agile organizational model* stresses the principles of agile software development methodologies including strong cross-functional collaboration, elimination of organizational silos, fast learning and decision cycles, and customer-centricity.

The *PMO*'s role in the digital product and service development context is to define, maintain, and enforce standards across the organization that are likely to ensure accelerated time to market and premium customer experience.

As to the *technological enabler*, it relates to the combination of technologies including AWS IaaS and PaaS, AWS Machine Learning, and AWS SageMaker big data solutions that your organization may use to meet the requirements of the business context challenges and opportunities.

The Digital Transformation Solutions

You should understand that digital transformation solutions, entries of the assessment matrix, are the formal answers that you provide to address the business context requirements from the human, operational, organizational, and technological perspectives.

Examples of digital transformation solutions addressing the business context requirement would include "Investing in big data infrastructure to get accurate market and customer insights" and, from the human enabler standpoint, "Hiring SageMaker experts with hands-on machine learning and Python programming practices."

Another example of digital transformation solutions addressing the business context requirement would include "Automating key IT operations to accelerate time to market and cut IT costs" and, from the technology enabler perspective, "Migrating the ecommerce on-premises infrastructure to AWS."

One final example of digital transformation solutions addressing the business context requirement would include "Undertaking multiple digital product development projects" and, from the organizational enabler perspective, "Implementing a PMO model."

Assessing Current Digital Product and Service Development

What's wrong with today's digital product and service development approach? The answers developed in this section will stir your interest for two reasons.

- You'll get a grasp on the good and bad of today's practices.
- By using the assessment framework to highlight these good and bad practices, you'll be taking your first steps into digital transformation management.

We'll evaluate the digital product development platform of a third-party chain of supermarkets in New York with the fictitious name of Julienne & Simone (J&S) Food. The company has been struggling in the changing supermarket industry, as its sales have dropped by 40 percent in only one year, and transforming the business to digital seems to be the safest option to save it.

The company uses the agile stage-gate process illustrated in Figure 3.1, and the goal of this assessment exercise is to capture the current business context and derive from it the problems with the current product development approach.

What Is a Digital Product and Service Development Platform?

Contrary to the widespread belief, a digital product and service development platform isn't limited to the technology stack underpinning the development effort. Figure 3.3 highlights the ingredients of a successful digital product and service development platform:

Figure 3.3: Ingredients of a successful digital product and service development platform

As illustrated in Figure 3.3, you should understand a digital product and service development platform as the ecosystem of performance enablers including people (human), processes (operational model), organizational structure (organizational model), technologies (technology), product development lifecycle, and innovation policy supporting digital product and service development.

People refers to the staff directly or indirectly involved in the digital product and service development endeavor. Direct contributors are involved in activities creating the digital product or service. Examples include customer development, product design and implementation, cloud migration, and cloud infrastructure monitoring. Indirect contributors are involved in activities supporting the product development effort, for example, social media marketing.

The *operational model* refers primarily to the digital product development lifecycle and the set of processes, practices, and methodologies that make it up. What's important to remember is that without the operational model, the digital product and service development effort would be messy. By organizing the development effort in phases and mobilizing proper staff, skills, methodologies, and tools in each phase, it alleviates the complexity of developing sophisticated technology systems and speeds up their delivery.

The organizational model relates to the organizational setting in which your digital product and service development function is immersed. Proper coordination between your product and service development team and the rest of your company brings significant added value, including breaking organizational silos, productive interactions and collaborations, and informed, easy, and fast decision-making. It contributes to simplifying and accelerating the product or service development effort.

The *technology stack* refers to the technology that supports the digital product development effort. This not only includes the infrastructure supporting the use of the digital product and service, including 4G/5G services, AWS IaaS, PaaS, and innovation as a service cloud services, but it also encompasses every single tool that supports the product or service development effort. The software integrated development environment (IDE) and web-based customer journey design solution are examples of a technology stack.

Digital product and service development lifecycle refers to the sequence of all the required activities that a company must perform to develop, manufacture, and sell a digital product or service. These activities include marketing, research, engineering design, quality assurance, manufacturing, and a whole chain of suppliers and vendors.

Understand *innovation policy* as the practice of bringing together research and technological development and business strategy that aims to create a conducive framework for bringing ideas to market.

Assuming that you're the one leading the assessment, let's use the assessment matrix for digital product and service development platforms to create a draft of an assessment reporting on J&S Food's product and service development platform.

Capturing Business Context

This first step of the assessment should have taken place following a meeting that your company's CEO might have asked you to organize. The CEO wants to discuss the expansion of the company's ecommerce business. The CEO considers digital expansion the safest option to save the company.

You involve sales, marketing, post-sales, and key business unit representatives in a two-hour videoconference. In agreement with the CEO, you put three questions on the meeting agenda:

- What challenges does the ongoing ecommerce industry disruption place on our business?

- What opportunities does this industry's disruption offer to our business?

- What are the specific legal and regulatory requirements with which our business must comply?

Table 3.1 summarizes the key decisions taken by the participants.

Table 3.1: J&S Business Context, Challenges, Opportunities, and Requirements

CONTEXT ELEMENTS	DESCRIPTION
Challenges	J&S must retain existing customers and acquire new ones to survive the industry disruption and thrive.
Opportunities	The growing demand for digital products and services and digital technology maturity offer the primary opportunities for J&S. They create the conditions for expanding the business's ecommerce efforts.
Requirements	Offering fit-for-purpose digital products and services by obtaining accurate insights into customer expectations, selling at competitive prices, providing a premium customer experience, and rapid go-to-market are the primary requirements.

Evaluating Your Digital Operating Model

Next you extend the conversation to "How do these requirements impact the way we work?" You should make it clear to the audience that when offering digital products and services, the main revenue stream brings significant changes for which the company is ill prepared.

You should offer to discuss the challenges of your current digital product and service development lifecycle versus the industry disruption-related requirements with the following questions:

Focus on digital product and service development: Is your organization's product development lifecycle (PDLC) designed to support digital products and services development?

Build on accurate customer insights: How well does our PDLC address customer development?

Sell at competitive prices: What financial latitude do we have to be competitive in terms of pricing?

Offer premium customer experience: How well does our PDLC address customer experience issues?

Rapid go-to-market: How effective is our PDLC at accelerating development and delivery?

Table 3.2 summarizes the participant's answers to these questions.

Table 3.2: The Weaknesses of the Current Digital Product Lifecycle

INDUSTRY DISRUPTION REQUIREMENTS	WEAKNESSES OF THE CURRENT PDLC
Focus on digital product and service development	The current PDLC isn't suited for digital and service product development. It's a technology-centric software development Lifecycle (SDLC) for business application development.
Build on accurate customer insights	Customer insights are not formally addressed in the current PDLC. Most practices are improvised.
Sell at competitive prices	The expensive on-premises infrastructure supporting the existing PDLC prevents the company from being competitive in terms of pricing.
Offer premium customer experience	Same weakness as the requirement "Build on accurate customer insights." This prevents any customer experience improvement initiative.
Rapid go-to-market	Despite the adoption of agile mechanisms, the automated IT operations don't accelerate the company's time to market.

Evaluating Your Technical Platform

Continue the conversation with the essential issue of technology: "How suited is the current technology stack for addressing the supermarket industry disruption-related requirements?" Offer to address the challenges of the current technology stack through the following questions:

Focus on digital product development: Is the current technology stack suited to digital product development?

Build on accurate customer insights: Is our enterprise data infrastructure and model suited to getting accurate customer insights?

Sell at competitive prices: Does our on-premises total cost of ownership (TCO) provide latitude to sell at competitive prices?

Offer premium customer experience: Is our data warehouse infrastructure efficient enough for getting customer insights that help to improve customer experience?

Rapid go-to-market: Does our technology stack enable rapid go-to-market?

Table 3.3 summarizes the participant's answers to these questions.

Table 3.3: The Challenges of the Current Technology Stack

INDUSTRY DISRUPTION REQUIREMENTS	WEAKNESSES OF THE CURRENT TECHNOLOGY STACK
Focus on digital product and service development	In addition to being complex with disparate solutions, the current technology stack lacks essential technology like IoT, machine learning, big data, and more.
Build on accurate customer insights	Our on-premises data warehouse platform is suited to obtaining accurate customer insights. Adopting a big data solution in the cloud, like migrating our data warehouse to AWS, would make it significantly faster and cheaper.
Sell at competitive prices	Our on-premises IT infrastructure is expensive and doesn't provide latitude for selling at competitive prices. Migrating to a cloud solution like AWS would make it significantly cheaper and allow J&S to be competitive in terms of pricing.
Offer premium customer experience	Same solution as the requirement "Build on accurate customer insights."
Rapid go-to-market	The current application delivery solution doesn't allow the required rapid go-to-market. A continuous delivery solution in the cloud would not only simplify the delivery effort, but it would also make it faster and cheaper.

Evaluating Your Organizational Model

Making sure that your digital product development function works in harmony and efficiently with the rest of your organization is the next topic of the conversation.

Offer to the discuss these issues via the following questions:

Focus on digital product development: Is the current project matrix suited to digital product development?

Build in accurate customer insights: How can a customer development team fit into the existing digital product and service development group?

Sell at competitive prices: How can a digital business strategist team fit into the existing digital product development group?

Offer premium customer experience: How can a customer development team fit into the existing digital product and service team structure?

Rapid go-to-market: Are we sure that J&S's continuous integration and continuous delivery (CI/CD) experts are efficiently used?

Table 3.4 summarizes the participant's answers to these questions.

Table 3.4: The Challenges of the Current Organizational Model

INDUSTRY DISRUPTION REQUIREMENTS	WEAKNESSES OF THE CURRENT ORGANIZATIONAL MODEL
Focus on digital product and service development	Making the digital product development function a subfunction hidden behind application development is incompatible with its importance in the overall digital strategy. An independent digital product and service development function built on an agile philosophy, principles, and practices must be created.
Build on accurate customer insights	A customer development team cannot fit into the current digital product development group. Such a team will fit into the independent digital product development function to be created.
Sell at competitive prices	A digital business strategist team cannot fit into the current digital product development group. Such a team will fit into the independent digital product development function to be created.
Offer premium customer experience	Same weakness as the requirement "Build on accurate customer insights."
Rapid go-to-market	A CI/CD team cannot fit into the current digital product development group. Such a team will fit into the independent digital product development function to be created.

Assessing Your Human Capital

"How suited is our human capital for meeting the supermarket industry disruption-related requirements?" is the final question for the meeting participants. Offer to address the issue based on the supermarket industry disruption-related requirements:

Focus on digital product development: Overall, does J&S have the workforce required for the proposed digital business competition?

Build on accurate customer insights: Does J&S have the data science experts that can help them obtain customer insights?

Sell at competitive prices: What resources can help J&S with making their prices competitive?

Offer premium customer experience: What resources can help J&S with improving the customer experience?

Rapid go-to-market: What resources can help J&S with rapid go-to-market?

Table 3.5 summarizes the participant's answers to these questions.

Table 3.5: Human Capital Asset Challenges

INDUSTRY DISRUPTION REQUIREMENTS	WEAKNESSES OF THE CURRENT WORKFORCE
Focus on digital product development	The current workforce has no experience working in a digital business context. Building a digital business workforce is a priority.
Build on accurate customer insights	Data scientists, machine learning scientists, senior data architects, and business intelligence (BI) developers are missing. Hiring them or training existing staff to do these jobs is another priority.
Sell at competitive prices	Digital business strategists and social media marketing specialists are missing. Hiring them or training existing staff to these jobs is a priority.
Offer premium customer experience	Data scientists, machine learning scientists, senior data architects, and business intelligence (BI) developers are missing. Hiring them or training existing staff to these jobs is another priority.
Rapid go-to-market	Cloud solution architects, cloud engineers, and continuous integration and continuous delivery (CI/CD) engineers are missing.

Challenges of Current Digital Product Development

The case of Julienne & Simone Food highlights the challenges common to most companies seeking to go digital. It teaches us that surviving digital disruptions is no stroke of luck; it's about properly dealing with the five requirements, as shown in Figure 3.4.

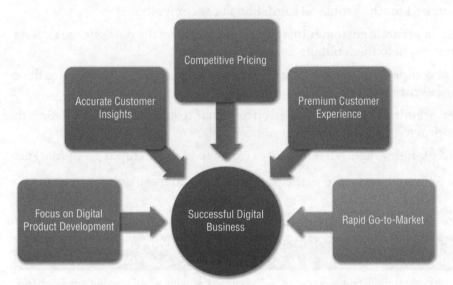

Figure 3.4: The five requirements model for a successful digital business

The five requirements model for a successful digital business is a model that determines the five pillars that businesses must successfully address to survive and prosper in the digital economy.

Focus on Digital Product and Service Development

The first of the requirements refers to the obvious notion that to survive and thrive in a digital disruption context, the first decision requires that the business focus on digital product and service development. The higher quality the digital products, the greater revenue.

Consumer habits are shifting to digital products and services because they make life easier and safer. Consequently, this makes developing and marketing these products and services one of your organization's primary revenue goals.

Accurate Customer Insights

A digital product's attractiveness is determined by the extent to which it meets consumer expectations. This makes customer development a strategic activity of your digital business. *Customer development* is the process of identifying potential customers and their expectations and figuring out how to meet them. A lot of companies spend the majority of time on their product and services but not enough on understanding the needs of customers. The more time and money that you spend on big data, machine learning, and data science, the more accurate customer insights you will gain, and the more attractive your digital product will be.

A company with a strong data science capacity is ideally equipped to survive and thrive in the disruptive digital economy.

Competitive Pricing

The next factor in the five requirements framework addresses the importance of pricing in your digital product and service competitiveness.

It's determined by the intensity of the competitive rivalry in your industry, how unique the features of your digital product and services are, and how much it would cost your company to develop and monetize them.

Competitive pricing makes big data, data science, and machine learning essential assets to surviving and thriving in the digital economy.

Premium Customer Experience

The ability to improve the customer experience continuously with your digital products and services is a strong competitive advantage. *Customer experience* refers to your customer's holistic perception of their experience with your business. It's the result of every interaction your customer has with your business, from navigating your website to talking to your customer service personnel and using your digital products and services. The better experience that customers have, the more they're likely to do business with your company and be repeat customers.

A company that has strong big data, data science, and machine learning capabilities is likely to improve the customer experience continuously and, as a result, survive and prosper in the disruptive digital economy.

Rapid Go-to-Market

The last of the five requirements focuses on the importance of accelerating your organization's time to market. Speedy delivery of high-quality digital products and services is a competitive advantage you can't neglect. Companies delivering high-quality digital products and services with fast time to market acquire more new customers and gain the loyalty of their existing customers.

Understanding the five requirements and how they make a digital business successful can help your company effectively go digital and generate substantial revenue.

Key Takeaways

At this point, you have fully entered the digital transformation world, learning its strategic, business, and technological fundamentals.

In Chapter 1, "The Digital Economy's Challenges, Opportunities, and Relevance of AWS," we elaborated on how the disruptive digital economy introduced new normals, including ecommerce, data science, and technological innovation. In addition to understanding the do's and don'ts of cloud computing, you also learned how Amazon Web Services (AWS) technologies were suited to help your organization take advantage of this new normal.

This chapter clarified the notion of digital product and service development. You learned about its fundamentals including the hybrid nature of today's practices, stage-gate principles, and elements of its ecosystem such as human factors, the PDLC, the organizational model, and the technology stack. I highlighted the use of two tools that will be part of your digital transformation practice: the assessment matrix for digital product platforms and the five requirements model for successful digital business.

In the next chapter, you will take a further step into the digital transformation discipline. You will learn about the lesser known yet important notion of industrialization of digital product development practices.

References

1   Linda Gorchels, "Product Management 2020," *LinkedIn* (January 22, 2020). https://www.linkedin.com/pulse/product-management-2020-linda-gorchels/?articleId=6625837990528761856

2   Kelsey Miller, "Eleven Data Science Careers Shaping Your Future," *Northeastern University* (June 04, 2020). https://www.northeastern.edu/graduate/blog/data-science-careers-shaping-our-future/

3   Anthony Marter, "Why we Need to Rethink Product Management in an Agile Practice," *Mind the Product* (June 04, 2020). `https://www.mindthe-product.com/why-we-need-to-rethink-product-management-in-an-agile-practice/`

4   Robert G. Cooper, Soren Kielgast, Tomas Vedsmand, "Integrating Agile with Stage-Gate: How New Agile-Scrum Methods Leads to Faster and Better Innovation," *Innovation Management* (August 26, 2016). `https://innovationmanagement.se/2016/08/09/integrating-agile-with-stage-gate/`
.

Industrializing Digital Product and Service Development

The First Industrial Revolution used water and steam power to mechanize production. The Second used electric power to create mass production. The Third used electronics and information technology to automate production.

—Klaus Schwab

Digital products and services are becoming part of the business revenue stream. This requires that their development approach guarantees not only rapid go-to-market but also reliability and quality. That's the purpose of the digital product and service development platform industrialization. While there are many ways to achieve the platform industrialization, the safest one is the strict application of relevant principles and practices of what is known as *mass production* (*MP*) techniques, particularly those of the assembly line. Make no mistake, these techniques are the foundation of software development approaches as widespread as continuous integration and continuous deployment, and most importantly, DevOps. Businesses must make them the basis of their digital product and service development platform.

After recounting the influence of Total Quality Management and mass production techniques on today's software development approaches, this chapter defines the notion of digital product and service development platform industrialization and shows you how to build on industrialization factors to implement DevOps as the digital product and service development platform. It then focuses on how industrialization factors are implemented using advanced AWS services and architectures.

The Total Quality Management and Mass Production Heritage

Make no mistake, without an industrial approach to digital product and service development, expecting success is wishful thinking; optimizing every single activity by automating tasks, using proven practices and methodologies, and relying on highly skilled staff are what it takes.

In this section, we'll discuss the foundations of the lesser known, yet essential, digital product and service development platform industrialization including Total Quality Management and mass production techniques.

What you must know is that Total Quality Management and mass production techniques have inspired dozens of industrial manufacturing and management approaches. Six Sigma, agile, continuous integration and continuous delivery, and DevOps are recent examples.

These techniques provide the insights needed to properly automate your development process, organize your development effort, and optimize your staff interactions and collaborations. Let's discuss them now.

Total Quality Management Principles Defined

Total Quality Management (TQM) is a management approach that provides the quality assurance that customers will get what they expect. From that perspective, TQM is in line with the idea that to succeed in the digital business, digital product and service development must shift its focus from product and technology to consumer concerns.

TQM is focused on the improvement of quality and performance in all functions, departments, and processes throughout the organization to provide services that exceed customer expectations.

The industrialization of the digital product and service development process draws on six of the eight TQM principles; they're needed to implement digital product and service development ecosystems that guarantee competitive digital products and services. The following sections sum up the information you should know about them.

Customer Focus

The belief behind this principle is the notion that the safest way to make your digital product and service profitable is to develop them based on functions and features expected by customers. This implies the existence of a data science culture, big data solutions, and infrastructure within your organization.

Workforce Commitment

This represents the idea that your staff workforce, skills, knowledge, and creativity play a vital role in your digital product and service attractiveness and profitability. This assumes the existence of staff policy, tools, and infrastructure for your digital development platform that creates the highest possible productivity.

Process Approach

The trust behind this principle is the notion that formalizing your organization's work procedures via a documented series of steps and decisions increases productivity. This means a total adherence of your organization's staff to your process and practice requirements for your digital product and service development platform to succeed.

Integrated System

The belief underpinning this principle is that the proper interconnection of your organization's departments and functions is a solid basis to succeed. This means that your digital product and service development platform must be understood as an ecosystem of people, processes, best practices, tools, and infrastructure, which is not narrowly limited to a technology stack.

Continual Improvement

This principle teaches that making customers happy by meeting their expectations isn't achieved in one day. This implies that for your digital development platform to succeed, the existence of policies, tools, and infrastructure are necessary for digital product and service development continuous improvement.

Transversal Communication

This principle underscores the need for everybody in the company to be on the same page on critical issues such as strategies, priorities, processes, and methodologies. This entails the existence of agile operational and organizational models for your digital product and service development platform that increase cross-functional collaboration and interactions effectiveness.

Mass Production Principles Defined

Mass production refers to the manufacture of large quantities of standardized goods by an automated mechanical process. It builds on automation or assembly lines to facilitate the high-volume production of similar products. The industrialization process draws on three principles of mass production to meet the requirements of the digital business. These include an assembly line, work specialization, and automation.

Assembly Line

Mass production involves several *assembly lines* where staff with various profiles perform routine tasks and one specific job. Examples include the assembly of complex products like automobiles, transportation equipment, and electronic goods where the worker is assigned a repeatable task and where the process moves to the next worker who performs another task until the product is completed.

Work Specialization

Work specialization, also known as *division of labor*, refers to the extent to which a company divides individual tasks into separate jobs. An example would be how adopting software continuous delivery would consolidate the division of your application delivery process into five jobs including software development, continuous integration (CI) testing, user acceptance testing (UAT), operational acceptance testing (OAT), and continuous deployment (CD).

Automation

Automation, referred to in this book as an *automated product line*, is a system of interconnected workstations designed to monitor and control the production and delivery of digital products and services. The perfect example would be how the AWS CodePipeline platform automates an organization's software continuous delivery processes from integration testing to stage testing and deployment to production.

Industrialization Factors

TQM and MP have in common the fact that they leverage a variety of optimization enablers referred to in this book as industrialization factors.

Industrialization Factor Defined

An *industrialization factor* is a belief, principle, best practice, methodology, tool, or infrastructure recognized for creating the conditions for the rapid delivery of quality digital products and services. It's not only about automation and speed, but it is also about customer expectations including fit-for-purpose and reliability.

Industrialization factors impact various aspects of your digital product and service development platform performance. Examples include the impacts on your development team's collaboration, on your staff's productivity, and on the agility of your digital product and service development process. Let's discuss the industrialization factor families that you will deal with across your company's digital transformation.

Families of Industrialization Factors

Bear in mind that industrialization factors are organized into four families including Principles, Design Patterns, Methodologies, and Technologies. Figure 4.1 illustrates the industrialization factor families:

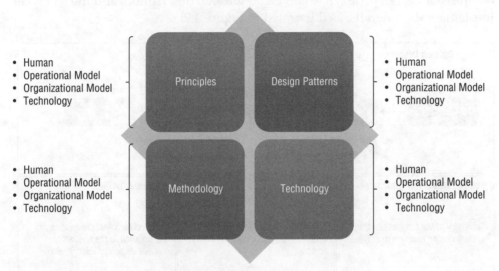

Figure 4.1: Overview of the industrialization factor families

As you can see, each family addresses at least one performance enabler of your digital product and service development platform including Human, Operational Model, Organizational Model, and Technology. Let's discuss them.

Principles Family

A *principle* represents a fundamental truth or proposition that serves as the foundation for a system of belief. This means that principles influence the way that people understand and analyze situations. More importantly, they guide the decisions that people make and the actions that they take.

For instance, the TQM principle, Customer Focus, illustrates the value of principles. It states a fact that is commonly admitted: The safest way to make a product profitable is to develop it based on functions and features expected by customers. It also suggests the decision to invest in big data solutions and the action to implement a data science team.

The information to keep in mind here is that principles are powerful systems design tools. By suggesting solutions, decisions to make, and actions to take, they accelerate systems design and implementation.

Design Patterns Family

A *design pattern* is a reusable solution to a commonly known problem, not only in software development but also in a variety of business areas including organizational design, team development, and cloud architecture.

Four elements characterize design patterns including the pattern diagram, the business or design problem to solve, the solution description, and the technical implementation details, as illustrated in Figure 4.2.

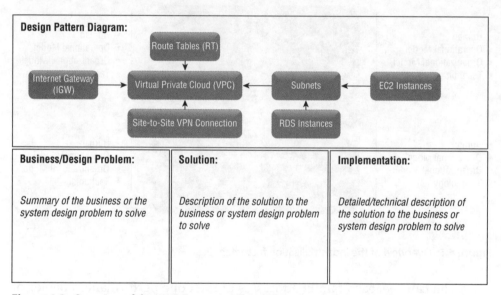

Figure 4.2: Overview of the AWS Enterprise Cloud Migration design pattern

The important point is that, just like principles, design patterns offer reusable solutions to commonly known business problems and help to accelerate systems design and implementation.

Methodology Family

Methodologies are frameworks combining assumptions, reasonings, rules, and tools designed to make it easier to solve a problem or address a complex issue. Table 4.1 summarizes the methodologies identified as industrialization factors that your transformation team will address.

Table 4.1: The Methodologies Identified as Industrialization Factors

METHODOLOGY FAMILY	DESCRIPTION
Software development	Software development methodologies include software architecture approaches as well as IoT, ML, and data science architectural and implementation frameworks.
Software testing	Software testing methodologies include frameworks for designing automated unit, user, and operational acceptance testing processes.
Continuous integration and delivery	Continuous integration methodologies include frameworks for designing continuous integration, delivery, and deployment processes.
Operations	Operations methodologies include IT operations frameworks of best practices and continuous improvement frameworks.

Always make sure that your industrialization team relies on proven methodologies; the structured approaches they offer accelerate complex systems design and implementation.

Technology Family

Technology covers all of the information technology tools and infrastructure used to support your digital product and service development platform. Table 4.2 sums up the technologies identified as industrialization factors that your transformation team will tackle.

Table 4.2: Technologies Identified as Industrialization Factors

TECHNOLOGY FAMILY	DESCRIPTION
Software development	Software development technologies include software implementation tools as well as IoT, ML, and data science architectural and implementation tools.
Software testing	Software testing technologies include automation solutions for unit, user acceptance, and operational acceptance testing tools.
Continuous integration and delivery	Continuous integration technologies include automation solutions for continuous integration, delivery, and deployment.
Operations	Operations technologies involve system, application, and infrastructure monitoring solutions including artificial intelligence (AI) driven monitoring tools.

Technology is essential to the automation of your digital product and service development platform.

Understanding DevOps as the Framework for Implementing Your Digital Product and Service Development Platform

In today's information technology practice, implementing DevOps is seen as the safest and fastest way to implement an industrialized digital product and service development platform.

DevOps is consistent with the requirements of digital product and service development platforms as defined in Chapter 3, "Digital Product and Service Development Challenges." They're both structured around a delivery lifecycle enabled by a technology stack and supplemented by operational and organizational best practices.

This section discusses the key concepts to know about DevOps and how the industrialization factors help to implement it as an industrialized digital product and service development platform.

DevOps Defined

DevOps represents the combination of software development (Dev) and IT operations (Ops) practices and tools designed to increase your organization's ability to deliver applications and services faster. DevOps seeks to accelerate your organization's software delivery lifecycle while providing high-quality software.

DevOps achieves that goal by removing the barriers between siloed development and operations teams so that they work together across the software delivery lifecycle and by automating tasks across the software delivery lifecycle.

Understanding DevOps Components

The best way to understand DevOps is to rely on a framework that highlights the means to achieve its objectives including people, processes, practices, and tools. Figure 4.3 gives an overview of a standard DevOps platform.

As illustrated, the key DevOps components include the software delivery lifecycle, toolchain, people, practices, and methodologies. Let's explore them.

Software Delivery Lifecycle's Importance

The *software delivery lifecycle (SDLC)* is primarily a vision of how your IT department organizes the software delivery effort. The SDLC seeks to optimize your organization's software delivery effort in terms of faster and higher volumes of software releases.

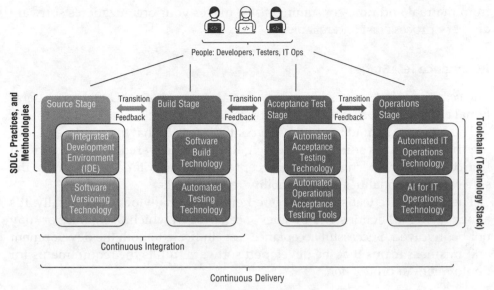

Figure 4.3: Functional overview of a standard DevOps platform

As Figure 4.3 illustrates, the SDLC is consistent with the division of labor popularized by assembly line mechanisms; it splits the software delivery effort into smaller and sequential steps including Source, Build, Acceptance Test, and Operations.

Source Stage

The *source stage* is where your organization's continuous delivery process starts. It's where changes to software sources are tracked, stored, versioned, and made available for the build stage. In addition, other checks such as automated code quality tests and code syntax reviews are carried out at this step.

The rationale underpinning this stage is that, by relieving your developers from the hassles of managing software versions, it not only makes them more productive and creative, but it also speeds up delivery and increases the number of releases that your organization can deploy.

Build Stage

The *build stage*, also known as *continuous integration stage*, is where automating the integration of the multiple code changes from your development team is carried out into a single and consistent release. It includes automated code compilation, integration, unit testing, and functional testing.

The logic behind this phase is that frequently testing the software early in the development lifecycle, and more importantly relieving your developers from manual and time-consuming tasks, makes your organization's software delivery process fast and reliable.

Acceptance Test Stage

The *acceptance test stage* is where the user acceptance tests (UATs) and operational acceptance tests (OATs) are performed.

The rationale behind the automation of these tests is that the end-to-end testing they provide is suited for rapidly getting the delivered software verified from the user perspective and later accepted based on criteria derived from the software functionalities and operability requirements.

The acceptance test step is triggered either manually or automatically. It's about trying all actions and business scenarios in which users may or may not be involved. Successful acceptance tests indicate to both the development and business teams that the developed software fulfills the requirements for deployment in production.

Operations Stage

The *operations stage* is not only where your organization's applications are operated and made available to users or customers, but it is also where, via continuous improvement practices, user and customer feedback is provided to continuously improve the conditions for successful software development, testing, deployment, and operations.

The operations stage refers to the Ops in DevOps. It includes processes as important as infrastructure provisioning, monitoring and control of applications, disaster recovery management, and compliance and security.

DevOps Practices Purpose

Each stage of the software delivery lifecycle is associated with best practices. These practices are factors that enable the achievement of the DevOps approach's objectives including a faster delivery of an ever-increasing number of software releases.

These practices vary according to companies and industries. In general, six of these practices are considered essential. The following sections discuss the key points that you need to know about them.

Understanding Agile Project Management

Agile project management is an iterative approach to managing software development projects. This approach uses iteration, collaboration, continuous integration, continuous delivery, and continuous improvement as factors for achieving the objectives of DevOps.

Bear in mind that these five factors create the conditions for faster development and deployment of high-quality software releases.

Understanding Shift Left

Shift left is a practice intended to identify software defects early in the delivery lifecycle. The bottom line is to improve quality and achieve production-ready releases by moving as many tasks as possible to the left in the software delivery lifecycle. This practice is the foundation of the continuous integration process.

By putting together and automating early in the software delivery process, particularly in the build stage tasks as critical as code compilation, integration, unit testing, and functional testing, the shift left practice allows your organization not only to save development and testing costs, but also to accelerate its time to market.

Understanding Automation

Automation is the process of replacing manual intervention and repeatable processes by software and systems that accelerate application delivery. The important point is that by simplifying the software delivery effort, automation increases your development team's productivity and allows your organization to meet the DevOps speed and high release rate objectives.

Understanding the Value of Infrastructure as Code

Infrastructure as code (IaC) is about managing and provisioning infrastructure resources via software code instead of manual and repeatable processes. IaC is based on configuration files that specify the features of the infrastructure to provision or upgrade. These files use descriptive languages like YAML Ain't Markup Language (YAML) and JavaScript Object Notation (JSON) to instruct your IaC system on how to generate the expected infrastructure.

Keep in mind that automation and infrastructure as code go hand in hand. IaC enables automation. It allows your operations team to create easy and reusable procedures that deploy virtual servers, launch databases, and configure network infrastructure, storage systems, and load balancers.

Continuous Delivery

Continuous delivery is the ongoing practice of building, testing, and delivering new software releases using automation. Continuous delivery differs from continuous deployment in that, in the latter, every change that passes the build and acceptance test stages is systematically deployed to a production environment and made available to users.

As illustrated in Figure 4.3, continuous delivery extends the build stage. It automatically deploys all code changes to the acceptance test environment and then to a production environment where applications are made available to customers.

Continuous delivery is a DevOps fundamental practice. It aggregates software version control, continuous integration, and acceptance test requirements into a coherent practice for accelerating software delivery.

Continuous Improvement

Continuous improvement is a practice whose objective is to create a culture where anyone in your development team can make improvement recommendations in areas as important as software development, software architecture, testing, deployment, and operations.

Continuous improvement is based on feedback loops, illustrated in Figure 4.3 by the left-arrow labeled feedback. *Feedback loops* are mechanisms where your organization's software delivery stakeholders receive ongoing feedback and share the identified strengths and weaknesses to improve specific practices.

The important point to keep in mind is that by gradually making your organization's software development processes efficient, increasing your products and services competitiveness, and establishing a proactive learning culture, continuous improvement mechanisms ensure the delivery of high-quality software and digital products and services. Continuous improvement is an essential practice.

Methodologies Benefit

Every stage of the software delivery lifecycle is supported by one or more methodologies. The bottom line is to provide the logic and the structured approach needed to address the challenges of software development, software architecture, testing, deployment, and operations.

Among the many methodologies that are used in DevOps, three stand out including Scrum, Extreme Programming (XP), and Kanban. Let's discuss them.

Understanding XP Benefits

Extreme Programming (XP) is an agile software development methodology whose primary objective is the delivery of high-quality software while making the development team responsive to a customer's changing requirements. Although XP is not often cited as a major DevOps component, it provides principles and practices of value including continuous integration, continuous delivery, continuous deployment, and test-driven development (TDD) (see Figure 4.4).

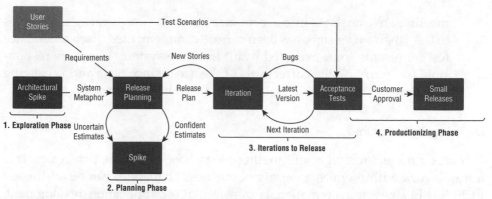

Figure 4.4: Overview of XP development lifecycle

Source: Lucidchart

The XP development process is based on the principle of iterative cycles. Each cycle consists of four essential steps including Exploration, Planning, Iterations to Release, and Productionizing. Let's discuss them.

Exploration   This is where users and customers specify sets of user stories defining the project scope. User stories are informal explanations of the features and functions expected from the software. They're written from the business perspective.

Planning   This is where your development team and the users, also known as the *stakeholders*, are involved in the planning game for two-session planning meetings including release planning and iteration planning. The objective is to create a release plan used to create an iteration plan.

Release Planning   Here your development team estimates the size of each story, acknowledges their priority and expected value, and then decides on the course of action based on the team capacity. A release encompasses the next one to two months of work.

Iteration Planning   This happens in the same or another meeting to produce the iteration's plan of programming tasks. Each iteration lasts between one and three weeks, and it is broken down into programming tasks. User stories intended to be part of the iteration are selected by users from the release plan based on their priority. Acceptance tests are also selected and broken down into testing tasks.

Iterations to Release   This is where your development team launches into a series of weekly programming cycles. Each weekly cycle starts with a meeting involving the developers and stakeholders to decide which stories will be delivered during the week. Stories are then broken down into tasks to complete at the end of the week. Developers and stakeholders then review progress and decide whether the expected benefits have been delivered.

Productionizing   In this phase, acceptance tests are created from user stories. During an iteration, the user stories selected during the iteration planning meeting are translated into acceptance tests. The user specifies scenarios to test when a user story has been correctly implemented. Each acceptance test represents some expected result from the system. Users are responsible for verifying the correctness of the acceptance tests and reviewing test scores to decide which failed tests are of highest priority.

Defining Agile Scrum

Scrum is a project management methodology based on agile principles. It is a framework within which a variety of business challenges can be addressed including business transformation, IT transformation, application development, and of course digital product and service development.

Scrum is based on the belief that to deliver the maximum business value, your organization's software development capability must consist of six principles including empirical process control, self-organization, collaboration, value-based prioritization, timeboxing, and iterative development. Here are the implications of these principles.

Control Over the Empirical Process   This relates to the practice of making decisions based on observation and experience rather than on detailed planning and documentation. It values transparency, inspection, and adaptation.

Self-Organization   This is the practice of letting the team choose what is the best to accomplish the work rather than directing them on how to plan and perform their activities.

Collaboration   This process encourages the team members to work together and interface with stakeholders to create and validate the project deliverables and meet the project objectives.

Value-Based Prioritization   This is the process for determining what must be done now, and what can wait until a later date.

Timeboxing   The bottom line is to define and limit the amount of time dedicated to an activity. It helps to spot open-ended or ambiguous tasks.

Iterative Development   This process breaks down the development of large software applications into smaller chunks. With this principle, feature code is designed, developed, and tested in repeated cycles.

To implement these principles and deliver high-quality software and products and bring the highest value to customers, Scrum offers the framework illustrated in Figure 4.5.

As Figure 4.5 illustrates, Scrum is based on a delivery lifecycle structured around five elements including product backlog, sprint backlog, daily scrums, review, and retrospective. Let's discuss them.

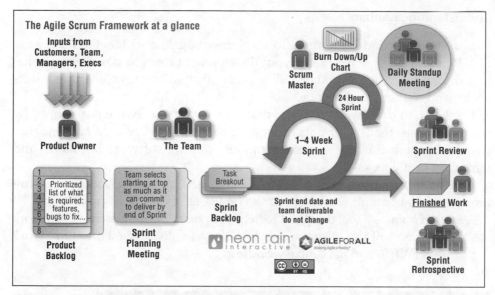

Figure 4.5: Scrum Agile software development lifecycle

Source: Neon Rain Interactive

Product backlog planning is where the Scrum project starts. The product backlog is a prioritized features list containing short descriptions of all the functionality expected from the software. It's the source of all the requirements for your development team.

The *sprint backlog* is the set of items your development team and stakeholders select from the product backlog to work on during the upcoming iteration, or *sprint* in scrum terminology.

A *sprint* represents the basic unit of software development in Scrum. It's developed in sprint planning sessions involving the product owner acting as application owner on the business side, the scrum master acting as the facilitator of the development effort, and the team including developers, testers, and operations. It lasts between one and four weeks.

Activities in a sprint include coding, unit testing, and acceptance and operational testing using XP practices as varied as TDD, continuous integration, continuous testing, and continuous delivery.

A *daily scrum* is a 15-minute meeting involving the development team to discuss progress toward the sprint goals and adapt the sprint backlog as necessary.

A *sprint review* is a meeting held at the end of a sprint where your development team, the product owner, and the scrum master inspect the release delivered during the last sprint and update the product backlog.

Retrospective is a formal meeting at the end of the sprint where the development team discusses their performance and the ways to improve it. A sprint retrospective is part your organization's continuous improvement approach.

Understanding Kanban

Kanban is a methodology used to implement agile and DevOps software development. Its goal is to allow your development team to visualize and analyze the software development and delivery effort at any time, identify bottlenecks, and maximize efficiency.

The Kanban driving principle is that high-quality software is achieved by using a system that continuously seeks to reduce delivery time and enhance customer satisfaction by smoothening out ongoing software initiatives and removing bottlenecks.

Kanban is structured around four key concepts including board, card, columns, swimlanes, and work in progress (WIP), as shown in Figure 4.6.

A *Kanban board* is a tool designed to help your development team depict work at various stages of the software delivery lifecycle, visualize work, limit work in progress (WIP), and maximize workflow.

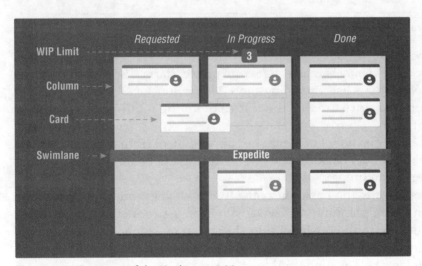

Figure 4.6: Overview of the Kanban activities

Source: Kanbanize.com

The *Kanban card* represents work items and helps your development team members communicate and share work items' status as they move through the workflow.

Kanban columns represent different stages of your workflow. The Kanban board has three columns including To Do, Doing, and Done. The To Do column contains all the cards that are next up, the Doing column contains all the cards on which your development team is currently working, and the Done column contains the cards that have been completed.

WIP represents the work items on which your development team is currently working. Its purpose is to frame the capacity of your team's workflow and allow it to manage software delivery in a way that creates a smooth workflow and prevents overloads.

Kanban Swimlanes are horizontal lanes used to separate different activities, teams, and classes of services.

DevOps Toolchain Importance

Also known as the *DevOps technology stack*, the *DevOps toolchain* is the combination of tools that support development, testing, deployment, and operations across the software delivery lifecycle.

As illustrated in Figure 4.3, the tools underpinning the software delivery lifecycle are organized into four categories including version control, continuous integration, acceptance testing automation, and infrastructure continuous monitoring. Let's discuss them.

Version Control Systems

Version control systems (VCSs) enable the source stage of the DevOps SDLC. VCSs are software tools that help your development teams manage changes to source code over time. A VCS's primary functions include keeping track of every modification to the code, organizing and controlling code revisions, and coordinating developer works.

In terms of the tools available on the market, AWS provides a versioning mechanism via its Simple Storage Service (S3) services. When enabled, S3 allows your development team to store, retrieve, and restore every version of every file automatically including source code in S3 buckets.

Additional VCS tools in which you might want to invest include Git, Concurrent Version Systems (CVS), and Apache Subversion (SVN). These VCS platforms are widely discussed in the J&S Food case study in Chapters 7–10.

Continuous Integration Platforms

Continuous integration platforms enable the build stage of the software delivery lifecycle. As the name suggests, the first goal of these platforms is to orchestrate the automation mechanisms for continuously building and testing your development team software projects.

Continuous integration platforms facilitate the automation of the parts of the software delivery lifecycle related to the build stage including code compilation, code integration, unit testing, functional testing, and deployment to acceptance test environment.

Three CI tools you might consider include Jenkins, TeamCity, and Bamboo from Atlassian. We will discuss these platforms throughout the J&S Food case study in Chapters 7–10.

Acceptance Test Automation Systems

Acceptance test automation systems enable the acceptance stage of the software delivery lifecycle. The main purpose of these systems is to provide business testers with the environment they need to design, develop, execute, and report their test scenarios and scripts.

Three acceptance testing automation tool options that you might consider include Selenium from Selenium, IBM Rational Functional Tester (RFT), and TestComplete from SmartBear. These systems are widely discussed and evaluated throughout the J&S Food case study in Chapters 7–10.

Infrastructure Continuous Monitoring Platforms

Continuous monitoring platforms enable the operations stage of the software delivery lifecycle. The primary goal of these platforms is to help your organization track, identify, understand your key infrastructure metrics, fix issues in real time, and suggest improvement recommendations

As to continuous monitoring platforms available on the market, Amazon offers CloudWatch. It's a system that collects monitoring and operational data in the form of logs and metrics that your operations staff can visualize using automated dashboards.

Two additional continuous monitoring platforms you might also consider include Nagios and Splunk from Splunk Inc. We will discuss these platforms throughout the J&S Food case study in Chapters 7–10.

AWS Industrialization Factors

Many AWS services, features, and architectural options are considered industrialization factors. They're used to optimize digital product and service development platforms.

The following sections discuss two categories of AWS industrialization factors and explain how these factors contribute to designing and implementing reliable digital product and service development platforms.

Understanding AWS Design Patterns: The Enterprise Cloud Migration Pattern

The *AWS Cloud Design Pattern* family is a collection of reusable solutions designed to address business and technology issues involving the AWS cloud. The primary purpose of the AWS design patterns family is to provide reusable solutions intended to accelerate the cloud architecture design and implementation processes.

This section focuses on the Enterprise Cloud Migration design patterns.

Defining AWS Enterprise Cloud Migration Pattern

The *Enterprise Cloud Migration (ECM) pattern* is a cloud architecture framework designed to guide, facilitate, and accelerate the implementation of AWS cloud environments.

Designed and popularized by the author of this book, the ECM pattern is based on the belief that using infrastructure as code to implement predefined enterprise cloud architecture models is the safest and fastest way to achieve a fully operational AWS enterprise cloud.

In this book, enterprise cloud refers to a unified computing environment combining as needed a public cloud, private cloud, and on-premises infrastructure designed to provide a single point of control for managing your organization's infrastructure and applications. Figure 4.7 gives an overview of the AWS ECM pattern:

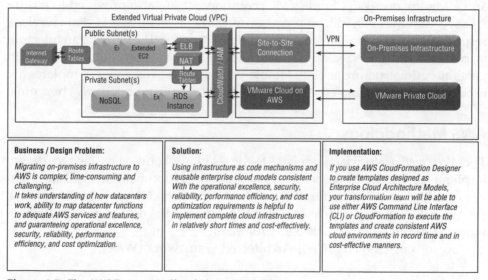

Figure 4.7: The AWS Enterprise Cloud Migration pattern

As illustrated, the AWS ECM pattern is composed of four elements including the baseline architecture, the business or design problem to solve, the solution to the problem, and the feature of the solution implementation. Let's discuss the baseline architecture.

Understanding the Baseline Architecture Purpose

To help your transformation team reduce implementation time, the ECM pattern offers an architecture baseline that is common to all AWS enterprise cloud architectures. The baseline sees the AWS enterprise cloud architecture through two building blocks: Extended Virtual Private Cloud (VPC) and On-Premises Infrastructure.

The *Extended VPC block*, a concept specific to the ECM pattern, is an aggregation of the AWS services and features. It's essential to building enterprise clouds. It includes the Internet Gateway that provides Internet access between your environment and the EC2 instances via route tables and public subnets. It also uses private subnets to secure data by preventing Internet access to the RDS instances and to all data storage devices under its control via a Network Address Translation (NAT) gateway. It finally leverages CloudWatch events and alarms that help to monitor the overall platform.

In addition to the authentication and authorization functions enabled via the Identity and Access Management (IAM) service, the Site-to-Site VPN connections and VMware on AWS Cloud (VMC) components are also provided to ensure robust communication with on-premises infrastructures and hybrid cloud services, respectively, involving VMware private cloud services. The baseline architecture is modeled using AWS CloudFormation Designer, a graphic tool that helps to generate infrastructure as code templates. The CloudFormation templates are executed to create complete AWS cloud environments in a relatively short time.

AWS Methodology

The *AWS methodology* family relates to the set of methodologies used to design, implement, and deploy either your AWS cloud environment or applications in your AWS cloud. The bottom line of the AWS methodology is to provide the framework, logic, approach, and tricks to simplify the design and implementation of solutions for the AWS environment.

Now let's discuss AWS Well-Architected Framework (WAF).

Defining AWS Well-Architected Framework

The *AWS Well-Architected Framework* is a structured approach for creating secure, high-performing, resilient, and efficient cloud infrastructure for applications. It is a library of architectural best practices structured around five pillars for designing, implementing, and operating reliable, secure, efficient, and cost-effective systems in the cloud.

These pillars are operational excellence, security, reliability, performance efficiency, and cost optimization, and they are associated with design principles from which best practices are derived. Let's discuss them.

Operational Excellence

Operational excellence is the first pillar of the framework. The concern in this area of focus is not only to make sure that your business takes advantage of the AWS cloud benefits, but also to ensure that the conditions for even more AWS benefits are continuously met.

The AWS benefits in question include high business value, secure and reliable applications, efficient operations, and innovation. Table 4.3 sums up the operational excellence design principles, their promised value, and derived best practice focuses.

Table 4.3: Operational Excellence Design Principles, Promised Value, and Derived Best Practice Focuses

DESIGN PRINCIPLE	PROMISED VALUE	BEST PRACTICE FOCUS
Perform operations as code	Managing infrastructure using infrastructure as code results in agile, efficient, and fast IT operations.	Operations planning, measuring, and improvements
Make frequent, small, reversible changes	Making infrastructure incremental changes prevents the deterioration of your staff experience with AWS cloud.	Operations measuring and improvement
Refine operations procedures frequently	Continuously improving procedures increases your organization's operations agility, efficiency, and speed.	Operations measuring and improvement
Anticipate failure	Regularly measuring your infrastructure failure scenarios results in proactive problem solving.	Operations measuring and improvement
Learn from all operational failures	Sharing across your organization's lessons learned from failures results in mature operations.	Operations improvement

Security

Security is the second pillar of the framework. Its focus is the use of risk assessments and mitigation strategies to protect data, applications, and infrastructure in your AWS cloud while delivering business value.

The security best practices cover areas including identity and access management, detective controls, infrastructure protection, data protection, and incident response. Table 4.4 sums up the security design principles, promised value, and derived best practices focuses.

Table 4.4: Security Design Principles, Promised Value, and Derived Best Practice Focuses

DESIGN PRINCIPLE	PROMISED VALUE	BEST PRACTICE FOCUS
Implement a strong identity foundation	Applying premium authorization and authentication mechanisms provides highly secure access control to your AWS resources.	Identity and access management
Enable traceability	The extensive use of log management practices and tools results in the capability to simplify security analysis, resource change tracking, and troubleshooting.	Infrastructure protection
Apply security at all layers	Holistic security approach integrating all elements designed to safeguard your infrastructure, protecting against all attacks.	Infrastructure protection
Automate security best practices	Implementing security controls based on infrastructure as code mechanisms provides highly secure architectures.	Infrastructure protection
Protect data in transit and at rest	Securing network and Internet traffic using mechanisms such as encryption and tokenization ensures effective access controls.	Data protection
Keep people away from data	Applying mechanisms that eliminate the need for direct access to data results in less loss and alteration of sensitive data.	Data protection
Prepare security for security events	Running security incident response simulations based on automation tools increases your organization's ability for rapid detection, investigation, and recovery.	Detective controls

Reliability

The area of focus of the *reliability* pillar is ensuring your AWS cloud and applications resilience through fault tolerance mechanisms. The reliability best practices cover areas including foundational requirements that impact your AWS cloud and applications reliability, change management, and failure management. Table 4.5 sums up the reliability design principles, promised value, and derived best practices focuses.

Table 4.5: Reliability Design Principles, Promised Value, and Derived Best Practice Focuses

DESIGN PRINCIPLE	PROMISED VALUE	BEST PRACTICE FOCUS
Test recovery procedure	Using automation to simulate different scenarios that lead to failures results in robust recovery systems.	Failure management
Automatically recover from failure	Relying on automatic notification and tracking of failure systems that trigger automated recovery processes, increasing your AWS platform reliability.	Failure management
Scale horizontally to increase aggregate system availability	Replacing large resources with multiple resources to reduce the impact of a single failure on the overall system increases your AWS platform reliability.	Failure management
Stop guessing capacity	Relying on mechanisms that monitor system utilization and automate the addition or removal of resources increases your AWS platform reliability.	Change management
Manage change in automation	Using automation and infrastructure as code to change or update your infrastructure is the safest way to keep your AWS platform reliable.	Change management

Performance Efficiency

The focus of the *performance efficiency* pillar is how well your organization takes advantage of the AWS computing resources to support the business objectives continuously and effectively. Performance efficiency best practices cover areas including selection of architectural options, review of architectural options for continual improvement purpose, monitoring of systems and applications, and trade-offs to ensure an effective architecture approach. Table 4.6 sums up the performance efficiency design principles, promised value, and derived best practices focuses.

Cost Optimization

The *cost optimization* area of concern is how your organization can take advantage of AWS cost-effective pricing options to deliver business value. Cost optimization best practices cover areas including expenditure awareness, cost effective

Table 4.6: Performance Efficiency Design Principles, Promised Value, and Derived Best Practice Focuses

DESIGN PRINCIPLE	PROMISED VALUE	BEST PRACTICE FOCUS
Democratized advanced technologies	Relying on as a service and managed solutions to take advantage of advanced technologies increases your team productivity.	Selection of architectural options
Go global in minutes	Adopting multiregion deployment results in low-latency AWS platforms and a better AWS experience for your team and customers.	Selection of architectural options
Use serverless architectures	Using serverless architectures not only removes the hassles of managing servers, but it also lowers operations costs.	Selection of architectural options
Experiment more often	Taking advantage of AWS virtual and automatable resources to perform comparative testing results in architectural choices that guarantee performance efficiency.	Review of architectural options for continual improvement purpose
Mechanical sympathy	Aligning your technology investment to your business objectives increases AWS platforms performance efficiency.	Trade-offs to ensure architecture effective approach

resources, matching supply and demand, and optimizing over time. Table 4.7 sums up the cost optimization design principles, their promised value, and derived best practices focuses.

You'll find detailed prescriptive guidance on design and implementation on the AWS Well-Architected Framework website.

Understanding the Industrialization Matrix for AWS

Industrializing a digital product and service development platform for the AWS environment is challenging. It's about planning, designing, and implementing your AWS cloud environment making complex architectural choices and then migrating your workload.

The following sections discuss the key information that you need to know about the AWS architecting process and the industrialization matrix.

Overview of the Industrialization Matrix for AWS

The industrialization matrix for AWS is a cloud migration framework designed to make the AWS cloud architecting process easy, effective, and fast (see Figure 4.8).

Table 4.7: Cost Optimization Design Principles, Promised Value, and Derived Best Practice Focuses

DESIGN PRINCIPLE	PROMISED VALUE	BEST PRACTICE FOCUS
Adopt a consumption model	Adopting a pay-as-you-go (PAYG) model can significantly help your organization cut its IT spending.	Expenditure awareness
Measure overall efficiency	Using measures like return on investment (ROI) to assess your AWS platform contribution to your business can help your organization adjust its spending.	Expenditure awareness
Stop spending money on data centers	Adopting cloud computing not only helps cut your IT spending, but it also helps your organization focus more on its customers.	Cost-effective resources
Analyze and attribute expenditure	Using measures like return on investment (ROI) and total cost of ownership (TCO) helps to understand your IT spending.	Optimizing over time
Use managed ad application-level services to reduce TCO	Using managed and application-level services not only removes the hassles of managing infrastructure, but it also offers lower costs.	Matching supply and demand

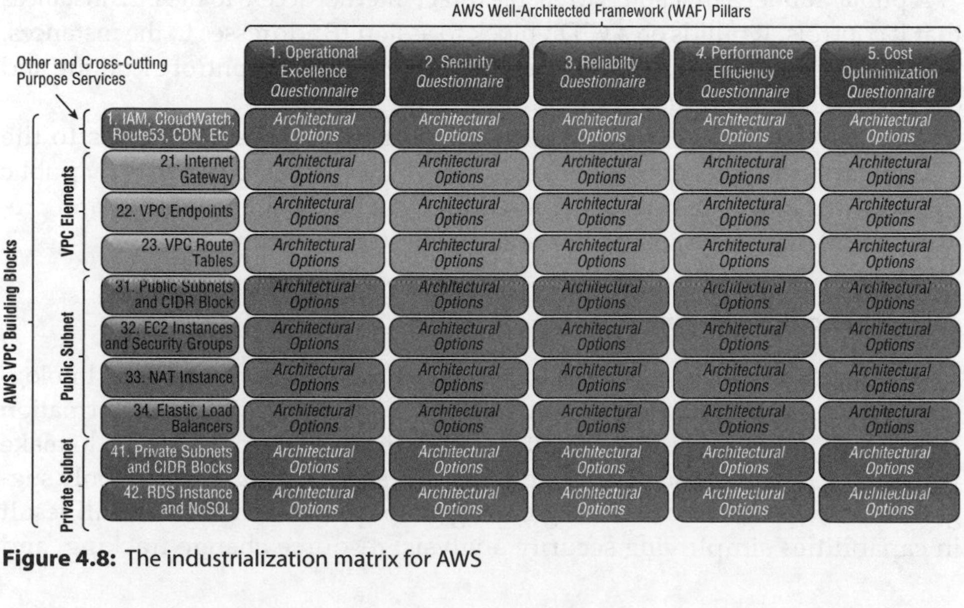

Figure 4.8: The industrialization matrix for AWS

The industrialization matrix combines the Well-Architected Framework elements and the core building blocks of the AWS cloud architecture into a matrix designed to offer architectural options and capture architectural decisions.

The AWS Well-Architected Framework Pillars

Each of the Well-Architected Framework pillars, including operational excellence, security, reliability, performance efficiency, and cost optimization, provides your transformation team with three pieces of information intended to simplify the design of your AWS cloud building blocks:

- Design principles
- Promised value
- Related architectural best practices

The design principles and the associated promised value guide the transformation team toward the best architectural options.

The VPC Building Blocks

The *Amazon Virtual Private Cloud (VPC)* building blocks represent the core elements of your AWS cloud including the VPC elements, public subnets, private subnets, and other services referred to in this book as *cross-cutting purpose services*.

The VPC elements ensure the connection between your AWS cloud and the Internet, and they secure the network traffic across your AWS environment. They include an Internet gateway, VPC endpoints, and VPC route tables.

A public subnet's function is to enable direct Internet access to the EC2 instances that it controls. It builds on a CIDR block to assign IP addresses to the instances, which in turn rely on security groups (virtual firewalls) to control incoming and outgoing network traffic.

A private subnet's function is to prevent direct Internet access to the EC2 instances that it controls. It builds on NAT gateways controlled by public subnets to enable instances under its control to connect to the Internet and prevent the Internet from initiating a connection with those instances.

The Architectural Options

The *architectural options*, entries of the matrix, represent the business, technological, and technical solutions upon which the members of your transformation team agree. An example of an architectural option is the rapid decision to make your AWS cloud consistent with the principle *enable traceability*. It not only suggests that the extensive use of log management practices and tools will result in capabilities simplifying security analysis, resource change tracking, and troubleshooting, but also recommends the combined use of Amazon CloudWatch and AWS CloudTrail services. CloudWatch monitors the health of your AWS resources while CloudTrail provides a log in user and API activity.

Key Takeaways

The objective of this chapter was to provide the basic knowledge needed to understand the design, implementation, and deployment of a digital product and service development platform in an AWS environment. You learned that, as the digital product or service is becoming a primary revenue stream for the business, industrializing its development is necessary.

We discussed TQM and mass production techniques as being the foundations of all manufacturing industrialization approaches for more than 75 years. TQM and mass production are the foundations of methods like Six Sigma, agile, and DevOps.

We moved on to identifying what's known as industrialization factors, then defined the notion of digital product and service development industrialization and explored the process for industrializing digital product and service development platforms along with the related design and implementation frameworks.

We finished this chapter by discussing AWS principle, design pattern, methodology, and technology industrialization factors.

This chapter marks the end of Part I of this book. In Part II, "Digitizing the Business Model Using AWS," you'll learn more about the digital transformation of businesses. More importantly, you'll build on the case study of J&S Food, Inc., to put into practice the digital product and service development platform implementation concepts, methodologies, practices, tools, and AWS services discussed in Chapters 1–4.

References

1   David L. Goetsch, "Quality Management: Introduction to Total Quality Management for Production, Processes, and Services," *Pearson International Edition* (January 22, 2006)

2   Gene Kim, "The DevOps Handbook: How to Create World-Class Agility, Reliability, and Security in Technology Organizations," *IT Revolution Press* (2016). https://hennyportman.wordpress.com/2017/02/15/book-review-the-devops-handbook/

3   Atlassian Agile Coach, "Kanban: How the Kanban Methodology Applies to Software Development," *Atlassian Agile Coach* (June 4, 2020). https://www.atlassian.com/agile/kanban/

4   Lucidchart Content Team, "What is Extreme Programming? An Overview of XP Rules and Values," *Lucidchart* (2000). `https://www.lucidchart.com/blog/what-is-extreme-programming`

5   Kanbanize Content Team, "What Is a Kanban Board?," *Kanbanize* (2000). `https://kanbanize.com/kanban-resources/getting-started/what-is-kanban-board`

6   Derek Belt, "The Five Pillars of the AWS Well-Architected Framework," *AWS* (May 15, 2018). `https://aws.amazon.com/blogs/apn/the-5-pillars-of-the-aws-well-architected-framework/`

Part

II

Digitizing the Business Model Using AWS

The digitization of the business model using AWS is based on a five-step process including understanding the industry's disruption impacts on the business, rethinking the business model to digital, designing the virtual private cloud (VPC) architecture and migrating IT to the AWS cloud, implementing DevOps as the digital products and services development platform, and deploying the digital business model across the company.

Part II, consisting of Chapters 5–9, builds on the case of Julienne and Simone (J&S) Food company, which is challenged by its competitors—Instacart, Amazon Fresh, Walmart Pickup, Thrive Market, Fresh Direct—to illustrate systematically the business digital transformation process using Amazon Web Services (AWS).

Chapter 5, "The J&S Food Digital Transformation Project," introduces the J&S Food's case, its origins, organization, growth periods, and current challenges. It then details the stages that led to the company's digital transformation plan including the digital food industry analysis, business impacts analysis, and digital business strategy development.

Chapters 6, "Rethinking J&S Food's Business," explains step-by-step the business model transformation to digital and introduces the digital business value chain framework that facilitates and accelerates business models configuration to digital.

Chapter 7, "Digitizing J&S Food's Business Model Using AWS—Implementing the VPC," presents, step-by-step, the AWS migration process. Important tasks and related tools and methodologies such as AWS migration strategy definition, specification of the AWS Virtual Private Cloud (VPC), and implementation of the VPC are methodically illustrated.

Chapter 8, "Implementing J&S Food's DevOps Platform Using AWS PaaS," describes the process for implementing DevOps in an AWS computing environment. It offers a DevOps implementation framework for AWS that facilitates CICD pipelines deployment along with that of agile software development activities underpinning the digital business value chain.

Chapter 9, "Developing J&S Food's Innovation as a Service Platform Using AWS," discusses the design and the deployment of a software engineering methodology for innovation development at J&S Food's. This methodology builds on the Unified Modeling Language (UML) and on the AWS Amplify framework to implement modern applications based on microservices architecture.

CHAPTER 5

The J&S Food Digital Transformation Project

The last ten years of IT have been about changing the way people work. The next ten years of IT will be about transforming your business.

—Aaron Levie

In this chapter, and through to the end of this book, a case study of a fictitious company, Julienne & Simone (J&S) Food, will be used to illustrate the digital transformation of an online grocery business. As the designated IT executive—chief information officer (CIO), chief technical officer (CTO), or enterprise architect—you'll be involved in the company's digital transformation.

During this journey, you'll be instructed on how to develop a transformation roadmap to help you lead the design and implementation of a universal AWS cloud architecture, including a digital product development platform. You will also be guided on how to drive the deployment of digital operating and organizational models throughout the business.

All along this journey, you'll deal with and apply the key principles, concepts, and tools of digital transformation using AWS to equip J&S Food with the world-class digital product development platform that it expects.

The following sections tell you all about the J&S Food Digital Transformation Project and guide your steps during the first stage of the J&S transformation journey: planning the transformation.

History of J&S Food, Inc.

Two cousins, Julienne and Simone, who were very passionate about the food business, had always dreamed of setting up a grocery chain. They imagined it as a series of grocery stores deployed across the New York state's most populous suburbs and engaged in retailing general food products.

In 1982, after investing all of their life savings, they opened their first store on Columbus Avenue, Rochester, NY. Because of a good health food section, a fast-food aisle, a wide array of frozen foods, and a decent bakery, the store didn't take long to attract people—actually, several hundred daily visitors.

Company's Evolution

J&S Food has grown steadily with some ups and downs marked by strategic adjustments including partnerships, mergers, and acquisitions. The company went through two primary milestones including what the current management team calls "Territorial Conquest and Diversification."

Territorial Conquest

After the business launch in 1982 and for five years thereafter, the company followed a strategy aimed at increasing its territorial presence. Several stores quickly opened in Harlem, the Bronx, Long Island, and Connecticut to the point that, as of 1984, 115 stores were opened generating an annual net income of $360 million.

As sales and investments proved insufficient to support the company's multiterritoriality ambition, J&S specialized in personal service and gourmet items for which it charged premium prices. Shipping items to customers around the world by air freight was also part of the company's business model.

The company partnered with Green Apple (another fictitious company) in 1988, and in 1990, the partnership consisted of an additional 35 stores, ranging in size from 7,000 to 17,000 square feet, and carrying 7,000 to 12,000 gourmet items including grapefruits, strawberries, and potatoes.

As shown in Figure 5.1, the company's operations were organized into front-office and back-office information systems whose primary goal was to provide the staff with the tools needed to increase productivity.

The front-office information system's purpose was to get in touch with customers and buyers and collect the information needed to gain insights into their profile, location, and expectations. The system was driven by front-office applications that provided the functionalities and data necessary to capture customer purchases and orders, record sales and payments, and provide customer service and support.

As to the back-office information system, its objective was to keep the business running by providing functions as vital as customer order fulfillment, distribution, shipping, inventory, analytics, finance, and accounting. This system built on a customer relationship management (CRM) system provided by PeopleSoft, a company acquired by Oracle Corporation in 2005.

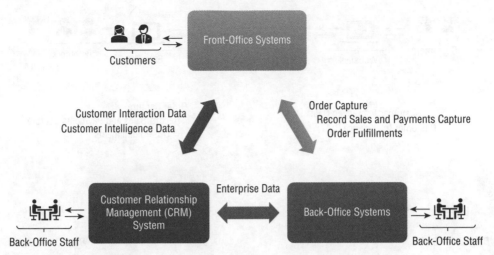

Figure 5.1: J&S front-office and back-office organizational model

Diversification

In 1991, J&S acquired Red Orange (one more fictitious company) to extend its supermarket chain with an additional 49 stores and to start a development new stage by diversifying its products. For 10 years, they offered nationally and regionally advertised brands and private label and generic brands. Their items included fresh meats, dry groceries, dairy products, baked goods, poultry, fish, fresh fruits, and vegetables.

In addition to the introduction of items such as soaps, paper products, and health and beauty aids, the most remarkable highlight was the operation of in-store pharmacies. The stores were opened seven days a week and on holidays from 8 a.m. to 9 p.m.

As shown in Figure 5.2, the company's operations were still consistent with the front- and back-office model.

The major change was the company's adaptation to then rising Internet technologies, particularly extranets and intranets. The extranet was used to implement a web portal that allows J&S to interact with its external vendors, partners, customers, and any other users who require access to restricted information. On the other hand, the intranet was used as a tool that enabled J&S staff to store, organize, and share information within the organization.

Company Culture

Every business builds on a set of shared values, goals, attitudes, beliefs, and practices that characterize the organization and make it successful. J&S Food was no exception. It relied on these four pillars: productivity, effectiveness, technology, and innovation. Let's discuss the value of each pillar.

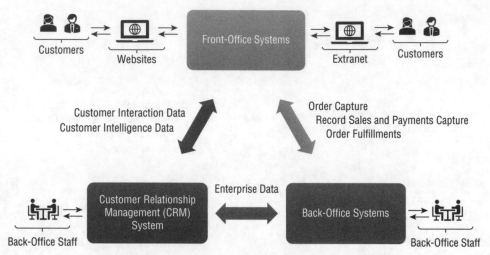

Figure 5.2: J&S front- and back-office information systems in the early 2000s

Productivity

In J&S founders' minds, the belief was that the more productive the staff, the better the quality of the service and the more satisfied the customers. The productivity principle was implemented via a policy aimed at providing staff with all of the tools they needed to make their work effective. Examples included training, tools, and seminars. Productivity is definitely the factor that allowed the company to grow and prosper over the past 28 years.

Effectiveness

For the J&S founders, *effectiveness* referred to the ability of workers always to do the right thing at the right moment. Workers were regularly reminded that they had to be methodical, pragmatic, and problem solvers.

Effectiveness is the feature about which the J&S customer support department was the most praised by clients. The Customer Satisfaction Score metric had never fallen below 98 percent in 28 years.

Innovation

For the J&S founders, innovation was the hand they played when it came to outperforming competitors. In addition to the company's data warehouse infrastructure, seminars involving top marketers played a vital role in providing the best ideas. In-store pharmacies, specialization in premium personal service, and gourmet offerings are examples of the beneficial results of these seminars.

Technology

At J&S, technology was considered the catalyst of productivity, effectiveness, and innovation. Investing in technologies likely to boost competitiveness was always a priority. The company adopted and adapted itself to the information technology innovations of the 30 past years including the enterprise resource planning (ERP) era in the 1980s, client server technologies in the 1990s, and the Internet in the early 2000s.

Transformation Journey's First Stage: Planning the Transformation

The *plan transformation stage* is about planning the digital transformation project. The bottom line is to deliver a comprehensive roadmap that will guide the transformation effort.

Without a proper digital transformation roadmap, chances are that your transformation team will not anticipate failure factors, and this affects your company's competitiveness and growth.

Alexander Graham Bell summarized the stake in this step as, "Before anything else, preparation is the key to success." Figure 5.3 highlights the planning activities to carry out.

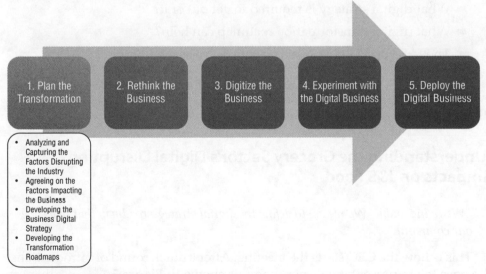

Figure 5.3: Planning the transformation stage

As recommended, the chief executive officer (CEO) will tackle the development of your business transformation roadmap as a four-round workshop including the following:

- Analyzing and capturing the factors disrupting the industry
- Agreeing on the factors disrupting the business
- Developing the business digital strategy
- Developing the transformation roadmap

Let's develop J&S Food's digital transformation roadmap.

The Kickoff Meeting

It's Friday, March 23. You're the freshly appointed CIO of J&S Food. The recently recruited CEO informs you that you'll lead the company's digital transformation:

"Finish your coffee and join us at the meeting in the main conference room."

You enter the room where the VP of marketing, the VP of IT infrastructure, three regional executive sales representatives, and an AWS consultant are all present. The video projector displays the meeting agenda on the projection screen:

- The grocery sector's digital disruption
- What digital strategy is required to get out of it?
- What digital transformation roadmap can help?
- The J&S Food Digital Transformation Project

The following sections discuss the issues that might have been addressed in such a meeting, the decisions that might have been made, and the challenges that you might have faced as CIO.

Understanding the Grocery Sector's Digital Disruption Impacts on J&S Food

"We're in trouble. We're here to define the digital strategy roadmap that will save our company."

This is how the CEO starts the meeting. After a quick round of introductions, he goes to the presentation's next page, as shown in Figure 5.4.

Figure 5.4: J&S Food sales over the past 9 years

The CEO comments on the chart and shares the highlights as follows:

- Sales have dropped by 72 percent in only 9 years.
- New competitors have been popping up every day.
- The business is moving into the platform economy.

A *platform economy* is the economic and social activity structured around and enabled by marketplace platforms. Examples of platforms include Amazon, Airbnb, Uber, and Netflix.

The CEO then elaborates as follows:

"The combined effect of the accelerated adoption of digital technologies and the emergence of the platform economy has been weakening our company's competitiveness. As the presentation shows, our sales have dropped by 72 percent in only nine years."

The CEO finishes by saying:

"What's happening is that online grocery delivery services like Instacart, AmazonFresh, Walmart Pickup, Thrive Market, and Fresh Direct are taking advantage of their brand value, wide distribution network, and competitive prices to increase their market shares. What else is affecting our competitiveness?"

The objective for all participants is to identify the supermarket industry's disruptors and to understand the impacts on the way that J&S Food does business.

Capturing and Analyzing the Factors Driving the Grocery Sector Disruption

A good practice for identifying disruption factors, performing a thorough analysis of the root causes of the industry's disruption, and understanding the impacts on the business is to rely on the framework and tools provided by consultants. One of these tools is the *Five Competitive Forces Matrix*, shown in Figure 5.5.

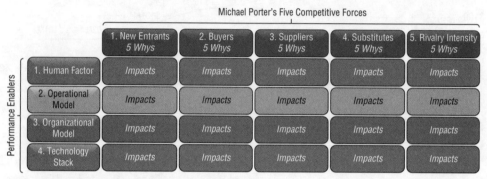

Figure 5.5: The Five Competitive Forces Matrix

The Five Competitive Forces Matrix is inspired by the framework of the same name, developed by Michael Porter of Harvard University. As illustrated, the framework is organized in a two-dimensional matrix of 29 cells associated with the *five whys* tool, which helps to capture the impacts of the five competition forces on your organization's performance enablers.

Understanding these forces is useful, as they determine the reactions of your industry players and in turn its attractiveness. These include new entrants, buyers, suppliers, substitutes, and intensity of rivalry.

New Entrants

New entrants are businesses entering or willing to enter your industry. The unique aspect of new entrants is that they force industry incumbents to take protective responses. A typical response is that they raise what's referred to as *barriers to entry*.

Examples of barriers to entry include using the company's brand value and customer loyalties as means to differentiate products and force new entrants to spend heavily in order to succeed (*product differentiation*). Making the cost of switching from one provider to another prohibitive for customers (*switching cost*) and making access to distribution channels difficult (*barriers to distribution channels*) are other barriers erected by incumbent companies.

The belief is that the new products, services, and technologies introduced by the new entrants are a potential existential threat to such incumbents; thus they pursue an aggressive strategy focused on winning market share.

In today's food industry, new entrants are bringing about what's referred to as the *digital food experience*, which involves a variety of products including organic, natural, and healthy foods ordered online and responsively delivered.

Buyers

Buyers, also referred to as *consumers* or *customers*, impact your industry as a whole and your business directly with a mindset focused on maximizing their experience when interacting with your business. The rationale underpinning this role is that they seek to force the prices of your organization's products and services down by stressing the best value for the money and insisting on quality. This is what's known as the *bargaining power of buyers*.

For today's buyers, the benefits of the digital food experience aren't negotiable: ordering organic, healthy, and dietetic foods online, responsively delivered, is their expected value.

Suppliers

Suppliers, also referred to as *providers*, impact your industry's attractiveness and profitability by their concern for controlling production costs, raising prices, and retaining loyal customers. Suppliers' logic today is that, in order to thrive, they need easy access to markets while reducing operational costs and making a profit. Doing business through digital business platforms is the safest way to achieve that goal.

Suppliers urge their buyers to join digital platforms; otherwise, they cannot guarantee product quality and affordable prices. This is what is known as the *bargaining power of suppliers*.

Substitutes

Substitutes refer to products and services from another industry that can perform the same function as the product in your industry. Substitutes that deserve your attention are those that are subject to trends resulting in improved quality, increased value for the money, and lower prices.

The logic behind substitutes is that they force incumbent businesses to compete with the industries producing them, intensifying competition.

Intensity of Rivalry

Intensity of rivalry refers to the extent to which businesses within an industry put pressure on one another to either maintain industry leadership or limit each other's profit potential.

The rationale of intensity of rivalry in today's food business is that the safest way to stay in business is to be part of the platform economy, by doing business either on a third-party digital platform or on a digital platform of your own.

The Five Whys Method

Five whys is an iterative and collaborative technique used to find the root cause of a given problem. As shown in Figure 5.6, the root cause of a problem is identified by asking a sequence of "why?" questions with each answer forming the basis of the next question.

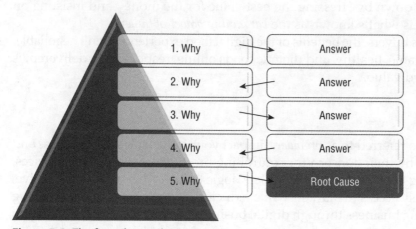

Figure 5.6: The five whys tool

The following illustrates the five whys method:

- Why is J&S Food's business weakening?
    - Because the supermarket industry is disrupting.
- Why is the supermarket industry disrupting?
    - Because most food businesses are adopting the platform economy.
- Why do businesses adopt the platform economy?
    - Because with the platform economy, businesses have access to global markets, their costs are cut, and profits are high.
- Why are they able to access global markets, cut their costs, and increase their profits?
    - Because clients around the globe are increasingly doing business online, cloud computing via virtualization, automation, scalability, metered billing, and security is taking operating expenses down and, as a result, increasing benefits.

- Why are clients increasingly doing business online, and why is cloud computing acting as a catalysts of business benefits?
  - Because digital business is the way to go, and cloud computing is the go-to technology in which to invest.

The reason why J&S Food's business is weakening is that the company's leadership underestimated the expansion of digital business and the benefits of cloud computing.

Discussing and Agreeing on the Factors Affecting J&S's Food Business

Discussions designed to identify the disruption factors for a case like J&S Food would normally assume that the accelerated adoption of digital business models, including ecommerce and digital platforms, by the company's competitors are making the company's performance enablers irrelevant.

These performance enablers include human factor, operational model, organizational model, and digital technology. An analysis of the company's business model elements using the Five Competitive Forces Matrix confirms this assumption. Let's discuss the various impacts on the J&S business model.

Determining the Factors Making J&S Food Staff Irrelevant

The conclusions regarding the causes of the irrelevance of J&S Food's human factor are summarized in the Five Competitive Forces Matrix shown in Table 5.1.

Table 5.1: The Factors Making J&S Food's Workforce Irrelevant

FIVE COMPETITIVE FORCES	IMPACTS ON THE HUMAN FACTOR AND PRIMARY DISRUPTOR
New entrants	New entrants bring in a digital food experience that involves ordering organic, natural, and healthy food products online and responsively delivered. J&S Food's workforce lacks the experience and skills needed to meet the requirements of the digital food experience.
Buyers	Buyers expect a digital food experience no matter what. J&S Food's workforce doesn't have the experience and skills needed to fulfill that expectation.
Suppliers	Suppliers prioritize working with a digital platform business. J&S Food's workforce lacks the digital platform business skills.
Substitutes	Today's substitutes leverage the requirements of the digital food experience. J&S Food's workforce lacks the experience and skills needed to deal with the requirements of the digital food experience.
Intensity of rivalry	The high intensity of rivalry in the online grocery sector reduces J&S Food's market share, as well as the company's activity, and forces it to reduce its staff.

The lesson to be learned from the impacts of the five competitive forces is that the combined effect of the expansion of the digital platform business in the supermarket industry and the consumer's increasing appetite for the digital food experience is making the J&S Food's staff incapable of preventing ongoing customer churn and market share loss.

Determining the Factors Weakening the Operational Model

The conclusions regarding the causes of the weakening of the J&S Food's operational model are summarized in the Five Competitive Forces Matrix shown in Table 5.2.

Table 5.2: The Factors Weakening J&S Food's Operational Model

FIVE COMPETITIVE FORCES	IMPACTS ON THE OPERATIONAL MODEL AND PRIMARY DISRUPTOR
New entrants	New entrants bring in a digital food experience based on digital business platform processes. J&S Food's poorly automated food business practices are inconsistent with the requirements of digital business platforms.
Buyers	Buyers expect a digital food experience that J&S Food isn't in a position to deliver. The company's poorly automated practices are inconsistent with the requirements of digital business platforms.
Suppliers	Suppliers expect to do business based on digital business platform processes. The J&S Food's rigid, hierarchical, and siloed operations, comprised of separate front-office and back-office teams, is inconsistent with suppliers' expected levels of agility.
Substitutes	Substitutes stress online ordering and responsive delivery of organic, natural, and healthy food products based on digital platforms. J&S Food's operations aren't designed to develop digital food products and services of that nature.
Intensity of rivalry	The logic of the intensity of rivalry factor is that the safest way to stay in business is to adopt a digital business model. J&S Food's operational practices are inconsistent with this logic.

The lessons that participants would derive from the impacts of the five competitive forces on J&S Food's operational practices is that the requirements of digital food experience, particularly the adoption of digital business platforms, make the company's processes incapable of preventing ongoing customer churn and market share loss.

Identifying the Factors Weakening the Organizational Model

The conclusions regarding the causes of the weakening of J&S Food's organizational model are summed up in Five Competitive Forces Matrix shown in Table 5.3.

Table 5.3: The Factors Weakening J&S Food's Organizational Model

FIVE COMPETITIVE FORCES	IMPACTS ON THE ORGANIZATIONAL MODEL AND PRIMARY DISRUPTOR
New entrants	New entrants bring in a digital food experience that requires organizational agility in order to respond quickly to any customer request. J&S Food's rigid, hierarchical, and siloed organization, comprised of separate front-office and back-office teams, is inconsistent with the organizational requirements of the digital food experience.
Buyers	Buyers expect a digital food experience that guarantees agility and responsiveness. J&S Food's organizational rigidity, hierarchies, and silos are incompatible with the digital food experience requirements.
Suppliers	Suppliers expect organizational agility enabled by the digital business platforms. Because of its rigid, hierarchical, and siloed nature, J&S Food's organizational model isn't likely to deliver this expected agility.
Substitutes	Substitutes stress online ordering and responsive delivery of organic, natural, and healthy food products based on digital platforms. J&S Food's organizational model isn't designed to support digital food products and services of that nature.
Rivalry intensity	The logic of the intensity of rivalry factor is that the safest way to stay in business is to adopt a digital business model. J&S Food's organizational model isn't consistent with this logic.

The key message participants that would receive from the five competitive forces is that J&S Food's organizational model isn't likely to help the company prevent massive customer churn and market share loss.

Determining the Factors Making the Technology Stack Irrelevant

The conclusions regarding the causes of the weakening of J&S Food's operational model are summarized in the Five Competitive Forces Matrix, as shown in Table 5.4.

The key piece of information that participants would receive from the five competitive forces is that J&S Food's technology stack is disconnected from the supermarket industry's trend. The company's basic ecommerce website in addition to its manual back-office processes cannot help the company stop massive customer churn and market share loss.

Table 5.4: The Factors Making J&S Food's Technology Stack Irrelevant

FIVE COMPETITIVE FORCES	IMPACTS ON THE TECHNOLOGY STACK AND PRIMARY DISRUPTOR
New entrants	The new entrants are pushing for the adoption of digital business models and the related digital business platforms in the supermarket industry. The J&S technology stack is inconsistent with that requirement.
Buyers	Buyers expect a digital food experience based on digital business platforms. J&S Food's technology stack, based on a basic ecommerce website, is inconsistent with the benefits provided by digital business platforms.
Suppliers	Suppliers expect to do business based on digital business platforms. J&S Food's basic ecommerce website unlikely to meet suppliers' expectations.
Substitutes	Substitutes emphasize online ordering and responsive delivery of organic, natural, and healthy food products based on digital platforms. J&S Food's technology stack is totally incapable of supporting the development, delivery, and management of products and services of that nature.
Intensity of rivalry	The logic of the intensity of rivalry factor is that the safest way to stay in business is to adopt a digital business model. J&S Food's technology stack is inconsistent with that logic.

Developing and Sharing J&S Food's Digital Mission and Digital Strategy

As you have realized, adopting a digital platform business model is the most reliable solution for J&S Food. The next step is to define the company's mission and from this mission derive its digital strategy and the roadmap to support the transformation effort.

Clicking the mouse to display the presentation's next page, the CEO announces the following:

"Building a leading online grocery shopping business is our target for the next two years with a pilot experiment starting next year... What will our digital strategy and transformation roadmap look like?"

Defining J&S Food's Mission

Once the root causes of your organization's disruption have been identified, along with the solution most likely to save it, the next step is to redefine its mission. Unlike the business vision statement that proclaims the current and future objectives of your organization, the mission statement is concerned about the who, what, and why of your future business. It's the basis on which the strategic objectives and a strategic plan are derived.

Nine elements will make your future business mission statement the pillar of your digital transformation strategy:

Customers: Who are the consumers interested in the digital food experience?

Products and services: What products and services will your organization sell through digital platforms?

Markets: On what digital business and social media platforms will your organization do business?

Technology: In what digital business platforms and other technologies will your organization invest?

Survival, growth, and profitability objectives: What are your organization's core objectives?

Philosophy: What will be the basic beliefs, core values, aspirations, and philosophical priorities of your future business?

Self-concept: What are your organization's strengths and competitive advantages?

Concern for public image: What will be your business's public image in the future?

Concern for staff: What will be your organization's attitude and orientation toward its staff?

The CEO announces J&S Food's next mission as follows:

- *"Taking advantage of digital business platforms and AWS cloud technologies to provide our staff with the best work environment they need to offer consumers a world-class digital food experience."*
- *"Making J&S Food a prosperous, leading online grocery shopping business."*

You're all set for developing J&S Food's digital strategy.

Developing J&S Food's Digital Strategy

The digital transformation of J&S Food's business is not a trivial initiative—it's not narrowly defined as changing the company's technology or providing staff with new IT tools. It's much more complicated than that.

J&S Food's Digital Business Strategy Defined

A *digital business strategy* is the combination of tactics that your company uses to mobilize human, operational, organizational, and technological resources to achieve specific online business objectives.

A digital business strategy is composed of two elements including the *objectives* and the *resources* needed to achieve these objectives. The objectives are varied—they can be financial, they can be customer-related, or they can focus on the improvement of your company's strategic processes.

On the resources side, these refer to the means mobilized to achieve the online business objectives. There are four categories of resources: human, operational, organizational, and technological.

- Human resources represent human capital, skills, competencies, and creativity.

- Operational resources relate to the set of processes and practices used to make human resources productive.

- Organizational resources refer to the mechanisms implemented to make people interactions and collaborations productive.

- Technological resources are the set of tools and infrastructure used to make human, operational, and organizational factors efficient.

Understanding the Strategy Map Tool

Another useful tool that a consultant can provide is the *strategy map*, specifically the strategy mapping tool created by Balanced Scorecard (BSC) pioneers, Harvard's Robert S. Kaplan, and David P. Norton.

The strategy map views the organization's strategy through two components: the objectives to be achieved and the resources needed to achieve these objectives (see Figure 5.7).

Internal processes represent the key processes your organization relies on to achieve the objectives while the organizational capacity spans people, organizational, and technological factors needed to enable processes' effectiveness and efficiency.

The strategy is developed by correlating the resources factors with the objectives to which they contribute using arrows. The logic behind the strategy map is that the organizational capacity (people, organizational structure, technology) enables the organization's internal processes, which in turn enable customer expectations, and that results in the expected profits.

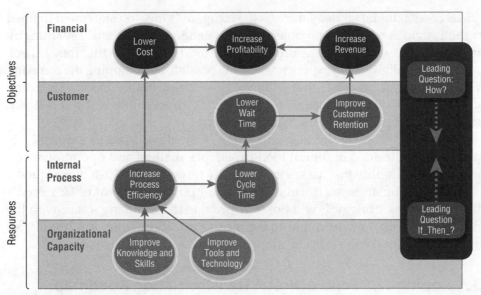

Figure 5.7: Overview of the strategy map tool

Source: Balanced Scorecard Institute

Understanding J&S Food's Digital Strategy

The strategy map illustrated by Figure 5.8 summarizes J&S Food's digital strategy resulting from the meeting discussed above.

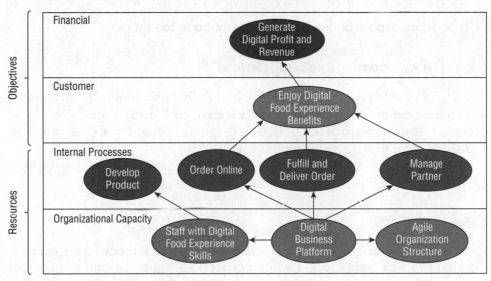

Figure 5.8: J&S Food's digital strategy

J&S Food's digital strategy mirrors the company's mission statement defined in the previous section. The objective is to generate profit and revenues by providing consumers with the unique digital food experience that they expect.

The unique digital food experience is made possible by equipping the company with the strategic processes that will make it a leading online grocery shopping business. These processes include online ordering, order fulfillment and delivery, product development, and managing partners.

The strategic processes are enabled by three competitive assets including highly qualified staff trained in digital food experience matters and operational and organizational agility that makes the company responsive to customer requests.

The digital business platform is the most important element of J&S Food's digital business strategy. It will not only provide the company's staff with the innovative tools they need and make the organization agile, but it will also automate and make the selected strategic processes more efficient.

Developing J&S Food's Digital Transformation Roadmap

Taking into account the factors disrupting the business, the organization's future mission statement, and the capabilities that J&S Food's digital strategy mobilizes to help the company survive, participants are ready to discuss the company's digital transformation.

The question that the participants must have in mind is the following:

"How to convert the digital strategy into an implementation plan?"

That's the purpose of the digital transformation roadmap.

Digital Transformation Roadmap Defined

The *digital transformation roadmap* is the bridge that links your digital strategy with the execution of the transformation. It answers the questions "what?" and "when?" The framework illustrated in Figure 5.9 provides an easy and fast transformation roadmap development approach.

A digital transformation roadmap consists of four elements: capabilities, workstreams, activities, and phases and milestones.

Capabilities

Capabilities are nothing more than the performance enablers discussed in Chapter 3, "Digital Product and Service Development Challenges," as well as the capabilities of the strategy map and the resulting digital strategy addressed in the previous sections of this chapter. Capabilities include the human factor, operational model, organizational model, and technology needed to transform the business. In addition to defining their related workstreams, capabilities are

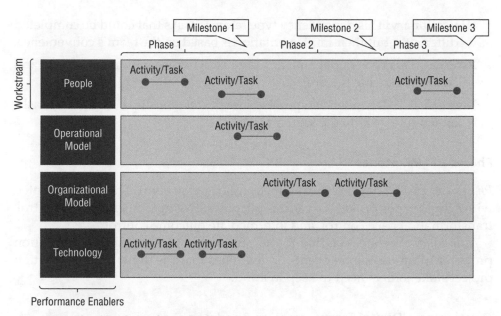

Figure 5.9: The digital transformation roadmap

used to put together the activities needed to implement these workstreams throughout the timeline.

Workstreams

Workstreams are the set of activities needed to implement or improve specific capabilities. Activities within a workstream are arranged according to priorities and order of precedence.

By default, the digital transformation roadmap includes four workstreams including human (or people), operational model, organizational model, and technology.

Activities

An *activity* is one or more tasks slated to be performed within a specific workstream. It has a start and end date, a duration, and dependencies.

Task dependency is a link in which a task or a milestone relies on other tasks to be performed. There are five types of dependencies:

Mandatory: This type of dependency indicates that a task must be carried out at a particular time.

Predecessor-successor: This dependency type is based on the relationship between the initiation and completion of individual tasks.

Discretionary: This dependency type refers to tasks that could be completed differently, but their implementation is based on the team's convenience.

External: This type of dependency defines activities within the project and activities outside the project.

Internal: This dependency type describes the relationship between two tasks or activities within the same project.

Phases and Milestones

Phases are specific stages of the digital transformation effort. They are associated with activities performed for various purposes. Examples include risk control, transformation pace control, and intermediate outcome control.

Milestones are dates relating to the progress of the digital transformation project. Milestones signal events or deadlines that the digital transformation project stakeholders need to keep in mind.

Developing a Digital Transformation Roadmap

The easiest and fastest way to develop a digital transformation roadmap is to follow the iterative process illustrated in Figure 5.10, which is based on the digital transformation framework.

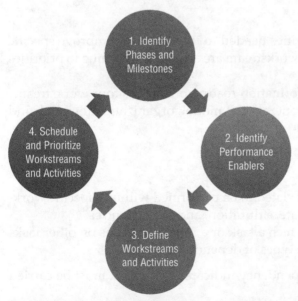

Figure 5.10: The simple digital transformation roadmap development

Four collaborative and iterative steps support the digital transformation roadmap including identifying phases and milestones, identifying performance enablers, defining workstreams and activities, and scheduling and prioritizing workstreams and activities.

Identifying Phases and Milestones

The intent of this step is to brainstorm with the participants about the phases and milestones that are likely to make the transformation successful. A good practice is to associate each phase and milestone with a tangible or meaningful deliverable. Examples of phases and milestones are architecture design, platform implementation, system testing, and system deployment.

Identifying Performance Enablers

Similar to the phases and milestones step, the objective is to brainstorm with the participants to identify the performance enablers that effectively support your digital business. A good practice is to spot the needed performance enablers among those identified as factors weakening your industry and company.

Other performance enablers, besides the four we already know (people, operational model, organizational model, and technology), could include content marketing and your organization's brand equity, that is, the commercial value that your organization derives from consumer's perception of your brand name.

Defining Workstreams and Activities

Defining a workstream and the related activities involves listing the activities and tasks to carry out for the implementation or improvement of the associated performance enabler. The rule is that every performance enabler is associated with a workstream, which is in turn associated with activities. The VP of IT infrastructure, VP of marketing, sales executives, and any other participants are responsible for providing a list of the activities and tasks of their respective business areas.

Scheduling and Prioritizing Workstreams and Activities

The goal of this step is to plan, schedule, and prioritize the activities and tasks of the different workstreams in a way that ensures a successful digital transformation effort. Properly linking and prioritizing activities and tasks is key to successfully developing a digital transformation roadmap.

A good practice for effective workstreams and activities scheduling and prioritization is to use techniques like the Critical Path Method (CPM) and Program Evaluation and Review Technique (PERT).

Understanding J&S Food's Digital Transformation Roadmap

Figure 5.11 illustrates the results of the digital transformation roadmap development process.

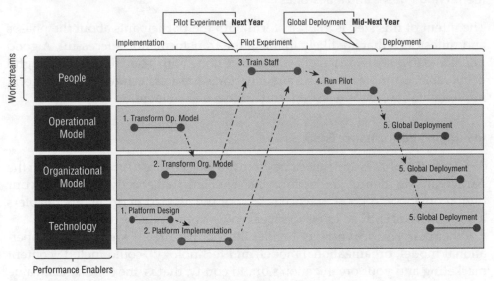

Figure 5.11: The J&S digital transformation roadmap

The following sections summarize the strategic decisions that participants made as part of the development of the digital transformation roadmap.

Mitigating Risks via a Pilot Experiment

Participants agreed that the slightest failure of the platform would have a significant impact on the company. Thus, managing that risk was a key decision. The decision is reflected in the Pilot Experiment phase on J&S Food's digital transformation roadmap.

Pilot experiments are small-scale trials involving actual staff in real business conditions. The intent is to confirm feasibility, estimate duration and cost, and identify potential pitfalls and the solutions to avoid them prior to full-scale deployment.

Participants agreed that the J&S Food grocery store in the city of Buffalo and its 150 employees would be selected to support the pilot experiment.

Anticipating Resistance to Change by Transforming Processes and Organizational Structure First

Another important issue that participants agreed upon was people's *resistance to change*, particularly to operational and organizational changes. Resistance to change is understood to be any act, speech, or attitude seeking to oppose modifications or transformations that disrupt current conditions. The participant's decision on this is reflected in the transformation roadmap in the implementation phase where the transformation of the operational and organizational models is started early on in the process.

Accelerating the Global Deployment to Catch Up with the Competition

One of the benefits of the pilot experiment that participants exploited was the ability to capture pitfalls and propose solutions proactively. This results in an accelerating effect on the large-scale deployment and helps the company catch up to its competitors. The parallel deployment of the operational and organizational models, as well as technology on the roadmap, reflects the participants' decision.

The J&S Food Digital Transformation Project's Statement of Work

As the meeting ends, it's the digital program leader's responsibility to formalize the transformation program's key decisions including scope, schedule, risks, team, and costs. The purpose of the Digital Transformation Project's statement of work is described in the following sections.

The Statement of Work Defined

The *statement of work (SOW)* is the narrative description of the transformation project's requirements. It defines the project scope, activities, timelines, roles and responsibilities, and deliverables.

The typical content of the SOW includes introduction, project objectives, scope of work, work requirements, schedule and milestones, acceptance criteria, and other requirements.

The following sections outline J&S Food's digital transformation project's statement of work that were drafted at the end of the meeting.

Introduction/Background

J&S Food's board of directors has recently approved the J&S Food Digital Transformation Project to support its strategic plan to reinvent the company's business. To provide prospective clients with the digital food experience that they expect, the J&S Food Digital Transformation Project will focus on implementing a digital business platform that will enable the company's key digital business processes. To accomplish this, J&S Food will rely on an internal team assisted by high-profile external digital business platform implementation and cloud computing experts. J&S Food anticipates that its new digital business model will move the company forward to keep existing clients and winning new ones while capturing additional market share.

Scope of Work

The scope of work for the J&S Food Digital Transformation Project includes all planning, execution, implementation, knowledge transfer, and training. The selected external consultants will assist J&S Food's team in the design and implementation of the platform.

Each stage of the project will require approval from J&S Food's management before moving on to the next stage. The selected external consultants must ensure that they provide adequate resources for designing, building, testing, and implementing the platform, and that it is staffed for training J&S Food's personnel as well.

Specific deliverables and milestones will be listed in the "Work Requirements" and "Schedules and Milestones" sections of the SOW.

Work Requirements

As part of the J&S Food Digital Transformation Project, the selected consultant will be responsible for performing tasks throughout the various stages of this project. The following tasks will result in the successful completion of this project:

Kickoff

- The project team leader will create and present a detailed transformation plan including schedule, work breakdown structure (WBS), testing plan, implementation plan, training plan, and transition plan.

- The project team leader, assisted by the consultants, will present the J&S Food Digital Transformation Project plan to J&S Food's board of directors for review and approval.

Implementation Phase

- The project team works with all stakeholders to gather requirements and establish metrics.

- The project team creates the platform's logical architecture based on the collected requirements.

- The project team leader, assisted by the consultants, will present logical architecture to J&S Food's board of directors for review and approval.

- The project team will implement the newly designed digital business platform based on the detailed architecture and implementation plan.
- The project team leader will present a written status report at a weekly meeting.

Pilot Experiment Phase

- External consultants will provide training in accordance with an approved training plan provided in the kickoff meeting.
- The project team leader will present a written status report at a weekly meeting.

Global Deployment Phase

- The project team will support the operational and organizational model's global deployment.
- The project team, assisted by the consultants, will ensure the successful deployment of the technological stack supporting the digital business platform.

Schedule/Milestones

Platform architecture approval: June 1

Platform implementation acceptance: December 1

Pilot experiment: Early next year.

Global deployment: Mid-next year.

Acceptance Criteria

For the J&S Food Digital Transformation Project, the acceptance of all deliverables will reside with J&S Food's VP of marketing acting as the project sponsor. The VP of marketing will maintain a small team of three advisors to ensure the completeness of each stage of the project and that the scope of work has been met.

Once the entire project is completed and the vendor provides its report/presentation for review and approval, the VP of marketing will either sign off on the approval for the next phase to begin or reply to the vendor, in writing, advising the vendor what tasks must still be accomplished.

Other Requirements

All vendor project team members will submit security forms to J&S Food for clearance and access badges to the facility. All vendor consultants and quality control team members will be granted access to J&S Food's IT infrastructure and all necessary IT functions. They will also be given temporary J&S Food accounts to be used only for work pertaining to the Digital Transformation Project. Upon completion of the project, these accounts will be closed.

The Next Step

A follow-up meeting will be scheduled with the entire project team to finalize the statement of work.

Key Takeaways

A major advantage of case studies in understanding issues as complex as the digital transformation of a business using AWS is that they engage the reader in discerning the key principles, concepts, and practices by abstracting from examples.

The guidance provided in this chapter on the development of J&S Food's digital business strategy and transformation roadmap not only illustrated the benefits of learning though a case study, but it also provided concrete meaning to what is meant by transforming the way that companies do business. The intent of the J&S Food's case throughout the remaining 11 chapters is to help you develop and understand the wide spectrum of digital transformation skills.

This chapter helped you to take your first steps into J&S Food's digital transformation journey. The next chapter will help you deal with the transformation of the company's business.

References

1   Chuen Seet, "What Is a Strategy Roadmap," *Jibility* (April 5, 2018). `https://www.jibility.com/what-is-a-strategy-roadmap/`

2   Michael E. Porter, "Competitive Strategy: Techniques for Analyzing Industries and Competitors," *The Free Press* (June 4, 1998). `https://hbr.org/1979/03/how-competitive-forces-shape-strategy/3`

3   Robert S. Kaplan and David P. Norton, "Translating Strategy into Action: The Balanced Scorecard," *Harvard Business School Press* (1996). `https://hbr.org/1992/01/the-balanced-scorecard-measures-that-drive-performance-2`

Rethinking J&S Food's Business

Digital Transformation is an illusion, unless it's backed by a genuine business transformation, rethinking the entire company, turning its ideas, strategies, and organization upside down and inside out.

—Jakob Vasehus

It's an open secret that a significant portion of digital transformation projects fail to deliver the expected benefits. An article in *Harvard Business Review*, "Digital Transformation Is Not About Technology," puts these numbers on the table: "70 percent of all digital transformation initiatives do not reach their goals. Of the $1.3 trillion that was spent on digital transformation in 2018, it was estimated that $900 billion went to waste."

Digital transformation should be seen as the rational deployment of digital technology across the organization in support of all areas of the business. This assumes that the weaknesses of the current business model versus the digital competition requirements are understood and that the solutions to fix them are defined.

The transformation of your business will result in changes to how it operates and how your organization can provide customers with the first-class digital business experience they expect.

In this chapter, in the role of the J&S Food's digital transformation project leader, you'll attend a business transformation workshop facilitated by an enterprise architect. You'll learn the essence of the concept of the digital operational model, why it matters for the digital business, how to design it, and how it would help J&S Food to transform its business model to digital.

Transformation Journey's Second Stage: Rethinking the Business

The *rethinking the business stage* is about developing the target digital business architecture (also referred to as *digital business model*) in terms of how the business will operate in order to deliver the digital experience expected by customers. Adapting the organization to the requirements of digital competition is the goal. Without that adaptation, your digital transformation project will look like an IT transformation effort, focused solely on IT matters. As long as your staff, processes, organizational, and governance structures haven't been aligned to the requirements of the digital economy, expecting business benefits from your digital transformation is wishful thinking.

Rockwell Automation's Rod Michael summarizes the stakes in this step as, "If you automate a mess, you get an automated mess." Figure 6.1 illustrates where the digital transformation team stands in the transformation journey:

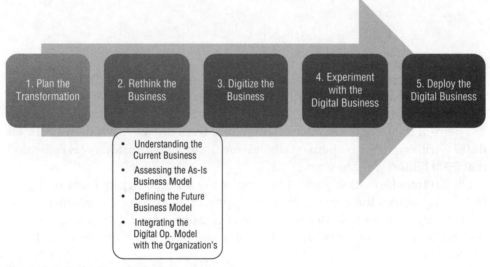

Figure 6.1: Rethinking the business stage

As Figure 6.1 indicates, the enterprise architect will tackle your business transformation effort as a four-round workshop including the following:

- Understanding the organization's current business architecture, also referred to as *operational model*.
- Assessing the as-is business architecture.
- Defining the organization's future digital business architecture.
- Integrating your digital operating model with the rest of your organization in order to ensure a cross-functional synergy.

Let's transform J&S Food's business for the digital economy.

Understanding J&S Food's Current Business

Following the usual introductions involving marketing, sales, customer service, software development, IT operations, and product development representatives, the enterprise architect starts the meeting with these words:

"The objective of our workshop is to reinvent altogether the business in a way that ensures a world-class digital food experience for our customers."

The enterprise architecture process starts with piecing together the baseline business architecture by capturing and modeling information about processes, practices, data, tools, and staff.

The baseline business architecture is a set of models describing the as-is business model. These include the process model, for example, the use case diagram that provides the big picture of the company's activities. The data model points out the data to consider for the purpose of market and customer insights, as well as for cloud migration issues.

The baseline business architecture is used as a collaborative tool that allows participants to discuss their business areas in terms of how it works, their weaknesses, data handled, desired improvements, as well as the new products and services to develop and the processes supporting their management.

Capturing the Current Business Model

This activity is about piecing together the as-is business model. The bottom line is to get the big picture of how the business works in terms of staff, processes, data, and underlying tools.

Attendees at the meeting should include relevant stakeholders from business and IT. For J&S Food's digital transformation project, sales, customer service, software development, product development, IT operations, and the webmaster should be in attendance.

Using a *use case diagram*, a business modeling tool of the Unified Modeling Language (UML) methodology, the enterprise architect pieces together the as-is business model based on the answers to the following questions provided by participants:

- What are the use cases of our current business platform in your business area?
- Who are the actors? What are their responsibilities?
- How do these use cases link together to make our as-is business model?
- What data is handled?

Understanding Use Cases

Use cases represent functionalities provided by a system that allow actors to perform specific actions. In the context of J&S Food's digital transformation project, their purpose in the use case diagram is to highlight the functions provided by the organization's business model.

The use cases are represented either by circles or ellipses. The example in Figure 6.2 is the use case Buy Online. It represents the buy functionality provided by J&S Food's current business model to allow customers to buy online.

Understanding Actors

Use cases are initiated or supported by people, applications, and systems. People, applications, and systems are what's known in UML terminology as *actors*. Their purpose in the use case diagram is to represent the stakeholders of the system. In the context of J&S Food's case study, we'll refer to actors as the stakeholders of the J&S Food's business model. They include your organization's staff, customers, partners, applications, and systems.

Understanding Links

The goal of links in a use case diagram is to highlight the dependencies between use cases. There are two types of links including *include* and *extend*.

An *include relationship* is one in which the base use case includes another use case (the inclusion use case). The include relationship supports the reuse of functionality. It's represented by an arrow starting from the base use case and directed to the inclusion use case.

An *extend relationship* is a type of dependency in which one use case (the client) requires another use case (the supplier) for implementation or operation. It's represented by an arrow starting from the supplier use case to the client use case.

The following section discusses the J&S Food's as-is business model as established by participants.

The Current Business Model Captured

Figure 6.2 represents J&S Food's as-is business model as it would result from the different contributions.

J&S Food's as-is use case diagram, as captured by the enterprise architect, shows that the company's business is structured around six key functions including buy, fulfill order, manage supply chain, perform customer service, maintain website, perform payment, and develop food product. Let's discuss them.

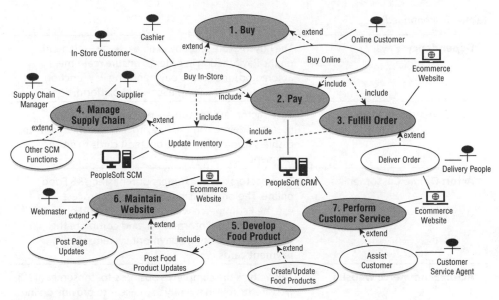

Figure 6.2: J&S Food's as-is use case

Buy

Initiated either by the *in-store customer* or by the *online customer*, the Buy use case enables the act of purchasing one or more of J&S Food's range of food products.

Table 6.1 summarizes the information that sales representatives would provide about the Buy use case, including its purpose, dependencies, stakeholders, and their roles.

Table 6.1: The As-Is Buy Use Case

Buy Use Case Purpose	The primary goal of the Buy use case is to enable in-store and online consumer purchases. It splits into Buy In-Store and Buy Online functions that depend on the update inventory, fulfill order, and pay functions in order to ensure the best buying experience.
Dependency: Update Inventory	The Buy In-Store and Buy Online use cases depend on the Update Inventory function to keep J&S Food's inventory consistent. The Update Inventory function is a module provided by the PeopleSoft SCM system.
Dependency: Fulfill Order	The Buy Online use case depends on the Fulfill Order function to ensure timely delivery of online consumer orders. The process is facilitated by the Fulfill Order system of the Ecommerce website. It interacts with the PeopleSoft SCM to perform inventory updates.

Continues

Table 6.1 (*continued*)

Dependency: Pay	The Buy In-Store and Buy Online use cases depend on the Pay function in order to ensure real-time, automated, and secure payment. The Pay function is a module of the PeopleSoft CRM platform.
Actor: In-store Customer	These actors are consumers purchasing J&S Food in-store. Their role in the Buy process is to interact with cashiers using cash, debit, or credit cards to ensure payment.
Actor: Online Customer	These actors are consumers purchasing J&S Food online. Their responsibility in the Buy process is to use the Ecommerce website to place food orders, provide delivery information, and complete the purchase using online payment systems via payment cards.
Actor: Ecommerce Website	This actor is the company's business-to-consumer (B2C) website. Its role in the Buy use case is to provide online customers with order taking and order tracking functions.
Actor: PeopleSoft SCM	This actor is the system supporting J&S Food's supply chain management activity. Its role in the Buy use case is to update in real time the company's inventory and keep it consistent.
Actor: PeopleSoft CRM	This actor is the system supporting the company's CRM activities. Its responsibility in the Buy use case is to provide in-store and online automated payment functions.
Actor: Cashier	Cashiers are J&S Food's staff. Their responsibility is to interact with in-store customers to collect payments based on cash registers enabled by the PeopleSoft CRM system.

Fulfill Order

Starting after the online order is issued by the online customer, the Fulfill Order use case starts the delivery process.

Table 6.2 summarizes the information that the sales representatives would provide about fulfill order, including its purpose, dependencies, stakeholders, and their roles.

Table 6.2: The As-Is Fulfill Order Use Case

Fulfill Use Case Purpose	The objective of this use case is to trigger order preparation and delivery as well as the company's food product inventory update. The Fulfill Order function is provided by the Ecommerce website.
Dependency: Update Inventory	The Update Inventory function is triggered to keep J&S Food's inventory consistent. The Update Inventory function is a module of the PeopleSoft SCM system.
Dependency: Deliver Order	The Deliver Order function is performed by the delivery person. It's relates to preparing the order and delivering it in a timely manner in order to ensure timely delivery of online consumer orders. The Deliver Order function is facilitated by the Ecommerce website.
Actor: Ecommerce Website	The company's B2C website's role is to provide functions that facilitate order preparations and delivery. These functions include fulfilling and delivering the order.
Actor: Delivery Person	The delivery person is J&S Food's partner whose responsibility it is to ensure timely order delivery.

Pay

The purpose of the Pay use case is to provide online payment functions via debit or credit cards as well as in-store payment functions using cash and payment cards.

Table 6.3 summarizes the information that the sales representatives would provide about the Pay use case, including its purpose, dependencies, stakeholders, and their roles.

Perform Customer Service

The Perform Customer Service use case represents the set of actions taken by J&S Food's customer service advisors to offer post-sales services to customers. As it contributes to improving a customer's experience with J&S Food's products, this use case is considered vital for the company's performance.

Table 6.3: The As-Is Pay Use Case

Pay Use Case Purpose	The main goal is to provide in-store and online payment functions. It supports both Buy In-Store and Buy Online functions in order to ensure the best payment experience. The Pay function is a PeopleSoft CRM system's module.
Dependency: Buy In-Store	The Buy In-Store use case depends on the Pay function to complete in-store customer purchases.
Dependency: Buy Online	The Buy Online use case depends on the pay function to complete online customer purchases.
Actor: PeopleSoft CRM	This actor is the system supporting the company's CRM activities. Its responsibility in the Pay use case is to provide automated payment functions.

Table 6.4 sums up the information that sales representatives would provide about the Perform Customer Service use case, including its purpose, dependencies, stakeholder roles, and responsibilities.

Table 6.4: The As-Is Perform Customer Service Case

Perform Customer Service Use Case Purpose	The primary goal of the Perform Customer Service use case is to provide customers with the help they need either to know more about J&S Food's products or to improve their experience with the company's products.
Dependency: Assist Customer	The Perform Customer Service use case depends on the Assist Customer function to help customers enjoy superior experience with the company's products. The Assist Customer function is provided either by phone via PeopleSoft call center technologies or via an Ecommerce chatbot.
Actor: Customer Service Agent	This actor is a J&S Food's external partner responsible for helping customers by phone or by email.
Actor: Ecommerce Website	This actor is the company's B2C website whose role it is to enable the Assist Customer function based on chatbot technologies.

Manage Supply Chain

The purpose of the Manage Supply Chain use case is to deliver end-to-end supply chain management (SCM) functionalities in support of J&S Food's activities.

Table 6.5 summarizes the information that the sales representatives would provide about the J&S Food's SCM use case, including its purpose, dependencies, stakeholders, and their roles.

Table 6.5: The As-Is Manage Supply Chain Use Case

Manage Supply Chain Use Case Purpose	This use case delivers five functions, including production, shipment, and distribution of food product as well as control and updating of internal inventories.
Dependency: Update Inventory	The Update Inventory function is part of the Manage Supply Chain use case. It's invoked every time a food product is purchased in-store or delivered following online payments. The Update Inventory function is a module of the PeopleSoft SCM system.
Actor: Supply Chain Manager	This actor is J&S Food's staff responsible for managing the company's grocery store inventories.
Actor: Supplier	This actor is J&S Food's external partner responsible supplying the company with food products.

Maintain Website

The Maintain Website is the set of activities performed to keep the website available and always up-to-date for online customers. Given the growing importance of online customers, the Ecommerce website maintenance activity is considered strategic.

Table 6.6 synthesizes the information that the sales representatives would provide about the Maintain Website use case, including its purpose, dependencies, stakeholders, and their roles.

Table 6.6: The As-Is Maintain Website Use Case

Maintain Website Use Case Purpose	The primary objective of this use case is to make sure that the Ecommerce website is operational. It splits into post-website updates and post-product updates respectively performed by a webmaster and supported by the Ecommerce website.
Dependency: Post Page Updates	As its name suggests, this use case covers all of the activities needed to update the Ecommerce website pages. These activities are carried out by the webmaster.
Dependency: Post Product Updates	The Post Food Product Updates cover the activities aimed at keeping J&S Food's product catalog up-to-date and consistent. These activities are carried out by the webmaster based on Ecommerce development tools provided by the Ecommerce website.

Continues

Table 6.6 (*continued*)

Actor: Webmaster	This actor is J&S Food's staff responsible for maintaining the Ecommece website.
Actor: Ecommerce Website	This actor is the company's business-to-consumer (B2C) website. Its role in the Maintain Website use case is to provide the web design and development tools needed to maintain the website.

Develop Food Product

The Develop Food Product use case represents the set of activities covering food products development. These are important activities in J&S Food's business model.

Table 6.7 summarizes the information that the sales representatives would provide about the Develop Food Product use case, its purpose, dependencies, stakeholders, and their roles.

Table 6.7: The As-Is Develop Food Product Use Case

Develop Food Product Case Purpose	This use case covers menu design, meal proposal, meal cooking as well as other food products. It depends on two functions including create and update food products and Post Food Product Updates delivered by the Ecommerce website.
Dependency: Create/Update Food Product	The Create/Update Food Product use case allows the food product developer not only to offer new meals but also to cook them in a way that provides a superior food experience to customers.
Dependency: Post Product Updates	The Post Food Product Updates cover the activities aimed at keeping J&S Food's product catalog up-to-date and consistent. These activities are carried out by the webmaster based on Ecommerce development tools provided by the Ecommerce website.
Actor: Product Developer	J&S Food's partner is responsible for supplying take-out prepared foods and other food products.

Understanding J&S Food's Current Data Model

The enterprise architect would draw J&S Food's current data model as shown in Figure 6.3.

What you need to know about the as-is data model is that it is captured to help develop data migration scenarios and, more importantly, to identify the data that will part of J&S Food's analytics process.

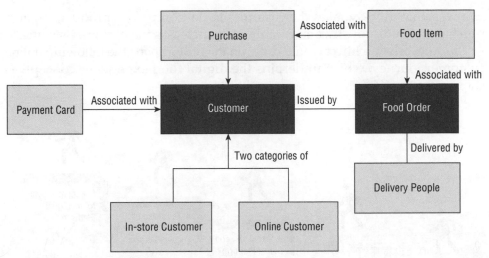

Figure 6.3: J&S Food's current data model

Figure 6.3 shows that Customer and Food Order represent the key data of J&S Food's current business model. Customer is an aggregation of several data including purchase, payment card, in-store customer, online customer, and food order. Food Order aggregates food item and delivery person information.

Assessing the As-Is Operational Model

After capturing and analyzing the organization's as-is business architecture, its processes, stakeholders, IT tools, infrastructure, and how it works, the next step the enterprise architect would take is to involve participants in assessing the existing business model. The objective is to evaluate how well the company's business model aligns with the disrupting industry's requirements and, more importantly, to identify the improvement areas. This is done in two steps including understanding the requirements to align with and then carrying out the actual assessment.

First let's discuss the requirements of the disrupting supermarket sector summed up in the concept of the digital food experience.

Digital Food Experience Defined

Digital food experience is a concept that summarizes the business model that any company willing to succeed in the online food business should adopt. "It's a set of practices in your industry that look like recommendations and standards," says the enterprise architect who summarizes his observations of the supermarket industry as "an optimization of the customer journey online in a way that quickly takes the customer to the company's product, triggers purchase, ensures loyalty, and continuously increases the customer's value."

The enterprise architect would draw on the posterboard the following online customer journey, which underpins the digital food experience concept, as shown in Figure 6.4.

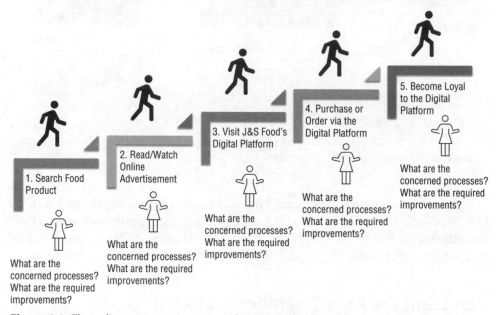

Figure 6.4: The online customer journey underpinning the digital food experience concept

What you must keep in mind is that the online customer journey is essential to building profitable digital business models. In line with the digital business requirement mantra, "focus on customer desires first," it helps to question, all along the five stages leading to the act of purchase, the customer's concerns and expectations as well as the organization's relevant processes and related improvement areas.

Assessing J&S Food's Operational Model

As you can imagine, assessment brainstorming sessions are passionate. For each stage of the customer journey, participants need to understand the customer's concerns and expectations and derive from them the company's relevant processes and related improvement areas.

Table 6.8 sums up the findings and recommendations that participants might agree upon.

Figure 6.5 illustrates, flagged as new, the functions identified as part of J&S Food's future digital business.

Table 6.8: Overview of the Assessment Findings and Recommendations

	FINDINGS	IMPROVEMENT RECOMMENDATIONS
Search Food Product	**Concerned Processes:** Prospecting, connecting, and presenting parts of the Buy use case.	Increase J&S Food's social media presence including the implementation of a social media and content marketing strategy.
Read/Watch Online Ads	**Concerned Process:** The presenting part of the Buy use case.	Same recommendations as previous.
Visit J&S Food's Digital Platform	**Concerned Process:** The approaching part of the Buy use case.	Same recommendations as previous.
Purchase/Order via Digital Platform	**Concerned Process:** The Pay and Fulfill parts of the Buy use case.	Implementation of a two-sided marketplace platform intended to optimize the Fulfill Order process. Implementation of a smart shopping bag intended to accelerate in-store purchases.
Become Loyal to the Digital Platform	**Concerned Processes:** Performing customer service and developing food product.	Implementation of a digital products and services development platform consistent with DevOps principles.

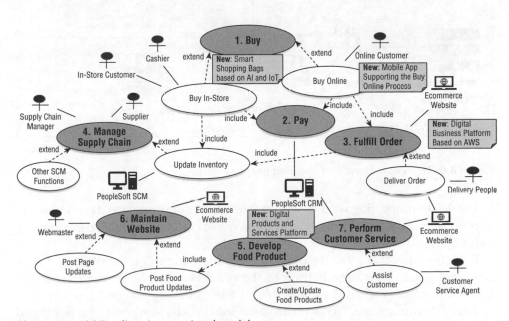

Figure 6.5: J&S Food's as-is operational model

The sales representatives, as well as the VP of marketing, would identify the following improvements that are expected to help the company outperform its competitors.

Defining the Digital Smart Shopping Bag

The VP of marketing would introduce the company's first digital food product, "Our next smart shopping bag will significantly improve our customers' digital experience."

Then the VP would explain, "Smart shopping bags use QR code (Quick Response) technology to enable customers to scan and pay for the food item they put in the bag as they shop without lining up at a cash register."

To make sure that all participants understand the requirements, the enterprise architect would draw the schematic diagram shown in Figure 6.6 on the posterboard.

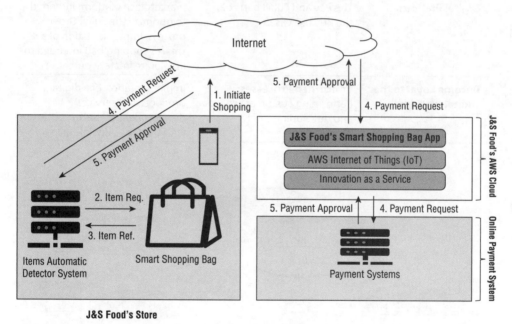

Figure 6.6: Overview of how the smart shopping bag works

The VP of marketing would describe the smart shopping bag as a "large bag that is connected to the Internet via the AWS IoT platform and the customer's debit or credit card."

First, the customer picks the inner bag to initiate the shopping process. As the customer places food items in the bag, the system counts them. As the customer leaves the grocery store, the credit card is automatically charged.

The VP would state, "This means that J&S Food's stores will be equipped with systems capable of remotely detecting and automatically counting food items in the bags."

Optimizing the Fulfill Order Experience Based on a Two-Sided Marketplace Platform

The second digital business asset that the VP of marketing would present is the company's next two-sided marketplace. The purpose of the two-sided marketplace platform is to facilitate interactions between J&S Food's customers and delivery people. It will make it easier, faster, and cheaper for J&S Food to find delivery people who will optimize the Fulfill Order process. Moreover, in addition to the exposure that delivery people will gain, the marketplace platform will generate a lot more business for delivery people than they would find on their own.

The two-sided marketplace platform will bring J&S Food's customers (also referred to as *buyers*) and delivery people (also known as *sellers*) together to create and exchange value including the benefits of being delivered in a timely manner to customers and the money paid by J&S Food (platform owner) to the sellers (see Figure 6.7).

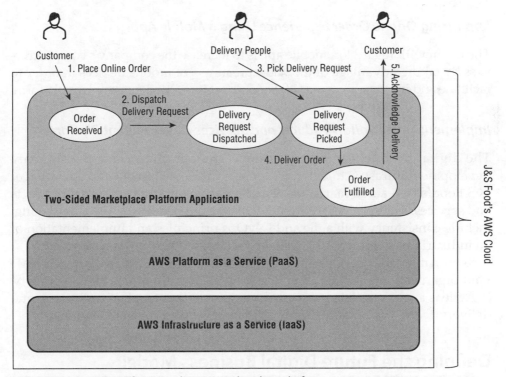

Figure 6.7: Overview of J&S Food's next marketplace platform

The VP of marketing would describe J&S Food's marketplace platform as an application hosted in the AWS cloud, consistent with cloud best practices, and providing four fundamental functions including Geolocate Delivery People, Dispatch Delivery Request, Track Delivery, and Acknowledge Delivery.

The *Geolocate Delivery People* function's primary purpose is to identify the delivery people who are the closest geographically to the customer who issued the online order.

What you need to bear in mind is that *geolocation* refers to the process of determining or estimating the geographical position of connected electronic devices using technologies like Global Positioning Systems (GPS) or IP addresses to identify and track their whereabouts.

The *Dispatch Delivery Request* function issues delivery requests to the delivery people who are geographically closest to the customer who placed the order online. Delivery people receive delivery requests on their electronic mobile devices including smartphones, tablets, and laptops. The Dispatch Delivery Request function builds on the geolocation function to determine the nearest delivery person.

The *Track Delivery* function allows customers to track their online order via their electronic mobile devices, while the *Acknowledge Delivery* function allows the customer to rate the delivery service.

Enhancing Online Order Experience Using a Mobile App

The intent with regard to a mobile app is to increase the company's competitiveness by taking advantage of the widespread use of mobile devices in order to facilitate and increase access to J&S Food's next two-sided marketplace platform.

Implementing a Digital Products and Services Development Platform

The digital products and services development platform is the software development infrastructure that will ensure the development and operation of J&S Food's two-sided marketplace and smart shopping bag digital products and services. The specific requirements, as formulated by the VP of marketing, include consistency with agile and DevOps principles and implementation of an industrialized approach to digital products and services development.

Keep in mind that DevOps is the combination of practices and tools that increase your organization's ability to deliver applications and services at high velocity.

Agile is an approach to software development that emphasizes incremental delivery, team collaboration, continual planning, and constant learning.

Defining the Future Digital Business Model

In this step, the enterprise architect will tackle the adaptation of the business to the digital competition. The bottom line is to redefine the business model in a way that guarantees a world-class digital food experience.

Reconfiguring J&S Food's Operational Model

Given the fact that the company's business model isn't tailored for the digital business, before moving forward, the enterprise architect will want to align the as-is J&S Food's business model's terminology to that of the digital value chain. The enterprise architect would achieve that by realigning J&S Food's existing value chain to the digital business value chain in terms of activities sequencing, process, and names. This is what is meant by operational model reconfiguration to digital.

The sections that follow define the differences between the value chain and the digital business value chain, and then it moves on with how to rethink J&S Food's business model.

Understanding Michael Porter's Value Chain

The *value chain* is the set of activities that an organization carries out to create value for its customers. In his book *Competitive Strategy: Techniques for Analyzing Industries and Competitor*s (Free Press, 1998), Michael Porter proposes a general-purpose value chain that companies can use to examine all of their activities and see how well they're performing. The rationale underlying Porter's value chain suggests that, on the one hand, to create value the organization must build on five activities that execute in a specific order. These activities include *inbound logistics, operations, outbound logistics, marketing and sales*, and *service*. On the other hand, these activities, referred to as primary processes, must be supported by four other activities, referred to as support activities. These activities include *firm infrastructure, human resource management, technology development*, and *procurement*, as illustrated in Figure 6.8.

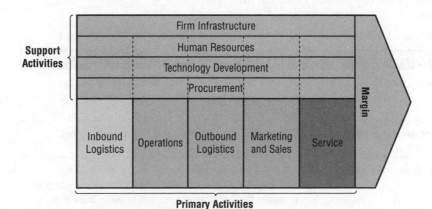

Figure 6.8: Michael Porter's original value chain

Source: Business Research Methodology

The Primary Activities

The purpose of the primary activities is to create a chain of added-value activities focused on creating value via the development of profitable products and services. Table 6.9 describes the primary activities.

Table 6.9: The Primary Activities of the Original Value Chain Framework

PRIMARY ACTIVITIES	DESCRIPTION
Inbound Logistics	The purpose is to provide the raw material needed to manufacture products. Activities include receiving, storing, and disseminating raw material to allow manufacturing.
Operations	The core purpose is to transform raw material into products. Activities include manufacturing, packaging, testing, and equipment maintenance.
Outbound Logistics	The goal is to take manufactured products to markets. Activities include collecting, storing, and distributing products to buyers and potential distributors.
Marketing & Sales	The objective is to attract buyers and trigger the purchase. Activities include advertising, promotion, and sales.
Service	The goal is to provide post-sales services for helping customers with the company's product and also to ensure loyalty. Activities include providing service to enhance the value of the product, installation, repair, and training.

The Support Activities

The intent with the support activities is to develop a chain of added-value activities that create the conditions for high-value products manufacturing. Table 6.10 describes the primary activities.

Table 6.10: The Support Activities of the Original Value Chain Framework

SUPPORT ACTIVITIES	DESCRIPTION
Firm Infrastructure	This encompasses a variety of enabling activities including strategic management, finance, accounting, legal, and quality management.
Human Resource Management	This includes activities such as recruiting, hiring, training, development, and compensation.
Technology Development	This involves research and development (R&D) activities aimed at selecting the technologies likely to improve the company's product quality, business processes efficiency, and staff productivity.
Procurement	This refers to the function of purchasing raw materials and the technology needed to manufacture products.

The Value Chain for Digital Business Defined

The digital business value chain described in this book is an adaptation by its author of the original version of the value chain. Like the original version, the digital business value chain is structured around two categories of activities: *primary* and *support* activities.

Unlike the original version of the value chain, which emphasizes product implementation and technology, the digital value chain considers customer concerns and expectations as a priority, and it uses these as a determinant of the digital products and services' expected features.

What you should keep in mind is that this paradigm shift introduces differences in the digital value chain (see Figure 6.9). These differences include the fact that, in the primary activities, *customer insights* (discovering customer concerns and expectations) are the starting point of digital products and services development, and also that *customer value increase* (the practice of selling customers offerings that complement purchases they've already made, known as *upselling*, or encouraging them to add on more expensive services, known as *cross-selling*) activities are considered strategic in digital business.

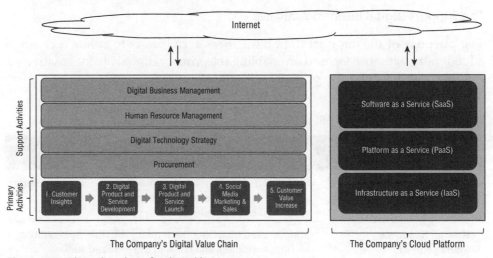

Figure 6.9: The value chain for digital business

The rationale underpinning the digital business value chain is that customer concerns and expectations are the primary determinant of value. The digital primary and support activities are described in the following sections.

The Primary Digital Business Activities

The goal of the primary digital business activities is to create a chain of added-value activities focused on creating value via the development of profitable digital products and services.

Table 6.11 describes the primary activities.

Table 6.11: The Primary Digital Business Activities of the Original Value Chain Framework

PRIMARY ACTIVITIES	DESCRIPTION
Customer Insights	Highlighting customer concerns and expectations using data science and big data solutions.
Digital Products and Services Development	Designing, developing, and testing digital products and services based on customer concerns and expectations provided as inputs by the customer insights activities.
Digital Products and Services Launch	Ensuring digital products and services deployment to production environments and go-to-market.
Social Media Marketing and Sales	Advertising and promoting on social media digital products and services to create brand awareness and trigger purchases.
Customer Value Increase	Taking advantage of interactions with clients to increase customer value via upselling and cross-selling operations.

The Support Digital Business Activities

The purpose of the support digital business activities is to create a chain of added-value activities focused on enabling the primary digital business activities. Table 6.12 describes the primary activities.

Table 6.12: The Support Digital Business Activities

SUPPORT DIGITAL BUSINESS ACTIVITIES	DESCRIPTION
Digital Business Management	Facilitating digital business primary activities by providing tools, methodologies, and approaches for delivering a superior digital experience.
Human Resource Management	Supporting digital business primary activities by recruiting, hiring, developing, and training the required staff.
Digital Technology Strategy	Enabling digital business primary activities by providing the methodologies and selecting the adequate technologies needed to deliver a superior digital business experience.
Procurement	Facilitating digital business primary activities by acting as liaison between digital products and services development teams and providers in terms of contract management and infrastructure purchases.

J&S Food's Digital Business Model Defined

The J&S Food's digital business model is the combination of its digital business value chain and its AWS cloud services, as shown in Figure 6.10.

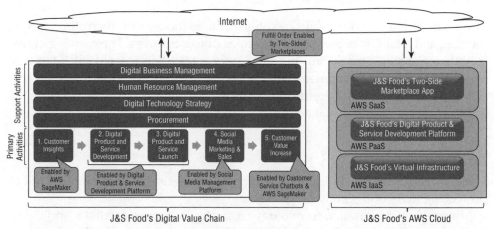

Figure 6.10: J&S Food's future digital business model

The digital business value chain highlights the set of activities intended to support its business while the AWS cloud platform hosts the applications, services, and platforms that enable the value chain. Let's discuss them.

Understanding J&S Food's Next Digital Value Chain

These activities will support the management of the digital business including optimizing J&S Food's digital business experience, providing high-quality human resources management, and making profitable relationships with customers, vendors, and partners.

Support Digital Business Activities

Support digital business activities consist of a number of activities enabling the primary digital business activities.

Digital Business Management

The digital business management activities would focus on managing the digital food experience management. Digital food experience management is about overseeing the digital food experience delivered and making sure that it increases customer value, stopping customer churn while acquiring new ones.

Digital food experience management would interact strongly with the digital products and services development teams to ensure that smart shopping bags and the two-sided marketplace platform are consistent with customer expectations.

Human Resource Management

The set of human resource (HR) activities will be focused on recruiting, hiring, training, and retaining digital experts in strategic business areas. These strategic areas include social media marketing, big data, Amazon Web Services (AWS), Internet of Things (IoT), agile development, and digital products and services development.

The human factor is a significant performance enabler, so J&S Food intends to create a clear competitive advantage with good HR practices.

Digital Technology Strategy

These activities are related to managing and processing information as well as protecting J&S Food's knowledge base.

Minimizing information technology costs, staying current with technological advances, and maintaining technical excellence would be considered sources of value creation.

Procurement

This is about what J&S Food would do to get the resources it would need to operate. This would include finding technology vendors, delivery people, and negotiating best prices.

Primary Digital Business Activities

These activities will support the design, development, operations, and selling of J&S Food's digital products and services including the smart shopping bag and the food products digital delivery.

The digital business value chain suggests that to deliver a superior digital food experience, the smart shopping bag and food products digital delivery service must be managed through a chain of clearly identified activities. These activities include customer insights, digital products and services development, digital products and services launch, social media marketing and sales, and customer value increase. Let's discuss them.

Customer Insights

Customer insights cover J&S Food's big data analytics. It's responsible for exploring and analyzing data to spot industry and market trends as well as customer concerns and expectations.

Data scientists in an agile team involving marketing, sales, customer service, as well as smart shopping bag and food products digital delivery service developers, will build a big data solution to guide the J&S Food's marketing and product developers in terms of new products and features as well as innovations to implement.

Digital Products and Services Development

These activities involve marketing, sales, customer service, and digital products and services developers in an agile team structure. They cover design, development, testing, and maintenance activities of the smart shopping bag and food products digital delivery service.

The activities will build on the digital products and services development platform that will provide a DevOps approach to make sure that digital products and services are consistent with agreed expectations.

Digital Products and Services Launch

These activities cover the technical deployment of the digital products and services to production environment as well as planning and coordinating to debut new digital products and services or features to the market and make them available for purchase.

Digital products and services launch activities involve in an agile team structure marketing, sales, customer service, digital products and services developers, and IT operations.

Social Media Marketing and Online Sales

Social media marketing refers to how J&S Food will use social media platforms to connect with its audience in order to build its brand, increase sales, and increase traffic to its Ecommerce website. The goal is to increase interactions with customers via relevant touchpoints in order to make customers aware of J&S Food's brand and to create the conditions for substantial purchases and orders.

These activities will include J&S Food publishing great content on its social media profiles, listening to and engaging its followers, analyzing the results, and running social media advertisements. Social media management tools will be used to help the company get the most out of the most popular social media platforms.

Customer Value Increase

These activities refer to the process designed to ensure that J&S Food's customers are satisfied with the products and services that they ordered. The goal is to improve customers' experience continuously with services.

In addition to helping customers to enjoy their digital food products and services delivery, these activities will help J&S Food take advantage of data analytics platforms with the goal of better understanding customer feedback data and anticipating customer expectations.

Understanding J&S Food's AWS Cloud Platform

This is the AWS cloud that will host J&S Food's Ecommerce activities. This could be the CEO's decision considering factors such as cost savings, automation, scalability, rapid development, and security benefits, advocated by the cloud computing consultant.

As the CEO makes clear:

"What tipped the balance in favor of AWS is the flexibility of its Virtual Private Cloud (VPC). The VPC offers options that make it possible to organize applications hosting while guaranteeing security and performance. This makes it the ideal environment to implement J&S Food's virtual datacenter (VDC)."

VDC is a single point of control for managing the organization's infrastructure and applications in the AWS cloud.

J&S Food's AWS Software as a Service

This is the web-based model via which J&S Food's online customers and delivery people will access the company's two-sided marketplace from their smartphones, tablets, personal computers, and voice-activated personal assistants. The benefits of the AWS SaaS model for J&S Food's stores and delivery people might include the ability to run via an Internet browser 24/7 from any device. From an operational management standpoint, no installation, equipment updates, or traditional licensing management is needed.

The J&S Food's Platform as a Service

The J&S Food's digital products and services development platform will be based on AWS PaaS services. These are the AWS services designed to support rapid development, running, and management of applications. It supports the development of applications, both desktop and mobile.

The benefits that J&S Food's development community might gain from AWS PaaS services are ease of use, various arrays of tools, unlimited server capacity, reliable encryption and security mechanisms, and managed IT services.

The J&S Food's AWS Virtual Infrastructure

This the AWS service that J&S Food may emphasize to support its Ecommerce infrastructure. The bottom line may be to implement a virtual datacenter

(VDC) used to replace physical resources, such as servers, with virtual resources hosted and managed by Amazon. The benefits for J&S Food can be substantial infrastructure cost savings, ease of use, scalability, flexibility, and security.

Integrating J&S Food's Digital Operational Model with the Organization

What is viewed as one of the main challenges faced by businesses engaged in a digital transformation is that of the organization of work. However, it's wrongly considered "challenging."

Given that the goal is to deliver a superior digital experience that generates revenue and that by smartly bringing together the company's value-added activities into what's referred to in this book as the *digital business organizational model* that makes it possible, why not consider the digital business value chain a shortcut that simplifies the design of the organization of people and work?

The following sections discuss the notion of the digital business organizational model and describe J&S Food's digital organizational model, including its stakeholders, collaboration, and decision-making structures.

The Digital Business Value Chain: A Shortcut to the Digital Business Organization

When it comes to organizational design, digital transformation experts have been wrong to underestimate the benefits of the value chain. The value chain as it's extended to digital business organizational design in this section is useful for a variety of reasons:

- It's based on principles founded on the creation of value leveraging the synergy of added-value resources (people, processes, practices, and technologies).

- It brings together your organization's added-value activities into a digital business organizational model.

- Consistent with the division of labor principles, it splits your organization's activities into primary and support.

Digital Business Organizational Model Defined

The digital business organizational model represents a synergy of your organization's added-value resources augmented with adequate collaboration and decision-making mechanisms (see Figure 6.11).

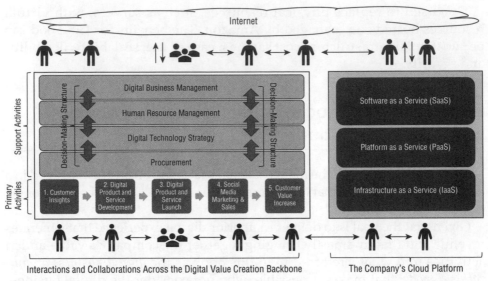

Figure 6.11: The digital business organization model

These resources include people, processes, practices, tools, and infrastructure while collaboration and decision-making mechanisms include the project management office (PMO) model, agile Scrum, and the project matrix defined in Chapter 3, "Digital Product and Service Development Challenges." The primary objective is to help the enterprise architect not only to define the organization of work in terms of processes, activities, people, roles, and responsibilities, but also to define the adequate interactions, collaborations, and decision-making structures.

The next section provides a simple tool to design your digital business organizational model intelligently.

Developing the Digital Business Organizational Model

To develop the digital business organizational model, the enterprise architect would brainstorm with participants based on the questionnaire shown in Table 6.13.

Table 6.13: Digital Business Organizational Model Design Questionnaire

DEPARTMENT	STAKEHOLDER ROLES & RESPONSIBILITIES	INTERACTIONS, COLLABORATION, AND APPROACHES	DECISION-MAKING STRUCTURES
	WHO? WHAT ROLES AND RESPONSIBILITIES?	*WHO INTERACTS/ COLLABORATES WITH WHO? AGILE? MATRIX?*	*WHAT IS THE ADEQUATE GOVERNANCE, REVIEW, AND DECISION-MAKING STRUCTURES?*
Digital Business Management			
Human Resource Management			
Digital Technology Strategy			
Procurement			
Customer Insights			
Digital Products and Services Development			
Digital Products and Services Launch			
Social Media Marketing and Sales			
Customer Value Increase			

The J&S Organizational Model Defined

Figure 6.12 shows the J&S Food's digital business organizational model that would result from the discussion between the enterprise architect and participants using the questionnaire.

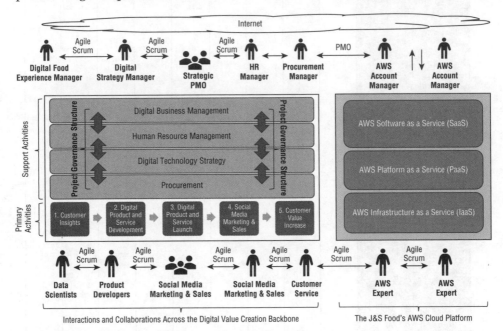

Figure 6.12: The J&S Food's organizational model

J&S Food's digital business organizational model highlights three elements including roles and responsibilities, interaction and collaboration mechanisms, and decision-making structures. Let's discuss them.

Roles and Responsibilities

The *responsibility assignment matrix*, also known as the *responsible, accountable, consulted, and informed (RACI) model*, illustrated by Table 6.14, describes the roles and responsibilities of J&S Food's business model's stakeholders.

Table 6.14: J&S Food's Responsibility Assignment Matrix (RAM)

ROLE	DIGITAL BUSINESS AREA	ROLE DESCRIPTION
Digital Food Experience Manager	Support — Digital Business Management	Interacts with the digital strategy manager and all actors involved in the primary activities designed to assess the performance of the company's digital food experience and recommend improvements for J&S Food's digital food experience.

ROLE	DIGITAL BUSINESS AREA	ROLE DESCRIPTION
Digital Strategy Manager	Support — Digital Business Management	Collaborates with the CEO, digital food experience manager, and all of the stakeholders of J&S Food's business on planning and monitoring the company's digital business strategy.
Strategic Project Manager	Support — Digital Business Management	Acting as the Scrum master, the strategic project manager facilitates digital products and services development prioritization, ensures that digital products and services development best practices are applied, and provides insights into development progress to the digital food experience and digital strategy managers.
HR Manager	Human Resource Management	Collaborates with digital food experience and digital strategy managers as well as with all actors involved in the primary activities designed to recruit, hire, develop, and train the staff needed in J&S Food's business.
Procurement Manager	Procurement Management	Collaborates with the stakeholders of J&S Food's primary activities to address infrastructure purchase, legal, and vendor management issues.
Data Scientist	Customer Insights	Collaborates with social media marketing and sales managers to explore and analyze data in an effort to identify digital food market trends and customer concerns and expectations.
Product Developer	Digital Products and Services Development	Collaborates with the digital food experience manager and with all stakeholders of the primary activities to develop digital products and services. Assumes operational responsibility of the digital products and services development platform as well as that of the two-sided marketplace platforms.
Social Media Marketer and Salesman	Social Media Marketing & Sales and Digital Products & Services Launch	Collaborates with all actors involved in J&S Food's primary activities as well as with the digital food experience and digital business strategy managers on digital products and services' rollout and sales.
Customer Service Agent	Customer Service	Collaborates with data scientists, product developers, and with digital food experience and digital strategy managers on increasing customer value.

Interaction and Collaboration Mechanisms

The methodologies and tools that participants would select to optimize interactions and collaborations across J&S Food's organizational model include agile Scrums and the project management office (PMO) model.

Agile Scrums are set of meetings, tools, and roles that work in concert to help teams structure and manage their work. The PMO model refers to a structure supporting the execution of the organization's business strategy by facilitating the delivery of strategic projects and promoting project management best practices across the company.

Table 6.15 summarizes their benefits.

Table 6.15: The Interactions and Collaboration Mechanisms Implemented

TOOLS/ METHODOLOGIES	INVOLVED STAKEHOLDERS	BENEFITS
Agile Scrums	All primary activities stakeholders and digital food experience and digital strategy managers	Quicker release of digital products and services to customers. Higher productivity across J&S Food's primary activities. Lower costs and higher quality.
Project Management Office (PMO) Model	All actors involved in J&S Food's support activities	Project portfolio management (PPM) used. Effective new product development governance process. Effective new digital products and services selection process. Objective focused on business goals. Better view of the big picture of J&S Food's digital food experience performance.

Key Takeaways

Successful digital transformation cannot be achieved without first adapting your business model to the requirements caused by your industry disruption.

In this chapter, you learned that your business model transformation requires that your organization address several issues and derive from them a business system that allows the company to offer the best possible digital experience.

These strongly interconnected issues include the identification of factors disrupting your industry, their impact on customers and the company, and more importantly, consideration of customer concerns and expectations without which no superior digital business experience is possible.

This chapter provided excellent techniques for making the business model transformation process simpler, easier, faster, and more importantly profitable. These techniques include the following:

- The five competitive forces framework used to capture the factors disrupting an industry and related transformation requirements.

- The digital customer journey used to capture consumer concerns and expectations at all stages toward purchase.

- The use case diagram utilized to capture and understand the key elements of the as-is business architecture.

- The digital business value chain used to assess the organization's staff, processes, practices, and tools versus the transformation requirements and processes used to derive the improvement areas.

- The digital business organizational model utilized to reconfigure the organization interaction, collaboration mechanisms as well as the decision-making structures.

In the next chapter, you'll be involved in the digitization of J&S Food's new business architecture facilitated by an Amazon Web Services (AWS) senior solution architect.

References

1. Spring Wise, "Smart Shopping Bag Could Eliminate Queuing," *Spring Wise* (April 6, 2016). `https://www.springwise.com/smart-shopping-bag-eliminate-queuing/`

2. Juho Makkonen, "Two-Sided Marketplace: Why and How They Succeed," *Sharetribe* (February 22, 2021). `https://www.sharetribe.com/how-to-build/two-sided-marketplace/`

3. Evan Tarver, "What Are the Primary Activities of Michael Porter's Value Chain," *Investopedia* (May 26, 2019). `https://www.investopedia.com/ask/answers/050115/what-are-primary-activities-michael-porters-value-chain.asp`

4. Ian Mitchell, "The Agile PMO," *The Home of Scrum* (March 05, 2017). `https://www.scrum.org/resources/blog/agile-pmo`

Digitizing J&S Food's Business Model Using AWS— Implementing the VPC

The increasing presence of cloud computing and mobile smart phones is driving the digitization of everything across both consumer and enterprise domains. It is hard to imagine any area of human activity which is not being reengineered under this influence, either at present or in the very near future.

—**Geoffrey Moore**

The stake in this step of the digital transformation journey is to implement the technology in a cloud environment in a way that not only makes the operational and organizational models efficient but also allows J&S Food to deliver a superior digital food experience. The challenge is to achieve the intelligent and efficient use of technology with a laser focus on the processes and practices that enable the expected digital experience.

This chapter will show you how an AWS Solutions Architect leverages the Enterprise Cloud Migration (ECM) design pattern to speed the implementation of J&S Food's AWS computing environment.

In this chapter, you'll be part of an operational model digitization session involving an AWS Solutions Architect, application developers, testers, and IT operations.

The workshop will address issues such as developing an AWS migration strategy, defining an AWS cloud architecture, re-architecting applications for AWS, and migrating applications to AWS.

Transformation Journey's Third Stage: Digitizing the Business Model

The digitizing the business stage is about implementing cloud technology in a way that enables the expected digital food experience. It's a three-phase process including the implementation of the DevOps platform (Chapter 8, "Implementing J&S Food's DevOps Platform Using AWS PaaS"), developing the innovation as a service platform (Chapter 9, "Developing J&S Food's Innovation as a Service Platform Using AWS"), and this chapter, which is about implementing J&S Food's Amazon Virtual Private Cloud (VPC) that will not only host the company's virtual infrastructure resources but also support the company's digital business.

Figure 7.1 illustrates where the digital transformation team stands in the transformation journey.

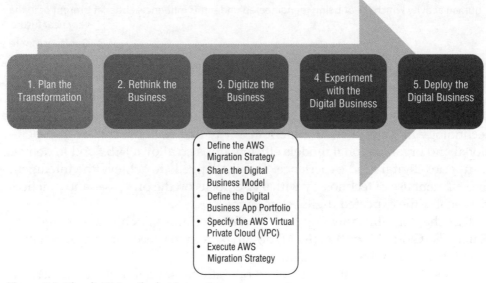

Figure 7.1: The digitizing the business stage

As Figure 7.1 indicates, the AWS Solutions Architect would tackle the digitization effort in these five steps:

- Defining the AWS migration strategy
- Sharing the digital business model
- Defining the digital business application portfolio
- Specifying the Amazon Virtual Private Cloud (VPC)
- Executing the AWS migration strategy

Let's see how the AWS Solutions Architect would go about digitizing J&S Food's business model.

Defining J&S Food's AWS Migration Strategy

The problem with today's practice is that cloud migration strategy development is overlooked. Developing an AWS migration strategy is not a trivial task that can be improvised or narrowed down to a matter of taking applications to the cloud and making them compatible with the requirements of the AWS computing environment.

What you need to know is that, in the context of a digital transformation project, developing an AWS migration strategy is primarily about pinpointing the key processes of the digital business model, making sure that the applications underpinning these processes are migratable, and then proceeding with the technical adaptation and deployment of these applications to the AWS computing environment. As you can see, the perspectives and objectives are different.

Figure 7.2 illustrates the kind of AWS migration strategy development framework the AWS Solutions Architect would use.

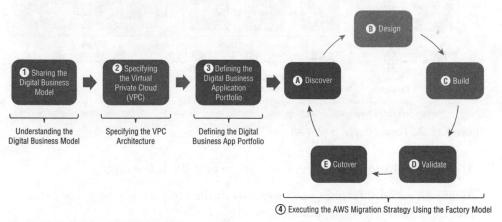

Figure 7.2: J&S Food's AWS migration strategy

The AWS migration plan recommended in Figure 7.2 includes four steps:

1. Sharing (with the implementation team) the digital business model
2. Specifying the VPC architecture
3. Developing the digital business applications portfolio
4. Executing the AWS migration strategy

The next sections elaborate on each of them.

Sharing J&S Food's Digital Business Model

The AWS Solutions Architect would start the meeting by sharing the new digital business model with the implementation team (see Figure 7.3):

"The goal here is to examine all of the pieces of the business architecture to identify the underpinning applications and systems."

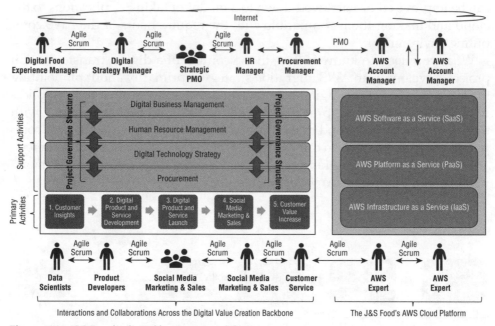

Figure 7.3: J&S Food's digital business model

The AWS Solutions Architect would then add the following:

"For each activity (primary and support) in the digital business value chain, provide the underlying applications, existing or new."

Table 7.1 outlines the application list that would result as part of J&S Food's new digital business model.

Table 7.1: Concerned Business Domains and Related Applications

BUSINESS DOMAIN ACTIVITIES	EXISTING APPLICATIONS	NEW APPLICATIONS
Customer Insights	PeopleSoft CRM	Big data solutions based on Amazon Elastic Map Reduce (EMR)
Digital Product and Service Development	No specific application or platform	Digital product and service development platform based on DevOps

BUSINESS DOMAIN ACTIVITIES	EXISTING APPLICATIONS	NEW APPLICATIONS
Digital Product and Service Launch	No specific application or platform	Digital product and service development platform based on DevOps
Social Media Marketing and Sales	None	Two-sided marketplace platform; ecommerce website; Hootsuite (a social media management platform)
Customer Value Increase	None	AI / ML solution based on Amazon SageMaker
Digital Business Management	None	Not applicable
Human Resource Management	Not applicable	Not applicable
Digital Technology Strategy	Not applicable	Not applicable
Procurement	Not applicable	Not applicable

Let's discuss the development of J&S Food's digital business application portfolio.

Defining the J&S Food's Digital Business Application Portfolio

This activity is about screening the applications identified in Table 7.1 that are migratable to the AWS computing environment. The application readiness for AWS is evaluated and the application migration strategy is determined accordingly.

Figure 7.4 explains the digital business application portfolio development process.

Each application in the application candidate list is evaluated against two main criteria: compatibility with the technical and technological requirements of AWS and the risks and constraints.

The application migration strategy refers to the adaptation of the application's code and architecture to the AWS computing environment requirements. It is determined based on the AWS 6R's model explained in Table 7.2.

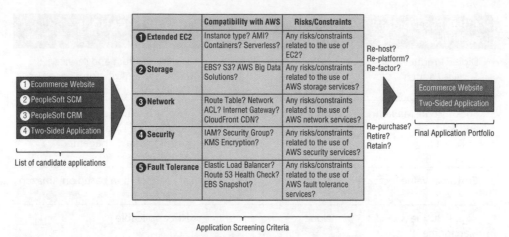

Figure 7.4: The digital business application portfolio development process

Table 7.2: The AWS 6R's Model

MIGRATION STRATEGY	DESCRIPTION
Re-host	Also referred to as *lift-and-shift*, this application migration approach is about moving the application in the AWS environment without changes.
Re-platform	Also referred to as *lift, tinker, and shift*, this migration method is about making few optimizations to achieve tangible benefits.
Re-factor / Re-architect	This migration approach is about re-architecting the application using AWS services and features to make it compatible with the AWS computing environment.
Re-purchase	This approach is about dropping the licensing method in favor of the software-as-a-service (SaaS) model.
Retire	This recommendation is about decommissioning the application if it's no longer needed.
Retain	This recommendation is about postponing the application migration or keeping it in the organization's on-premises infrastructure.

Applying the screening criteria and deciding on the adequate application migration strategies, participants would determine that the ecommerce website and the future two-sided marketplace application are part of the J&S Food's digital business application portfolio.

The PeopleSoft CRM and SCM ERPs would not migrate to the J&S Food's AWS computing environment, and the ecommerce website would be re-factored to make it compatible with the AWS computing requirements.

Specifying J&S Food's Virtual Private Cloud Architecture

In this step, the AWS Solutions Architect would warn as follows:

"This is a major and challenging step in the digitization of the business model: We have to define the company's cloud architecture."

The Solutions Architect would also reassure the audience as follows:

"We'll build on the enterprise cloud migration (ECM) framework for AWS to make the architecture effort effective, easy, and fast."

Understanding the Enterprise Cloud Migration Model For AWS

The *enterprise cloud migration (ECM)* architecture for AWS, as discussed in Chapter 4, "Industrializing Digital Product and Service Development," is a cloud architecture design pattern developed by this book's author. The ECM design pattern seeks to simplify, facilitate, and speed the implementation of an enterprise cloud in the AWS environment.

This framework organizes the most commonly used AWS services into five key areas, forming what's known as the organization's *virtual private cloud (VPC)*. It suggests a VPC architecture specification in three steps:

- Deriving the organization's VPC architecture from the ECM design pattern diagram
- Removing any useless AWS service and feature or adding any new AWS service and feature
- Describing the purpose and role of each AWS service, component, and feature in the overall architecture

Let's pay attention to what the AWS Solutions Architect would say about J&S Food's next VPC.

J&S Food's Virtual Private Cloud Specified

The proposed J&S Food's AWS cloud architecture is projected on a screen, as represented in Figure 7.5.

The consultant would start by clarifying the following:

"The VPC is the virtual facility hosting your virtual infrastructure and applications in the AWS computing environment."

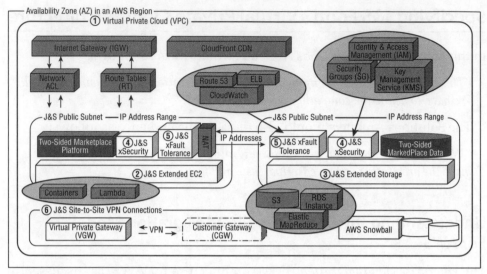

Figure 7.5: The J&S Food's VPC

As the diagram on the screen is fairly complex, the consultant would reassure the participants as follows:

"For your convenience, I've numbered 1 to 6 the key areas on which you should focus. The numbers are circled. These key areas include the virtual private cloud (VPC), the extended elastic cloud computing (EC2), the extended storage, the extended fault tolerance, the extended security, and the site-to-site VPN connection building blocks."

The next sections elaborate on how the Solutions Architect would justify the architectural options.

The Availability Zone

The availability zone purpose and benefits cannot be understood without knowing what an AWS region is. *AWS regions* are separate geographic areas that AWS uses to house its infrastructure.

An *availability zone (AZ)* is one or more discrete data centers with redundant power, networking, and connectivity in an AWS region. They provide inexpensive, low-latency network connectivity to other availability zones in the same AWS region. Each region is completely independent.

The Solutions Architect would explain as follows:

"J&S Food's cloud platform will take advantage of AZs to implement disaster recovery (DR) options."

The Solutions Architect would further justify as follows:

"These options will provide better availability for the two-sided marketplace platform and the ecommerce website while protecting them against failure of the underlying AWS platform including physical server, network, and storage."

In fact, the AWS availability zones are designed for physical redundancy and provide resilience, allowing for uninterrupted performance, even in the event of power outages, Internet downtime, floods, and other natural disasters.

Amazon CloudFront and the Content Delivery Network

Then the Solutions Architect would proceed with Amazon CloudFront,

"Understand Amazon CloudFront as a worldwide network of data centers called edge locations. The goal is to securely deliver to your customers data, videos, applications, and APIs at the lowest possible latency."

Being specific, the Solutions Architect would add,

"We'll need to create a CloudFront distribution, a content delivery network (CDN), to reduce the volume of application origin (location where content is stored) requests. It causes content to be stored in CloudFront edges and regional caches and fetched only when needed. That's how low latency is obtained."

J&S Food's Virtual Private Cloud

The AWS Solutions Architect would tell participants to think of the VPC as follows:

"The VPC is the virtual facility hosting the virtual infrastructure resources that will allow the two-sided marketplace platform to run efficiently, safely, and contribute to the expected superior digital food experience."

The Solutions Architect would further clarify as follows:

"The efficient and safe computing environment is made possible by the combined effects of six components including the Internet gateway (IGW), route tables (RT), network access control list (ACL), public subnet, private subnet, and the site-to-site VPN."

Let's review what the Solutions Architect would say about how these six elements contribute to J&S Food's AWS cloud architecture.

The Internet Gateway, Route Tables, and Network Access Control List

The Solutions Architect would ask participants to imagine the Internet gateway as a component that connects the VPC to the Internet and to other AWS virtual infrastructure resources and services.

He would certainly make clear how the Internet gateway works:

"The Internet gateway builds on route tables (RT) to enable and direct traffic from J&S Food's AWS virtual infrastructure resources to the Internet."

From the perspective of the Internet gateway's role in J&S Food's AWS cloud, the primary purpose of route tables will be to control and enable outgoing network traffic, more specifically, the traffic from J&S Food's virtual infrastructure to the Internet.

The Solutions Architect would certainly remind the participants about the following:

"Subnets, public or private, and route tables are strongly related, they form the mechanism that filters outgoing traffic."

Route tables contain the information needed to forward traffic along the best path toward its destination. The destination includes either the Internet or other virtual infrastructure resources within J&S Food's AWS cloud.

As to network ACLs, like route tables, their role is to secure network traffic within J&S Food's AWS cloud. Participants might ask the following:

"Why use Network ACLs if they provide the same services as route tables?"

Be aware that network ACLs provide additional security levels, unlike route tables that are focused solely on outgoing traffic, network ACLs are concerned about inbound and outbound traffic.

The Public Subnet Structure Elements

The public subnet is one that's associated with a route table that has a route to an Internet gateway.

The Solutions Architect would explain the public subnet as follows:

"Imagine the public subnet as server racks that house servers designed to enable direct access to the Internet or to be directly accessible from the Internet."

J&S Food's VPC will build on public subnets to allow direct access to the two-sided marketplace platform.

What you need to know is that, in addition to IP address ranges assigned to the AWS resources under their control, public subnets are associated with a network address translation (NAT) gateway.

NAT gateways enable instances, or any other AWS virtual infrastructure resources in a private subnet, to connect to the Internet or to other AWS services. They prevent the Internet from initiating connections with those instances and resources.

The Private Subnet Structure Elements

Unlike public subnets, private subnets route traffic through a NAT gateway in the public subnet. The NAT gateway forwards traffic to the Internet gateway.

The Solutions Architect would state the following:

"J&S Food's AWS cloud platform will rely on private subnets to protect business data including customer, order, and payment card information from Internet access."

The Site-to-Site VPN Connection

A *virtual private network (VPN)* connection refers to the connection between your VPC and your own on-premises network. Site-to-site VPN supports Internet Protocol Security (IPsec) VPN connections.

Your AWS site-to-site VPN is a permanent connection designed to function as an encrypted link between your AWS cloud and remote sites.

In J&S Food's AWS cloud, the site-to-site VPN connection will enable secure communications between the AWS resources in the VPC with your on-premises infrastructure.

J&S Food's Extended Elastic Compute Cloud Building Block

The *extended EC2* is a construct representing the idea of a virtual application server in the AWS computing environment.

By analogy, a virtual application server is a type of server designed to install, operate, and host applications and associated services in the most effective and efficient way possible.

The goal is to bundle the many and scattered AWS resources involved in efficiently hosting and running applications into a single, logical concept that facilitates not only understanding but also the architectural design effort.

The extended EC2's intent is to host and run the application supporting J&S Food's two-sided marketplace platform. Figure 7.6 shows the AWS services and features that comprise the extended EC2.

The following sections elaborate on what the AWS Solutions Architect would say about the features of the extended EC2.

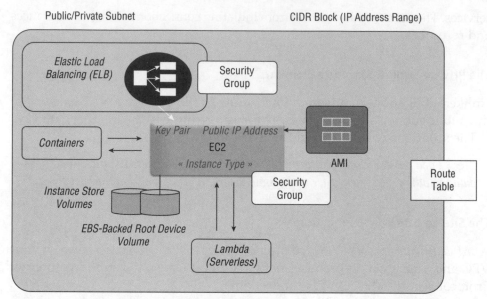

Figure 7.6: Overview of J&S Food's extended EC2

Instance Type

The concept of instance type is the hardware configuration underpinning the EC2 instance. The AWS Solutions Architect would propose to use the *T2.2Xlarge instance type*, which is appropriate for applications with large resource requirements. Table 7.3 describes a T2.2Xlarge instance type.

Table 7.3: The Characteristics of T2.2Xlarge Instance Type

CHARACTERISTIC	VALUE	DESCRIPTION
vCPUs	8	AWS instances support multithreading, which enables multiple threads (a thread is simply a process) to run in a single CPU. Each virtual central processing unit (vCPU) is a thread of a CPU core.
RAM (GiB)	32	Random access memory (RAM) is the memory capacity of the EC2 instance. The larger the RAM, the faster the processing.
CPU Credits/hr	81	CPU credits allow T2 instances to have CPU performance beyond the baseline performance provided by the EC2. One CPU credit is equal to one minute of a full CPU core.

To the question why not any other instance type, the Solutions Architect would advocate his choice:

"IBM WebSphere Liberty, the solution that will support the two-sided marketplace application, is based on Java EE. It's known for consuming a lot of system resources."

Amazon Machine Image

The role of the *Amazon Machine Image (AMI)* is the software configuration of the instance intended to support the two-sided marketplace platform. The AWS Solutions Architect would propose to use the WebSphere Liberty AMI, as described in Table 7.4.

Table 7.4: Features of the AMI Supporting WebSphere Liberty

FEATURES	DESCRIPTION
AMI type	64-bit (x86) Amazon Machine Image
Operating system (OS)	Linux/Unix, Ubuntu
Other software	WebSphere Liberty

Anticipating the question, "Why continue with IBM WebSphere?" the AWS Solutions Architect would reply as follows:

"The code audit we performed shows that the existing application, which is based on WebSphere, is well designed. We're going to extend its scope to the functionalities of a marketplace platform."

The AWS Solutions Architect would conclude as follows:

"Furthermore, WebSphere Liberty is a fast, dynamic, and easy-to-use Java application server that combines IBM technology with open-source software."

Key Pair

By default, AWS requires what's known as a *key pair*, which consists of a private and a public key. A key pair is a set of security credentials that will be used to prove your organization's user identities when connecting to an instance. Amazon EC2 will store the public key, and your organization will store the private one. The key pair mechanism eliminates the hassle of using a password to access the EC2 instances securely.

IP Addresses

By default, the EC2 instance supporting the two-sided marketplace will be assigned a public IP address. The IP address is automatically picked from the IP address range associated with the public subnet controlling the instance.

Elastic Block Store–Backed Instance

The instance hosting the two-sided marketplace application will be an *Elastic Block Store (EBS)*–backed instance that offers easy backup and restore solutions.

As discussed in Chapter 1, "The Digital Economy's Challenges, Opportunities, and Relevance of AWS," EBS provides raw block-level storage, and it supports uses such as formatting devices with a filesystem. An EBS-backed instance means that the root volume is an EBS volume, and storage is persistent. EBS-backed instances can be stopped without losing data.

The AWS Solutions Architect would promote the architectural choice as follows:

"With AWS incremental snapshots stored in S3, point-in-time states of the instance are captured and saved incrementally. The snapshot deletion process is designed so that you need to retain only the most recent snapshot in order to restore the volume."

Containers

The AWS Solutions Architect would argue the importance of containers as follows:

"We plan to develop microservices that will provide reusable services across business applications."

The AWS Solutions Architect would justify the architectural option as follows:

"This will facilitate the maintenance, and more importantly, the evolution of the two-sided marketplace application. The application code will be limited to invoking the appropriate microservices. The time saving is substantial. Containers are the environments in which the microservices will run."

Drawing participants' attention, the AWS Solutions Architect would add the following:

"There will be microservices for each of your key business concerns including customer, order, delivery person, and food product. The code of each microservice, and the related data and functions, will be bundled with configurations and dependencies systematically in containers."

Lambda Functions

As to serverless, the AWS Solutions Architect would explain the following:

"While microservices is way to organize your applications into reusable set of services focused on business concerns, serverless is another way to implement and host microservices. Using microservices will result in more modular applications, therefore easy and fast development, testing, deployment, and maintenance."

The AWS Solutions Architect would further clarify as follows:

"Lambda is an AWS service that allows your developers to upload codes. Lambda then automatically runs them in response to events received via message queue systems like Amazon simple notification service (SNS)."

To conclude, the AWS Solutions Architect says the following:

"The serverless model will generate the two-sided market application code executed on-demand in response to triggers that application developers have configured ahead of time. Serverless dramatically increases the speed at which developers can deliver applications."

J&S Food's Extended Storage Build Block

The *storage building block* specifies the storage solutions that will be used in J&S Food's AWS cloud. While Simple Storage Service (S3) will not be a key component of the application storage infrastructure, Relational Database Service (RDS) and Elastic MapReduce (EMR) will be the hub of J&S Food's storage capability.

Relational Database Service Instances

In addition to providing the services needed to store, update, and retrieve the two-sided market application's data, the RDS instance offers managed database management tasks, such as migration, backup, recovery, and patching.

To avoid useless and expensive changes, Oracle is selected as the relational database management system (RDBMS).

The AWS Solutions Architect would advise as follows:

"To get the best out of an RDS instance, automatic backups will be enabled for the two-sided marketplace application's Oracle database, and the backup window will be set to occur during the daily low in write input/output operations per second (IOPS). Backups will be least disruptive to your database usage at that moment."

The AWS Solutions Architect would add the following:

"To identify performance issues caused by insufficient resources and other common bottlenecks, available metrics will be monitored for the RDS DB instance with a focus on memory, CPU, and storage usage metrics."

Elastic MapReduce (EMR)

The *Elastic MapReduce (EMR)* platform will support J&S Food's data analytics activities. The AWS Solutions Architect might say the following:

"The data analytics activities will focus on key data including online customer, online order, delivery person, and food product. We'll build on Amazon EMR. It's the industry-leading cloud big data platform for processing vast amounts of data."

The consultant would the explain a number of precautions that would be taken:

"We'll ensure that AWS EMR clusters use the latest generation of instances for performance and cost optimization. More importantly, we'll make sure that in-transit and at-rest encryption is enabled for Amazon EMR clusters to secure data."

J&S Food's Extended Fault Tolerance Building Block4

The purpose of J&S Food's AWS platform's fault tolerance services is to ensure high availability for the two-sided marketplace application. These services include *Elastic Load Balancing (ELB)* and Route 53. Let's discuss their role.

Elastic Load Balancer

ELB allows for the monitoring of the health of the two-sided marketplace application and its performance in real time based on CloudWatch metrics, logging, and request tracing.

To offer a highly available application and deliver the expected superior digital food experience, three best practices would apply. These include app-tier ELBs health check, ELB access log, and ELB cross-zone load balancing enabled.

App-tier ELBs health check is the mechanism that determines the availability of registered EC2 instances and their readiness to receive traffic. Any downstream server that does not return a healthy status is considered unavailable and will not have any traffic routed to it.

ELB access log is the system that ensures that your AWS elastic load balancers use access logging to analyze traffic patterns and identify and troubleshoot security issues.

ELB cross-zone load balancing enabled is an option that ensures high availability for your ELBs by using cross-zone load balancing with multiple subnets in different AZs. Cross-zone load balancing is the idea that each load balancer distributes traffic across registered EC2 instances in all enabled availability zones.

Route 53

Amazon Route 53 will help to connect the requests of online customers to the infrastructure running in J&S Food's AWS cloud. It will help to configure DNS health check to route traffic to a healthy endpoint. Moreover, it offers the ability to individually monitor the health of the two-sided marketplace application and its endpoints. What you need to know is that Amazon Route 53 is a cloud Domain Name System (DNS) web service that connects user requests to infrastructure running in the AWS computing environment.

J&S Food's Extended Security Build Block

The purpose of J&S Food's security services is to secure the access to the two-sided marketplace platform and secure the network traffic within the company's AWS cloud. These services would include identity and access management (IAM) and encryption services. Let's discuss them now.

Identity and Access Management

AWS Identity and Access Management (IAM) will help to securely control access to the two-sided marketplace platform and underpinning virtual infrastructure resources. IAM will be used to control authenticated (signed in) and authorized (has permissions) online customers.

The Solutions Architect would clarify this as follows:

"In addition to the implementation of an identity federation mechanism that will make it easier to manage the authentication and permissions of external resources like delivery persons, we'll ensure that there are no IAM groups and IAM users with full administrator permissions within your AWS account, except for sys admins and DBAs."

To finish with identity and access management, the Solutions Architect would add the following:

"We'll make sure that AWS IAM access keys are rotated on a periodic basis as a security best practice (45 Days), and that security challenge questions are enabled and configured to improve the security of your AWS account. We will also implement many other security measures such as making sure that IAM policy for EC2 IAM roles for the app tier and web tier is configured."

Security Groups

A *security group* will be used to act as a virtual firewall for the EC2 instance hosting the two-sided marketplace application. The goal is to control incoming and outgoing traffic. Inbound rules of the security group control the incoming traffic to the EC2 instance, and outbound rules control the outgoing traffic from the instance.

Key Management Service

J&S Food's security services will build on *AWS Key Management Service (KMS)* to create and control encryption keys used to encrypt data. KMS uses envelope encryption in which data is encrypted using a data key that is then encrypted using a master key.

Executing J&S Food's AWS Migration Strategy

This activity in the AWS migration plan is where the actual application migration work takes place. The goal is to adapt the applications selected as part of the two-sided marketplace platform to the requirements of the AWS computing environment.

The Solutions Architect would focus on an iterative process underpinning the technical migration effort. This process is known as the *migration factory process*.

Understanding the AWS Application Migration Process

The Solutions Architect would warn the participants as follows:

"Many AWS Solutions Architects give in to the temptation of using piecemeal migration approaches. By doing so, they waste valuable time needed to optimize and modernize applications in a way that would help them take advantage of the AWS benefits."

The factory model is the circular part of the migration plan, as illustrated in Figure 7.2. It is the application of the industrialization principles defined in Chapter 4. These principles seek to accelerate the migration process and guarantee that applications fully adhere to the requirements of the AWS computing environment.

In a migration factory approach, applications move through what looks like an assembly line of five steps including *discover*, *design*, *build*, *validate*, and *cutover*. Let's briefly discuss these steps before applying them to the migration of J&S Food's ecommerce website.

Discover

This step is where the application's current architecture is pieced together and assessed versus the requirements of the selected migration strategy. Application development stakeholders including developers, testers, and technical architects are involved in discussions around the following questions:

- What are the current hardware features including CPU, RAM, storage capacity, and network interfaces?
- What is the current software configuration including operating system (OS), database, and ERPs?

Design

In this step, the application is redesigned according to its related migration strategy. The goal is to make sure that the application will enable the expected digital business experience.

Build

This step is where the new functions and architectural changes are implemented. The goal is to make sure that the application will run as expected in the AWS computing environment and that it effectively contributes to the desired digital business experience.

The activities carried out by the application development stakeholders include the following:

- Provisioning the target computing environment
- Deploying the application to the target computing environment
- Implementing the architectural changes
- Performing unit tests to assess the application readiness for the validate step

Integrate

In this step, the development stakeholders implement the application's external connections. The goal is to implement the mechanisms to ensure that the application can efficiently and safely communicate with your organization's on-premises infrastructure or with other external cloud platforms.

The activities carried out by application development stakeholders include the following:

- Configuring the site-to-site VPN connections
- Establishing the dedicated network connections between your AWS environment and your on-premises infrastructure using AWS direct connect
- Setting up hybrid cloud environments using VMware cloud on AWS (VMC)

Validate

In the validate step, the application undergoes a series of tests including build verification, functional, performance, disaster recovery, and business continuity tests. The goal is to make sure that it's compatible with the AWS computing environment requirements and that they can contribute to the expected digital business experience.

Cutover

In the cutover step, the AWS migration team executes the cutover plan that was agreed upon with the application owners. Performance user acceptance test (UAT) and operational acceptance tests (OAT) are performed at this stage to ensure a successful cutover.

The next sections illustrate the AWS migration factory process as the Solutions Architect would apply it to migrate J&S Food's ecommerce website and extend it into a two-sided marketplace platform.

Migrating J&S Food's Ecommerce Website Into a Two-Sided Marketplace Platform

The AWS consultant would present the objective as follows:

"Let's implement the company's AWS computing environment that'll support the digital business."

The consultant would further clarify as follows:

"The AWS computing environment is one specifically designed to help your applications get the most out of AWS services and features."

Then the consultant would write the workshop's agenda on the whiteboard as follows:

- *Implementing J&S Food's AWS computing environment*
- *Discovering the as-is ecommerce website*
- *Designing the two-sided marketplace*
- *Building the two-sided marketplace platform prototype, validating it, and deploying it.*

Starting with the implementation of J&S Food's VPC, let's see how the Solutions Architect would migrate the ecommerce website to the AWS computing environment.

Implementing J&S Food's Virtual Private Cloud

As Figure 7.7 shows, the VPC creation process leverages AWS CloudFormation designer and infrastructure as code techniques to speed the implementation of the company's AWS computing environment.

The Solutions Architect would explain the implementation of the VPC architecture as follows:

"The implementation of the VPC architecture is as simple as dragging from the left pane the desired virtual infrastructure resources, dropping them on the top pane, and properly linking these infrastructure resources. The related infrastructure code is generated on the bottom pane. A simple mouse click triggers the creation of the VPC as instructed in the CloudFormation template."

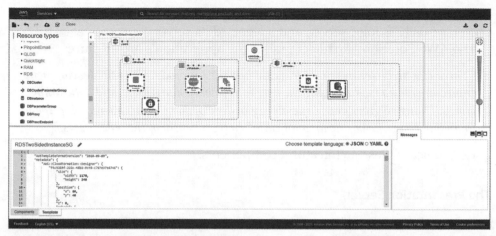

Figure 7.7: Implementation of J&S Food's VPC architecture using AWS CloudFormation Designer

What you should bear in mind is that the combined use of the enterprise cloud migration (ECM) design pattern and AWS CloudFormation designer reduces the implementation time, not in days but in weeks.

Discovering the Ecommerce Website Three-Tier Architecture

The Solutions Architect would draw the participants' attention as follows:

"We're entering the discovery phase of the AWS migration factory process."

In this step of the factory model, the goal is to understand the application's architecture as well as the source code. Figure 7.8 provides an overview of J&S Food's application architecture.

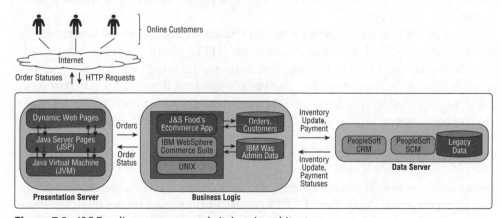

Figure 7.8: J&S Food's ecommerce website's as-is architecture

The application is based on a three-tier application including a presentation server, a business logic server, and a legacy data server.

The AWS Solutions Architect praises the application's architecture:

"Three-tier architectures provide many benefits for production and development environments by modularizing the user interface, business logic, and data storage layers. Doing so gives greater flexibility to development teams by allowing them to update a specific part of an application independently of the other parts."

Let's discuss these architectural components.

The Presentation Server

The *presentation tier* is the visible part of the application. The role of the *presentation server* is to display information related to services such as browsing merchandise, purchasing, and shopping cart contents. The presentation layer communicates with other tiers by outputting results to the browser/client tier and all other tiers in the network.

The presentation server is based on Jakarta Server Pages (JSP), formerly Java Server Pages. JSP is a collection of technologies that provide the mechanisms needed to create dynamically generated web pages based on HTML, XML, and SOAP. JSP enables developers to mix up static HTML with dynamically generated content of servlets.

The Business Logic Server

The *Business Logic Server* is responsible for performing business functions such as online order capture and order fulfillment. The business functions are primarily based on Java server. Servlets are Java programs that run inside a Java-capable HTTP server.

Dynamic JSP pages can invoke a servlet implementing these business functions by issuing a specific URL from the browser (HTTP client). Servlets are used to handle the request obtained from the dynamic JSP page via the web server, process the request by invoking the PeopleSoft function via an API, produce the data obtained in response, and then send the response back to the JSP page via the web server.

The Legacy Data Server

Legacy data is essential enterprise information that is stored in a computer system. J&S Food relies on PeopleSoft ERPs to store, update, and retrieve legacy data.

Extending the Ecommerce Website Architecture to a Two-Sided Marketplace Platform

As in the discover phase, the Solutions Architect would remind the participants the following:

"We're about to start the design step of the AWS migration factory process."

Figure 7.9 represents the architecture of J&S Food's digital business platform in the AWS cloud. This architecture resulted from the discussions involving the AWS Solutions Architect, the enterprise architect, your developers, and IT operations.

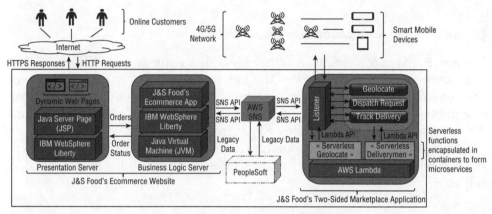

Figure 7.9: Overview of J&S Food's two-sided marketplace platform

The AWS version of J&S Food's digital business platform is composed of four components including the *presentation server*, the *business logic server*, the *AWS Simple Notification Service (SNS)*, and the *two-sided marketplace application*. Let's discuss them now.

The Presentation Server

As in the J&S Food's on-premises environment, the digital business platform would be based on a three-tier architecture. The presentation server is the first tier. Its scope covers hosting the web pages of the digital business platform, showing the online customers the web pages needed to either input or read information about orders, food, delivery persons, and customers.

The presentation server builds on JSP pages to invoke servlets in the business logic server to either input or get orders, food product, and delivery people's information.

The Business Logic Server

The second tier of the digital business platform architecture is *business logic server*. In addition to interacting with the PeopleSoft module in the on-premises environment via APIs built on a VPN connection to get or update data, the business logic server's scope covers various functions including capture orders, show orders, and trigger delivery persons searches.

A key piece of information to know is that the interactions between the digital business logic server and the two-sided marketplace application are supported by an Amazon SNS platform. The business functions build on servlets to invoke APIs that allow them to interact with PeopleSoft ERP to either get or update information about orders, customers, food products, and delivery persons.

The AWS Simple Notification Service

The *Amazon Simple Notification Service (SNS)* is a managed publish/subscribe (also known as *pub/sub*) service. The key thing to know is that this system enables communication between systems that are not directly connected. One side publishes messages to a shared communication channel, called a *topic*, and the other side subscribes to the messages from this topic.

The digital business logic application and the listener component of the two-sided marketplace application are subscribers to three topics, as described in Table 7.5.

Table 7.5: The J&S SNS Topics and Messages

TOPICS	MESSAGES	SENDER, RECEIVER, ACTION
Delivery person	Delivery person requested	Sent by the digital business logic application to the listener of the two-sided marketplace application. The listener triggers the geolocate function to dispatch the "delivery person requested" message.
Order	Order fulfilled	Order fulfilled message is sent by the listener to the digital business logic server. The digital business logic server updates the order information stored in the PeopleSoft CRM system.
Tracking	Order tracking requested	The order tracking requested message is sent by the listener to the digital business logic server. The digital business logic server retrieves order tracking information and sends it back to the listener. The listener orchestrates the display of the order tracking information to the customer mobile devices.

The Two-Sided Marketplace Application

The primary purpose of the two-sided marketplace application is to connect online customers with delivery persons. To achieve that goal, the application builds on four fundamental functions including listener, geolocate, dispatch request, and track delivery.

The *listener function* listens to requests that the online customer sends via a laptop or mobile device and triggers one of these functions: geolocate, dispatch request, and track delivery.

The listener interacts with the business logic server of the ecommerce website and with the two-sided platform via an AWS Simple Notification Service (SNS) message queue to capture online customer requests and accordingly trigger the two-sided marketplace platform's functions.

The listener builds on Amazon SNS to receive and send messages back and forth.

Amazon SNS, as illustrated in Figure 7.10, is a managed service that provides message delivery services from publishers to subscribers (also known as producers and consumers).

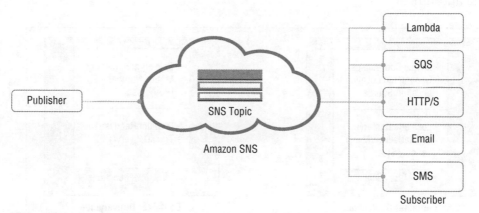

Figure 7.10: Amazon SNS

Source: Amazon

Publishers communicate asynchronously with subscribers by sending messages to a topic that consumers subscribe to prior to getting messages.

SNS is a logical access point and communication channel that supports various purposes including sending and receiving short message service (SMS), email, and HTTP/S requests, as well as invoking serverless functions via the AWS Lambda service.

The *geolocate function* builds on location technologies such as GPS or IP addresses to identify and track the whereabouts of connected electronic devices. The core objective of the geolocate function is to connect online customers and delivery persons in an effort to get online orders delivered.

The geolocate function interacts with the listener to capture messages published and associated with the topic "delivery person's geolocation" and then build on Lambda API to invoke the lambda serverless function Geolocate.

The *dispatch request function*'s purpose is to dispatch an SMS to J&S Food's delivery network.

The dispatch request function interacts with the listener to capture messages associated with the topic "delivery person requested." It then builds on the Lambda API to invoke the Lambda serverless function delivery person.

The *track delivery function*'s goal is to provide the online customers with tracking order information.

The track delivery function interacts with the listener to capture messages published and associated with the topic "delivery persons" and then build on the Lambda API to invoke the lambda serverless function Delivery Person.

J&S Food's Digital Business Microservices: Reusable Modules

Serverless functions are encapsulated in containers to form J&S Food's microservices. They include Geolocate and Delivery Person. Figure 7.11 illustrates their data and functions.

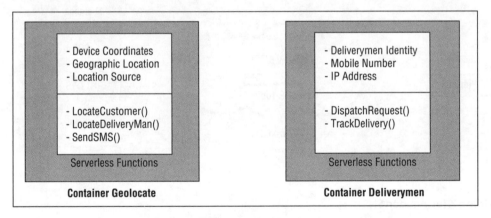

AWS Lambda Functions

Figure 7.11: J&S Food's digital business microservices

The microservices logical representation is based on the Unified Modeling Language (UML) class diagram formalism. The class diagram highlights the serverless functions to implement and the data that they handle.

The microservice encapsulated in the geolocate container handles three primary data and functions, as outlined in Table 7.6.

Table 7.6: Data and Functions of the Microservice Geolocate

DATA AND FUNCTIONS	DESCRIPTION
Device coordinates	Refers to the electronic device's position expressed in latitude and longitude coordinates.
Geographic location	Refers to the geographic location associated with device coordinates.
Location source	The source that provides the device coordinates and geographic location. This could be satellite, Wi-Fi, and mobile network.
LocateCustomer()	This function locates the geographic area and full address of the online customer.
LocateDeliveryMan()	Based on the geographic area and address of the customer, this function locates delivery people geographically closest to the online customer.
SendSMS()	This function issues an SMS to the delivery person geographically closest to the online customer. These SMSes notifies the need for a delivery person at a specific area.

The microservice encapsulated in the Delivery Person container handles three primary pieces of data using three functions, as described in Table 7.7.

Table 7.7: Data and Functions of the Delivery Person Microservice

DATA AND FUNCTIONS	DESCRIPTION
Delivery Person Identity	Refers to the delivery person information including full name, address, and taxpayer identification number (TIN).
Mobile Number	Delivery person mobile number.
IP Address	Delivery person mobile's IP address.
DispatchRequest()	This function issues an SMS to the delivery persons geographically closest to the online customer. These SMSes notifies the need for a delivery person at a specific area.
TrackDelivery()	Based on online order identification provided as input, this function returns the order tracking information.

Implementing J&S Food's Two-Sided Marketplace Platform

This is the build step of the AWS migration factory process. The bottom line for the development team is to migrate the existing ecommerce website to J&S Food's AWS computing environment and adapt it to the technical and technological requirements.

Migrating J&S Food's Existing Ecommerce Website to the AWS Computing Environment

Before starting the implementation, the Solutions Architect would recommend migrating the existing ecommerce website to the EC2 instance of J&S Food's virtual private cloud VPC (see Figure 7.6). The process will be based on the AWS Elastic Beanstalk service.

AWS Elastic Beanstalk is an easy-to-use service for deploying and scaling web applications and services developed with Java, .NET, PHP, Node.js, Python, Ruby, and Go. Figure 7.12 illustrates the application migration process using AWS Elastic Beanstalk.

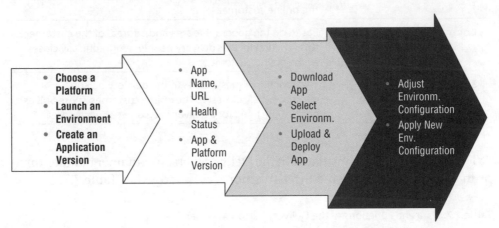

Figure 7.12: Overview of the application migration process with AWS Elastic Beanstalk

The developer simply uploads the application's code, and Elastic Beanstalk automatically handles the deployment, from capacity provisioning, load balancing, and auto-scaling to application health monitoring.

Overview of the AWS Modern Application Development Framework

To ensure the delivery of an application that meets the requirements and challenges of J&S Food's digital food experience, the Solutions Architect would recommend an ingenious approach inspired from AWS modern application development principles, as illustrated in Figure 7.13.

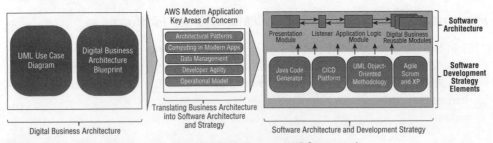

Figure 7.13: The modern application development on AWS framework

The framework builds on three pillars to facilitate the rapid development of secure, resilient, elastic, modular, and fit-for-purpose applications in the AWS computing environment. The following sections discuss the framework's elements and how it would help to deliver the two-sided marketplace software.

The Digital Business Architecture Element

The importance of the digital business architecture in the development of software is that the diagrams and architecture blueprints it provides highlight the software's goal in terms of functions to implement and interactions between these functions, as well as the data that they handle.

With the goal, functions, and data in sight, the software architecture, AWS computing environment, and operational requirements to deal with, as well as the development team's productivity, are ready to be discussed to elaborate a software development strategy.

The Solutions Architect would explain the next steps as follows:

"The elements of the business architecture are used by the AWS modern application development framework key areas of concern to determine the software architecture as well as the software development strategy."

Translation Rules: From the Business Architecture to the Software Architecture and the Software Development Strategy

The AWS modern application development framework is a set of key areas of concern that help to determine not only the software architecture but also its development strategy.

These areas of concern include architectural patterns, computing in modern application: containers and serverless, data management, developer agility, and the operational model. Let's discuss their role and importance.

Architectural Patterns   These are architectural principles that will help determine the best possible architecture for the software that will help to determine the best possible architecture for the software. Examples of such software architectural patterns include n-tier, event-driven, and microservices.

As illustrated in Figure 7.12, participants would agree that the best architecture for the two-sided marketplace platform is a combination of n-tier, event-driven, and microservices approaches.

Computing in Modern Application—Containers and Serverless   This concern encourages developers to take advantage of containers and serverless to make applications more modular and increase their portability. As Figure 7.12 shows, J&S Food's software development stakeholders would agree that basing the two-sided marketplace platform on containers and serverless would make its development and maintenance easier.

Data Management This concern emphasizes the need for the application to rely on the right datastore (SQL or NoSQL) but, more importantly, to decouple the application from its database by having them housed in separate microservices. The participants' recommendation was to keep legacy Oracle database in J&S Food's on-premises environment and give access to it via a site-to-site VPN connection APIs.

Developer Agility This concern stresses the need to provide the development team with the mechanisms for high productivity. These mechanisms include tool, infrastructure, methodologies, and work organization. The participants cited application code generators like AWS Amplify, continuous testing tools, Scrum agile, and Extreme Programming (XP) methodologies, as well as the UML object approach and serverless/AWS Lambda, as the factors likely to increase their productivity.

Operational Model In this concern, the emphasis is placed on making the operational model ever more effective, efficient, and fast. Participants would praise mechanisms such as microservices, containers, serverless, and even tools like serverless/AWS Lambda, AWS Amplify, AWS Elastic Beanstalk and CodeDeploy as essential catalysts of the operational model performances.

The Resulting Software Architecture and Development Strategy Element

Discussions about the implementation of the two-sided marketplace software, based on the principles of AWS modern application development, would result in the architecture and development strategy summed up in Table 7.8.

Table 7.8: Two-Sided Marketplace Software Module Architecture and Development Strategies

MODULES	DESIGN PATTERN	AWS API	DEVELOPMENT STRATEGY ELEMENTS
Listener	Event-driven	Simple Notification Service (SNS)	Code generator, continuous testing platform, and XP methodology
App Logic Server Module	N-tier	SNS, Lambda, Elastic Container Service (ECS)	Same as above
Digital Business Reusable Modules	Microservices	Same as above	Same as above

Validating the Two-Sided Marketplace Platform

Validating is the last step in the migration of the application before its deployment in the experimentation phase. It's about performing a series of tests including build verification, functional, performance, disaster recovery, and business continuity tests. Table 7.9 summarizes the validation tests that the two-sided marketplace application will pass.

Table 7.9: The Two-Sided Marketplace Validation Tests

VALIDATION TESTS	PURPOSE AND EXPECTED RESULTS
Build verification	This is a set of tests run on the application build in the AWS computing environment to verify that the build is testable before it is released to a test team for further testing.
Functional	This is a testing of the two-sided marketplace software that validates the application against the functional requirements/specifications.
Performance	This is a testing process used for testing the two-sided application's speed, response time, stability, reliability, scalability, and resource usage under a particular workload.
Disaster recovery	The disaster recovery test (DR test) examines each step in the two-sided marketplace application's disaster recovery plan as outlined in an organization's business continuity/disaster recovery (BCDR) planning process.
Business continuity tests	This test verifies how effective the business continuity plan is in real-time scenarios. The bottom line is to look for weaknesses or gaps in the plan. Once weaknesses are identified, the teams can work together to improve them.

Key Takeaways

Digitizing a business model is not a simple matter that would consist in deploying applications. It's a complex job that can be long and risky and that requires both a solid understanding of the business model and the technology.

In this chapter, you learned about the benefits and value of a number of AWS migration tools that guided and facilitated the cloud migration process. These tools included the following:

- The AWS migration strategy framework that provided an actionable migration plan that helped save precious time.
- The digital business application portfolio development process that helped to rapidly identify the applications migratable to AWS.

- The VPC blueprint that proves to be a powerful tool not only for specifying the company's AWS cloud architecture but also for implementing it using AWS infrastructure as code tools like CloudFormation designer.

- The AWS Modern Application development framework, which offers software engineering mechanisms that help to quickly determine the software architecture of the applications to migrate to AWS.

In the next chapter, you'll be involved in the second phase of J&S Food's digital business model digitalization. This second phase is focused on the implementation of the DevOps platform that supports the development of digital products.

References

1. Amazon Web Services, "AWS Cloud Adoption Framework (AWS CAF)," *Amazon Web Services* (2021). `https://docs.aws.amazon.com/whitepapers/latest/aws-migration-whitepaper/the-aws-cloud-adoption-framework-aws-caf.html`

2. Amazon Web Services, "Introducing AWS CloudEndure Migration Factory Solutions," *Amazon Web Services* (June 03, 2020). `https://aws.amazon.com/about-aws/whats-new/2020/06/introducing-aws-cloudendure-migration-factory-solution/`

3. Amazon Web Services, "The 6 R's: 6 Application Migration Strategies," *Amazon Web Services* (2021). `https://docs.aws.amazon.com/whitepapers/latest/aws-migration-whitepaper/the-6-rs-6-application-migration-strategies.html`

Implementing J&S Food's DevOps Platform Using AWS PaaS

DevOps and its resulting technical, architectural, and cultural practices represent a convergence of many philosophical and management movements (including): Lean, Theory of Constraints, Toyota production system, resilience engineering, learning organizations, safety culture, Human factors, high-trust management cultures, servant leadership, organizational change management, and Agile methods.

—**Gene Kim**

The stake in this second phase of J&S Food's operating model digitalization is to equip the company with a digital products and services development platform that guarantees online customers a superior digital food experience.

The challenge, as you know, is not to implement the technology; it is rather to set up an ecosystem of people, processes, practices, and values supported by technology in a way that enables the company to deliver innovative products and services continuously.

The implementation of such an ecosystem is not easy. It involves mobilizing and teaming up a variety of people, tools, methodologies, and skills. This takes time and energy.

The safest solution is to rely on a framework that can simplify and speed up DevOps implementation.

In this chapter, in the role of the chief information officer (CIO), you'll be involved in a workshop to define the architecture and implementation of the platform that will underpin J&S Food's digital product and service development platform.

In this meeting, led by the AWS Solutions Architect and the enterprise architect, you'll be part of the dialogue involving the VP of marketing, sales representatives, customer service, developers, testers, and IT operations. The goal is to ensure that the platform to be implemented meets the stakeholders' vision.

Transformation Journey's Third Stage: Implementing J&S Food's DevOps Platform

The second phase of J&S Food's digital business model digitization is about implementing DevOps. As discussed in Chapter 4, "Industrializing Digital Product and Service Development," DevOps is the combination of software development (Dev) and IT operations (Ops) practices and tools designed to increase the organization's ability to deliver applications and services faster.

The bottom line is to get a digital product and service development platform that enables the expected digital food experience.

Figure 8.1 illustrates where the digital transformation team stands in the business model digitization.

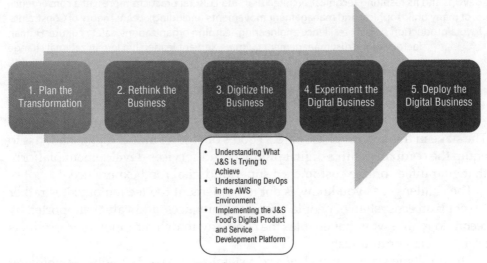

Figure 8.1: The DevOps implementation phase

As Figure 8.1 shows, the AWS Solutions Architect would address the DevOps implementation effort in these three steps:

- Understanding what J&S Food is trying to achieve
- Understanding DevOps in the AWS computing environment
- Implementing J&S Food's digital product and service development platform

Let's see how the Solutions Architect would go about implementing J&S Food's digital product and service development platform.

Understanding What J&S Food Is Trying to Achieve

In the next day's workshop, the Solutions Architect starts by saying this:

"What is your vision of the digital product and service development platform? How do you see it working on a daily basis?"

The VP of marketing replies as follows:

"I see our digital product development platform primarily as an ecosystem of men and women mobilized to developing innovative digital products and services relying as much as possible on artificial intelligence (AI) and Internet of things (IoT)."

Jotting down the technological concerns (AI and IoT), the Solutions Architect asks for further clarification:

"Why specifically AI and IoT?"

The VP of marketing delivers the requested clarification as follows:

"Our next lead digital product, the smart shopping bag, is a high-tech product. We want to make sure that the platform supports highly innovative technology products."

The consultant asks the following:

"From your perspective, what are the key success factors to the implementation of such a platform?"

As the project leader on the business side, the VP of marketing replies:

"To achieve this, I see three conditions: interactions between stakeholders based on agile principles, a strong focus on customer expectations, and the shortest possible time to market."

The next sections explain why DevOps is the platform that will help meet J&S Food's digital business expectations and more importantly how to implement it.

Understanding the DevOps Implementation in the AWS Computing Environment

As you must realize, what the VP of marketing expects is much more than a technical and technological platform that will miraculously deliver the digital products and services expected by customers.

The challenge for the Solutions Architect and the enterprise architect is to set up a consistent ecosystem of people, processes, practices, and tools that allows the delivery of J&S Food's digital food experience.

This section discusses the whys and wherefores of the DevOps implementation in the AWS computing environment including the common challenges and mistakes and, more importantly, the DevOps implementation framework for AWS.

Discussing the Challenges

Seeking to engage the implementation team, the Solutions Architect says the following, provocatively:

"As surprising as it sounds, the biggest challenge of most DevOps implementations is the ability to implement a platform that truly supports the business. . .and we must meet this challenge."

Trying to clear up the development team's apparent confusion, the enterprise architect clicks the mouse to display the diagram shown in Figure 8.2.

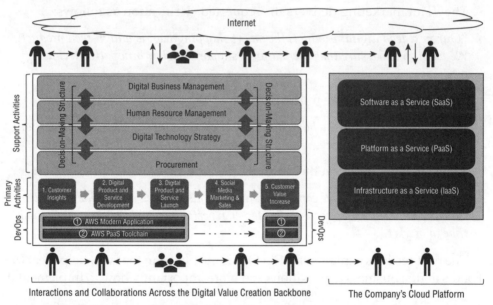

Figure 8.2: DevOps as part of the digital business value chain

The enterprise architect then clarifies:

"The fundamental purpose of DevOps is to optimize the way that we develop and deploy software. Therefore, DevOps improves the way we work in IT."

The Solutions Architect adds to the enterprise architect's explanations as follows:

"DevOps implementation in the context of this digital transformation project is about leveraging relevant AWS services and features across the company's value chain activities as well as the AWS modern application principles. The goal is to optimize all aspects of the development process that will underpin the company's smart shopping bag digital product."

Understanding the Common Mistakes

Proceeding with the dos and don'ts, the Solutions Architect makes the following clear:

"In this project we'll avoid four common mistakes of DevOps implementation projects in the AWS environment:

1. *We won't approach DevOps as a software deployment automation toolbox.*

2. *Accelerated deployment won't be the only benefit we expect from DevOps.*

3. *We won't narrow this DevOps platform to AWS CodePipeline.*

4. *We'll intelligently use AWS services with a laser focus, not only on deployment issues but on all activities identified as key for the business."*

Anticipating the participants' questions about that broad approach of DevOps implementation in the AWS computing environment, the Solutions Architect says the following:

"Let's discuss the DevOps architecture for AWS."

The DevOps Implementation Framework for AWS

Clicking the mouse to move to the presentation's next page, the DevOps blueprint for AWS is displayed, as illustrated in Figure 8.3.

The Solutions Architect explains the following:

"The blueprint represents the DevOps pipeline for AWS. It's the set of automated activities and tools in the digital business value chain that allows developers and operations to collaborate on building and deploying code to a production environment."

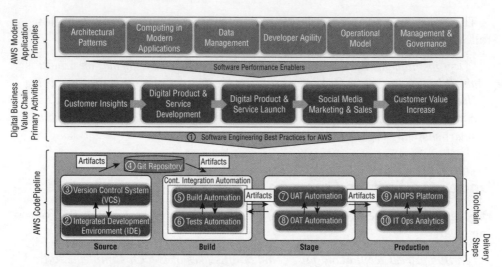

Figure 8.3: The DevOps implementation framework for AWS

The Solutions Architect then adds this:

"The fundamental intent is to make DevOps implementation in the AWS computing environment easy and fast."

The Solutions Architect next elaborates on the three primary building blocks of the DevOps implementation framework for AWS.

The Digital Business Value Chain Primary Activities and AWS Modern Application Influence

The Solutions Architect reminds the participants of the following:

"Primary activities are ones focused on the development of software associated with the digital product and service."

The purpose of the primary activities in the framework is to help, through a questionnaire, software development stakeholders to agree on the software development activities necessary for the implementation of digital products. Two important points to know are the role of the AWS modern application characteristics and that of the change management function.

Be aware that AWS modern application development (MAD) refers to the performance enablers discussed in Chapter 4. Their role is to recommend software engineering best practices for the AWS computing environment to ensure software delivery in line with the quality requirements of the company within ever shorter timeframes.

As for the software engineering best practices for AWS, its role is to infuse and consolidate in the delivery pipeline, technical and operational best practices that make the delivery process continuously efficient.

Table 8.1 illustrates the digital business primary activity specification matrix.

Table 8.1: The Digital Business Primary Activity Specification Matrix

	SOFTWARE DEVELOPMENT ACTIVITY #1?	SOFTWARE DEVELOPMENT ACTIVITY #2?	SOFTWARE DEVELOPMENT ACTIVITY #3?
Purpose	What's the purpose of the activity?	Same question as activity #1	Same question as activity #1
Stakeholders and roles	Who are the stakeholders? What's the role of each?		
MAD: Culture of ownership	What actions must be taken?		
MAD: Architectural patterns	How well to use microservices?		
MAD: Computing in modern applications	How well to use containers and Lambda functions?		
MAD: Data management	How can data management leverage microservices to address scaling, fault tolerance, and speed?		
MAD: Developer agility	What are the best practices to deploy to increase productivity?		
MAD: Operational model	How to leverage serverless to make IT and application operations agile?		
MAD: Management and governance	How to leverage programmatic guardrails that make governance checkpoints that slow down innovation?		

The AWS CodePipeline Service

The Solutions Architect states the following:

"Think of AWS CodePipeline as a pipeline structured and designed to facilitate the flow of software releases."

CodePipeline is an AWS continuous delivery service that enables you to model, visualize, and automate the steps required to release your software. The Code-Pipeline role in the DevOps implementation framework is to act as the DevOps pipeline.

The *DevOps* pipeline is the set of automated processes and tools that allows developers and operations to collaborate on building and deploying code to the production environment.

Two main components make up AWS CodePipeline: the delivery stages and the toolchain. Let's discuss them now.

Understanding AWS CodePipeline Delivery Stages

The *AWS CodePipeline delivery stages* refer to the software delivery lifecycle (SDLC) discussed in Chapter 4.

Stages including Source, Build, Stage, and Production are built-in features of the AWS CodePipeline service. Each stage contains actions that are performed on the application artifacts. Artifacts can be anything ranging from built, tested applications or updated containers.

Table 8.2 sums up the purpose of the AWS CodePipeline stages.

Table 8.2: Functions of the AWS CodePipeline Stages

	PURPOSE	DESCRIPTION
Source	Manages changes to software	In this stage, three functions are performed: creating the development environment, tracking the changes in software, and committing changes to the changes repository.
Build	Manages the continuous integration and continuous deployment (CICD) process	In this stage, four functions are automated: detecting new release in the changes repository, building the software (compiling and linking), testing, and deploying to the stage environment.
Stage	Manages acceptance tests	In this stage, four functions are performed: user acceptance test (UAT), operational acceptance test (OAT), acceptance tests approval, and deployment to production.
Production	Operates production environment and applications	In this stage, three primary functions are automated: production environment and application monitoring, operations logs analysis, and operational practices continuous improvement.

Note that the steps outlined in Table 8.2 are not set in stone. Other steps may be introduced depending on the needs of the business.

Defining AWS CodePipeline Toolchain

The *AWS CodePipeline toolchain* refers to the combination of tools mobilized across the delivery pipeline to implement stage functions.

Table 8.3 summarizes the type of tools supporting the functions of the delivery pipeline stages.

Table 8.3: The Technology Mobilized Across the Delivery Pipeline Stages

	TYPE OF SOLUTIONS	EXAMPLES OF MARKET SOLUTIONS
Source	Version control system (VCS) and integrated development environment (IDE)	Git and AWS CodeCommit (VCS), Eclipse (IDE)
Build	Continuous integration (CI), build, and unit test	Jenkins (CI), Ansible and Maven (Build), and Junit (Unit Test)
Stage	User acceptance test (UAT) and operational acceptance test (OAT) automation	Selenium and IBM Rational Functional Test (automated UAT) and JMeter (automated OAT)
Production	Cloud monitoring and management solution	AWS CloudWatch, Nagios, and Splunk

Links to DevOps tools in the AWS environment are provided in the reference section of this chapter.

Understanding DevOps Implementation for AWS

The implementation of the AWS DevOps blueprint depicted in Figure 8.4 is a three-step process.

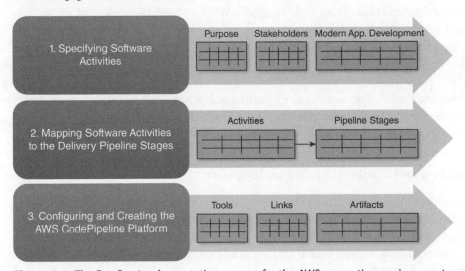

Figure 8.4: The DevOps implementation process for the AWS computing environment

These steps include specifying the software development activities, mapping the development activities to the stages of the delivery pipeline, configuring and creating the AWS CodePipeline platform, and deploying the primary activities of the digital business value chain. Let's discuss them.

Specifying the Software Development Activities

The Solutions Architect states the following:

"Software development activities are the value-adding activities of your company's future digital business. We must carefully identify them and define their features."

This activity consists of identifying the software development tasks that will constitute the value chain. The objective is to specify these software development tasks in terms of the actors to involve as well as the necessary best practices recommended by the AWS modern application likely to make them efficient.

The digital business activity specification matrix is a useful tool that allows software development stakeholders to capture, evaluate, and agree on the software development tasks to select.

Mapping the Development Activities to the Delivery Pipeline Stages

This activity is about mapping the software development tasks to the actions that are likely to automate them in the AWS CodePipeline platform. The bottom line is to associate each software development task with the corresponding stage in the delivery pipeline and then identify the AWS services or AWS partner services likely to automate them.

An example of an action and its related AWS service is the EC2 instance creation and deployment and the related AWS service Elastic Beanstalk, which is invoked to provision development, testing, or production environments. Another example of an action is the installation of Maven, an open source build tool for enterprise Java projects designed to take much of the hard work out of the build process.

A last example of an action is the build software that invokes the external Maven service to build (compile and link) the software in the build stage of the delivery pipeline.

Configuring and Creating the AWS CodePipeline

This task consists of configuring the delivery pipeline from the AWS CodePipeline console wizards or from the CloudFormation designer. The challenge is to automate the software delivery process from end to end. For each stage of the pipeline, including source, build, staging, and production, the following essential information is configured:

- The desired action
- The AWS service or AWS partner service to invoke
- The AWS service or partner service configuration information

Following the configuration of the production stage, the AWS CodePipeline delivery pipeline is ready to process software releases.

Implementing J&S Food's Digital Product and Service Development Platform

The objective is to design and implement a platform that addresses the technological, organizational, and operational issues.

This section discusses the design of J&S Food's DevOps toolchain and agile operating model.

J&S Food's Digital Product and Service Development Platform

Figure 8.5 illustrates the architecture of J&S Food's digital product and service development platform.

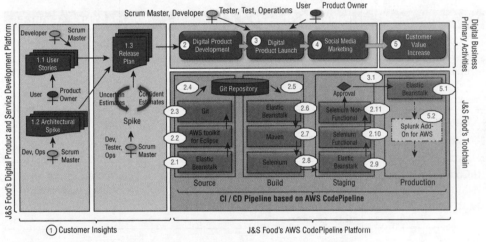

Figure 8.5: J&S Food's digital product and service development platform

The platform is based on the AWS CodePipeline service and is structured around two components: digital business primary activities and associated best practices and the toolchain.

The Solutions Architect discusses how the platform works:

"The platform is an event-driven system reacting to four events. First, it reacts to the event signaling changes in the software committed to the Git repository, (2.4) and (2.5) in the figure, to trigger the build process. The platform reacts to the event signaling the end of the build process, (2.8), to trigger the staging test including user acceptance tests and operational acceptance tests. Then it reacts to the event signaling the end of staging tests, (3.1), to trigger the application deployment to the production environment."

J&S Food's DevOps Toolchain

J&S Food's toolchain mobilizes four environment types including source, build, staging, and production.

The following sections outline the configuration of these stages.

The Source Environment

The *source environment* is the set of compute infrastructure and tools necessary for the software coding and unit testing activities. It's the environment that the development team will leverage to develop the ecommerce website, the smart shopping bag software components, and the two-sided marketplace application.

Table 8.4 sums up the automated action and related services of the source environment.

Table 8.4: The Source Platform's Actions and AWS Services

ACTIONS	PURPOSE	AWS/PARTNER SERVICES
Create development environment	Creates the extended EC2 instances intended to support the development environments for the ecommerce website, two-sided marketplace, and smart shopping bag applications	AWS Elastic Beanstalk
Install AWS toolkit	Installs in the extended EC2 instances the complete AWS toolkit for Microsoft Visual Studio	AWS Toolkit for Visual Studio
Commit changes	Posts changes in ecommerce website, two-sided marketplace, and smart shopping bag software to the Git repository	Git integrated with AWS CodePipeline via a plugin

The Build Environment

The *build environment* is the platform that will be generated by the AWS CodePipeline service to support the automation of the continuous integration and continuous delivery process.

Table 8.5 summarizes the actions that will be orchestrated to achieve the CICD process for the ecommerce website, two-sided marketplace, and smart shopping bag applications.

The Staging Environment

The *staging environment* is the platform that will be generated by the AWS CodePipeline service to automate the user acceptance test and operational acceptance test processes for each of the ecommerce website, two-sided marketplace, and smart shopping bag applications.

Table 8.5: The Build Platform's Actions and AWS Services

ACTIONS	PURPOSE	AWS/PARTNER SERVICES
Create the build environment	Triggered once changes in software are committed to the Git repository. This creates the environment intended to support the CICD processes.	AWS Elastic Beanstalk
Build the applications	Compiles, links, and generates executable files for the ecommerce website, two-sided marketplace, and smart shopping bag applications.	Maven integrated with AWS CodePipeline via a plugin
Perform unit tests	Performs automated unit tests for the ecommerce website, two-sided marketplace, and smart shopping bag applications.	Selenium integrated with AWS CodePipeline via a plugin
Deploy applications	Deploys the ecommerce website, two-sided marketplace, and smart shopping bag applications to the staging environment.	AWS Elastic Beanstalk

Table 8.6 outlines the actions that will be orchestrated to achieve the acceptance test for the ecommerce website, two-sided marketplace, and smart shopping bag applications.

Table 8.6: The Staging Platform's Actions and AWS Services

ACTIONS	PURPOSE	AWS/PARTNER SERVICES
Creates staging environment	Creates the extended EC2 environments needed to perform user acceptance tests and operational acceptance tests	AWS Elastic Beanstalk
Performs user acceptance tests (UATs)	Performs automated functional tests	Selenium Functional integrated with AWS CodePipeline via a plugin
Performs operational acceptance tests (OATs)	Performs automated performance tests	Selenium Non-Functional integrated with AWS CodePipeline via a plugin
Approval	Approves acceptance tests report and deployment to production of the ecommerce website, two-sided marketplace, and smart shopping bag applications	Non applicable

The Production Environment

The *production environment* refers to the setting where the ecommerce website, two-sided marketplace, and smart shopping bag applications will be made live and operated for use by the intended users.

Table 8.7 sums up the actions and AWS and partners services that will be leveraged to deliver the expected J&S Food digital experience.

Table 8.7: The Production Platform's Actions and AWS Services

ACTIONS	PURPOSE	AWS/PARTNER SERVICES
Creates production environment	Creates the extended EC2 environments that will host and operate the ecommerce website, two-sided marketplace, and smart shopping bag applications	AWS Elastic Beanstalk
Measures digital food experience	Analyzes the extended EC2 logs to evaluate J&S Food's digital food experience from the IT operations perspective	Splunk Functional integrated with AWS CodePipeline via a plugin
Continuously improves operations practices	Finds operations dysfunction, identifies the root causes, corrects the root causes	Same as above

J&S Food's Digital Business Primary Activities

Discussions about J&S Food's digital business primary activities concluded that five primary activities would support the development of three applications. Table 8.8 sums up the primary activities mobilized for each application along with the recommended AWS modern application best practices to focus on.

Table 8.8: The Primary Activities of J&S Food's Business Model

ACTIVITY	BIG DATA APPLICATIONS	ECOMMERCE WEBSITE	TWO-SIDED MARKETPLACE
Business requirements analysis	Discuss requirements with the product owner. UML use case or agile user story is the recommended best practice.	Same as big data applications	Same as big data applications
Software architecture design	Discuss the software architecture. Modular architecture based on microservices combining serverless and container is recommended.	Same as big data applications	Same as big data applications
Software coding	Java based on Microsoft Visual Studio Code is the recommended language.	Same as big data applications	Same as big data applications
Software testing	Automated CI based on Test-Driven Development (TDD) using a Selenium solution is the recommended practice.	Same as big data applications	Same as big data applications
Application deployment	Continuous deployment to production based on automatic UAT and OAT approvals is the recommended practice.	Same as big data applications	Same as big data applications

Designing the Agile Operating Model

The goal is to make the chain of primary activities agile by intelligently and appropriately deploying the principles and philosophy of agile methodologies such as Scrum and Extreme Programming (XP).

However, the Solutions Architect might temper the development team's enthusiasm as follows:

"Deploying agile for the sake of deploying agile doesn't make sense — agile isn't the goal, agile is the means. The goal is to deliver a digital food experience that meets expectations."

The Usual Challenges and Solutions

In the following sections, the enterprise architect discusses the do's and don'ts of agile operating model deployment.

Understanding the Challenges

The enterprise architect reminds the participants of the following:

"The implementation of an agile operational model always faces resistance, which actually means difficulty in dropping command-and-control cultures or silos mentality."

In addition to these old cultures and mentalities, the challenge will be to use a deployment approach that simplifies issues like defining accountabilities, interactions across the delivery pipeline stages, and rapid decision-making structures.

The enterprise architect provides the most effective approach:

"Methods such as Scrum and Extreme Programming are frameworks that we will use to transform the organization of our software development processes at a lower cost and, above all, quickly."

Understanding the Solutions

Agile methodologies are helpful as they provide actionable organizational and operational frameworks. These frameworks offer software development lifecycles that underpin delivery pipelines. They define roles and responsibilities, interactions between stakeholders, and also decision-making structures across the software delivery lifecycle.

The next section describes the agile operating model that resulted from the decision to base J&S Food's DevOps platform on Scrum and XP.

J&S Food's Agile Operating Model Defined

Figure 8.6 illustrates the agile operational model piece of J&S Food's DevOps platform.

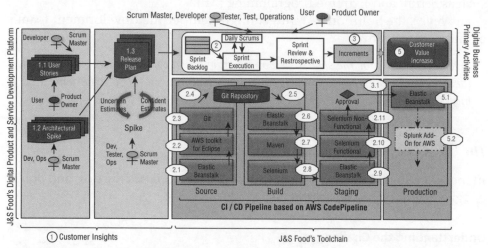

Figure 8.6: J&S Food's next agile operating model

Figure 8.6 shows that the Scrum approach facilitates software development and product launch activities. Scrum clarifies roles and responsibilities; through daily Scrums, this approach supports collaboration and decision-making.

Table 8.9 summarizes the roles and responsibilities in J&S Food's next digital product and service development team.

Table 8.9: J&S Food's Digital Product and Service Development Team

	ROLES AND RESPONSIBILITIES
Product owner	Defines stories (expected software functions), prioritizes product backlog (set of business requirements), and anticipates acceptance criteria for acceptance tests
Scrum master	Facilitates interactions, the Scrum events, including daily Scrums and sprint review, to accelerate the development effort and guarantee quality
Developer	Leverages the DevOps toolchain and AWS modern application principles to deliver high-quality software
Tester	Oversees and monitors automated tests during the build and staging phases of the software development effort
IT operations	Relies on AWS CloudWatch, Nagios, and Splunk services to monitor the DevOps toolchain and guarantee superior customer experience

The enterprise architect praises the benefits of Scrum and XP methodologies to the participants:

"Agile methodologies will help organize our software experts into cross-functional teams operating in rapid learning and short problem-solving and decision-making cycles. This is made possible by daily Scrums, sprint reviews, and sprint retrospectives."

Daily Scrums are meetings held daily involving the software development stakeholders. The purpose of such meetings is to set the context for the coming day's work. Benefits of daily Scrums include the following:

- Increased collaboration and ownership
- Improved progress visibility and exposure
- Increased control of the software development effort
- Reduced risk
- High quality

Sprint reviews are the meetings that take place at the end of the sprint. A *sprint* is a time-boxed period where the Scrum team works to complete a set amount of work. The purpose of the sprint review is to evaluate the latest features and to consider the plan for the software in the future.

As to the *sprint retrospective*, it's an "improvement" meeting held to identify improvements in all aspects of the software development process. The meeting is attended by the product owner, Scrum master, development team members, and other relevant stakeholders.

Key Takeaways

This chapter demonstrated that DevOps is a catalyst of the digital business performance provided that its implementation considers operational and organizational matters.

In this chapter, you learned about the big picture of DevOps, which integrates, as a whole, technological, organizational, and, more importantly, business performance issues through the AWS Modern Application.

In the next chapter, we will complete the study of the DevOps implementation by addressing the innovation services that J&S Foods will need to develop its lead digital product: the smart shopping bag.

References

1. Ernest Mueller, "What is DevOps and How Does it Work?" *The Agile Admin* (August 02, 2010). `https://theagileadmin.com/what-is-devops/`

2. Amazon Web Services, "AWS CodePipeline: Automate Continuous Delivery Pipelines for Fast and Reliable Updates," *Amazon Web Services* (November 22, 2017). `https://aws.amazon.com/codepipeline/`

3. Aditya Sridhar, "An Introduction to Git: What is it, and How to Use it?" *FreeCodeCamp* (August 12, 2018). `https://www.freecodecamp.org/news/what-is-git-and-how-to-use-it-c341b049ae61/`

Developing J&S Food's Innovation as a Service Platform Using AWS

Microservices are important simply because they add unique value in a way of simplification of complexity in systems. By breaking apart your system or application into many small parts, you show ways of reducing duplication, increasing cohesion, and lowering your coupling between parts, thus making your overall system parts easier to understand, more scalable, and easier to change. The downside of a distributed system is that it is always more complex from a systems standpoint. The overhead of many small services to manage is another factor to consider.

—**Lucas Krause**

Like most companies in the food industry, J&S Food must responsively innovate to survive and grow.

Artificial intelligence and machine learning (AI/ML) and Internet of Things (IoT) are the technologies that can help them, and this is what the company is about to do with the development of its smart shopping bag digital product.

Cloud computing has made technology accessible to most businesses, and most can meet the technology challenge.

However, to meet the market responsiveness challenge, companies must rely on microservices that are revolutionizing the software development approach in the cloud as well as that of digital products and services.

In this chapter, in the role of J&S Food's Digital Transformation leader, you will be involved in the development of a new software engineering approach and the tools supporting the implementation of innovative digital products and services for the AWS computing environment.

Transformation Journey's Third Stage: Developing J&S Food's Innovation as a Service

The third phase of the J&S Food's digital business model digitization is about designing and developing a new approach and tools supporting the development of innovations in the AWS computing environment. The bottom line is to get a set of microservices that makes the development of innovative digital products and services easy and responsive to market needs.

Figure 9.1 illustrates where the digital transformation team stands in terms of digitizing the business.

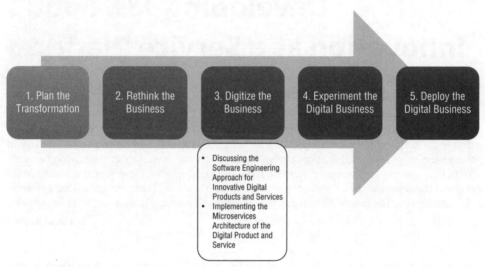

Figure 9.1: The microservices development phase

As Figure 9.1 shows, the AWS Solutions Architect would address the microservices development effort in two steps:

1. Discussing the software engineering approach for innovative digital products and services development

2. Implementing the microservices architecture of the digital product and service

Let's see how the Solutions Architect would go about developing the J&S Food's digital business objects.

Software Engineering Methodology for Innovations Development in the AWS Cloud

AI/ML, IoT, and big data are booming, but their practices lack the operational maturity required to meet the responsiveness challenge. Most companies must deal with a talent shortage combined with the absence of formal and reliable approaches.

The following sections discuss a methodology for developing innovative digital products and services in the AWS computing environment.

Software Engineering Methodology for Innovations Development

The software engineering approach for innovations development is a methodology for rapidly implementing innovative technology products and services in the AWS cloud. The methodology was developed by this book's author by combining the best of the *Unified Modeling Language (UML)* and that of microservices, containers, and AWS Amplify. The goal of this approach to innovation is to ensure an easy and rapid development of innovative products and services around AI/ML, IoT, and big data.

The following sections discuss the driving principles of the software engineering approach as well as its development lifecycle, while clarifying the essential role played by AWS Amplify.

Driving Principles Explained

The software engineering methodology is based on five principles. To help you understand its purpose and underlying philosophy, the following sections discuss these principles.

Improvisation and Innovation Are Incompatible

Building and running applications that exploit the benefits of the AWS computing environment is still a challenge. The lift and shift as well as the lift, tinker, and shift approaches, and the improvised software changes that go with them, result in applications that have latency and performance issues.

Planning the software development project in terms of effort to mobilize, tools to leverage, and challenges to be faced is the safest way to make the software delivery predictable and to mitigate the risks to the expected benefits and agreed upon schedule.

Modularizing Increases Quality, Responsiveness, and Cost-Effectiveness

Until recently, software programs have been built as monolithic systems in which all applications are dependent on one another within a single software program and hardware environment. The problem with monolithic software architectures is twofold: size and complexity. Monolithic software architectures raise a number of problems. For example, the size and complexity of the code make understanding, maintaining, and scaling it long, difficult, and expensive.

Conversely, decomposing software into small, meaningful, and understandable modules through microservices increases the development team's productivity, creativity, and responsiveness.

Abstracting Complexity Increases Quality, Responsiveness, and Cost-Effectiveness

Technologies such as AI/ML, IoT, and big data have a long learning curve that is incompatible with urgency. Using abstraction as a complexity reduction mechanism is the safest way to facilitate the use of these technologies.

Using the UML Models Helps to Abstract Technology Complexity

Reinventing models to abstract technological complexity is a difficult and unnecessary task. Common sense is to rely on proven methodology such as UML.

In addition to being a powerful guide for the development of innovative technological products, UML via models, such as the use case diagram, class diagram, and package diagrams, provide a structured approach that supports the design and implementation of microservices.

Using Microservices to Implement Modularity in the AWS Computing Environment Increases Quality, Productivity, and Responsiveness

The UML abstraction mechanisms are proven solutions to reducing and managing technical and technological complexity. Implementing UML abstraction mechanisms using the triplet (microservice, containers, and AWS Lambda) fosters the software modularity, increases operational agility, and accelerates the company's time-to-market.

Using AWS Amplify to Accelerate Modern Application Development

Developing modern applications in the AWS computing environment is challenging. They're built on a combination of modular architecture patterns, serverless operational models, a variety of AWS services, and agile processes. Application generators are needed to simplify and accelerate the development process.

AWS Amplify is a serverless framework platform for building secure and scalable mobile and web applications. It makes it easy to authenticate users, securely store data and user metadata, authenticate selective access to data, integrate machine learning, analyze usage metrics, and implement server-side code.

Key Concepts to Understand

This section introduces the key concepts that you need to know to understand the software engineering methodology for innovations development in the AWS computing environment.

The UML Class Diagram

The *UML class diagram* is the main building block in UML modeling. It's primarily used to highlight the meaningful business entities handled by the application, including their attributes, operations, and the relationships among them. Figure 9.2 depicts a typical class diagram.

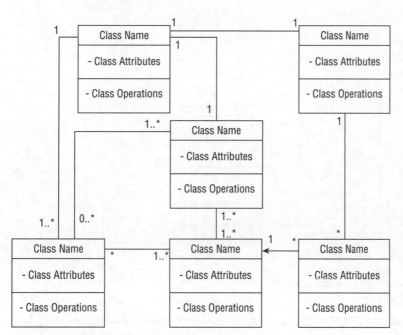

Figure 9.2: Typical UML class diagram

Even though the class defines what an entity handled by the application can do, it's primarily used in the methodology to identify the data that will be handled by the application.

A *class* is characterized by *attributes*, which define its features, and *operations*, which determine its behavior and the services it provides. The links between classes highlighted by the class diagram defines *dependencies* in terms of data and expected services.

The UML Package Diagram

A *UML package diagram* is used to group classes into packages. A *package* is a collection of logically related classes. Figure 9.3 shows a business model in which the classes are grouped into packages. Packages appear as rectangles with small tabs at the top. They will be used in the methodology to model the real-world modular structure of the system being modeled.

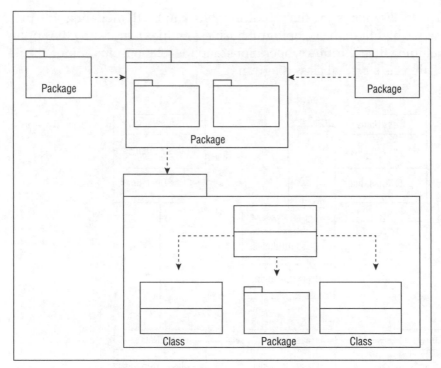

Figure 9.3: A typical UML package diagram

When organizing source code, packages will be used to represent the different layers of the source code such as the presentation layer, business logic layer, and data access layer.

AWS Lambda

AWS Lambda is an event-driven, serverless computing platform. It's a computing service that runs code in response to events and automatically manages the infrastructure computing resources required to run the code.

The only thing that developers need to do is to upload the code to Lambda, and it takes care of everything required to run and scale its execution and fulfill conditions and high availability requirements.

Lambda is then used to encapsulate the desired functions into dedicated archive files or containers to form the microservices.

Microservices Anatomy

Microservices are an architectural style that structures an application as a collection of services where each service implements different capabilities or roles.

Microservices will be used in the methodology to modularize your applications in a way that enables developers to build applications from independent, reusable modules, using different services and invoking functions with various parameters to obtain the desired end results.

AWS Amplify

Using AWS Amplify's Admin UI and CLI's intuitive workflows to set up scalable backends with authentication, storage, and data, developers not only can easily manage content but also can rapidly configure and deploy back-end applications. Figure 9.4 illustrates its constituent pieces.

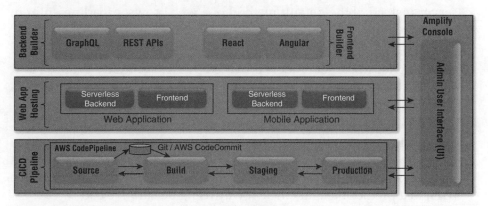

Figure 9.4: The blueprint of the AWS Amplify platform

Figure 9.4 shows that AWS Amplify is an application development accelerator. It is based on four building blocks that facilitate the development of mobile and web applications: Amplify console, application builders (backend and frontend), web app hosting, and the continuous integration and continuous deployment (CICD) pipeline.

The Amplify Console   The *AWS Amplify Console* provides access to the full range of Amplify services via an administration user interface, the *Admin UI*. The Amplify Console provides two chief services including hosting and the Admin UI:

- The hosting service provides a Git-based workflow for hosting full-stack serverless web apps with continuous deployment (CICD pipeline). Other repositories such AWS CodeCommit, Bitbucket, and GitLab may also be suitable.

- The Admin UI, via its visual interface, gives access to the application builders that developers leverage to create and manage web application front ends and back ends.

Full-stack web apps are serverless applications consisting of a back-end component built with cloud resources such GraphQL or REST APIs and of a front-end piece developed with single-page application (SPA) frameworks.

GraphQL is a query language and server-side runtime for application programming interfaces (APIs) that prioritizes giving clients exactly the data that they request and no more.

The Representation State Transfer application programming interface (REST API) is the standardized building block of interactive services.

As for SPAs, this refers to web applications that interact with the user by dynamically rewriting the current web page with new data from the web server instead of the default method of a web browser loading entirely new pages.

The Application Builders   The *application builders* (or development accelerators) refer to the set of tools provided by AWS Amplify to speed and simplify the development and deployment of web application front ends and back ends.

An example of application back-end builders is GraphQL, a query language with a syntax that describes how to ask for data, generally used to load data from a server to a client. An example of an application front-end builder is React, a JavaScript library that helps to create user interfaces (UIs) in a predictable and efficient way using declarative code.

Web Applications Hosting   *Web applications hosting* refers to the fully managed service offered by AWS Amplify for deploying and hosting full-stack web applications with built-in CICD pipelines that accelerate application delivery.

The CICD Pipeline   The *CICD pipeline* refers to the application deployment workflow delivered by AWS Amplify as part of its web application hosting services.

AWS Amplify will be used in the software engineering methodology as the mechanism for accelerating the application development and deployment process.

Understanding the Innovative Digital Product Development Lifecycle

The development of innovative technological products can be defined as an attempt to provide customers with a superior customer experience.

The digital product and service development effort addresses various issues (look and feel, safety, fit for purpose) and mobilizes various staff, skills, methodologies, and tools. Most failing projects don't reach their goal because of a lack of a formal and structured development process. Generally, they're based on improvisation.

This section offers a structured approach designed for the development of innovative digital products in the AWS computing environment.

The Five-Step Development Lifecycle

As shown in Figure 9.5, the successful digital product development project is an iterative five-step effort.

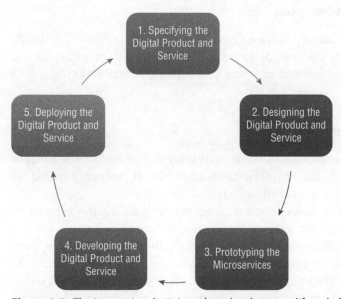

Figure 9.5: The innovative digital product development lifecycle for the AWS environment

The digital product development effort is about clarifying the product's functions, designing the product with a laser focus on the customer experience, designing and developing relevant microservices, developing the product itself, and organizing its go-to market. Let's take it a step further.

Specifying the Innovative Digital Product Using a UML Use Case Diagram

The purpose of the innovative digital product specification step is to identify the various use cases of the digital product and to identify the features that are likely to create a superior customer experience.

Marketing, sales, IT, the cloud solutions architect, the product designer, and the software developers take part in the workshops discussed below this activity.

The product development team will collaboratively carry out the following tasks:

- Identify the digital product's use cases
- Define the user experience
- Identify the digital product's functions
- Define the digital product's data model

The following sections elaborate on the digital product and service specification tasks.

Identifying the Digital Product's Use Cases

In this task, participants identify and describe the actors of the digital product's ecosystem using the UML use case diagram. For each actor, the concerned use cases are identified and described in terms of purpose, functional scope, and timing.

Defining the User Experience

Based on the described use cases, sales and marketing define each actor's buyer persona. A *buyer persona* is the representation of the ideal customer based on market research and actual data about existing customers.

Personas help marketing, sales, product, and services understand the ideal customer to attract. Participants then derive from the personas the user experience elements that the digital product development will leverage to implement the features that will make the product innovative.

The user experience is the customer's feelings and perceptions about using a particular product. It encompasses every aspect of the customer's interactions with the company's products and services. It describes how satisfied the customer is with the company.

Identifying the Digital Product's Functions

In this task, as illustrated in Figure 9.6, after identifying the business objects (concepts and material meaningful for the business) handled by the digital product, participants develop the UML sequence diagram to describe each use case.

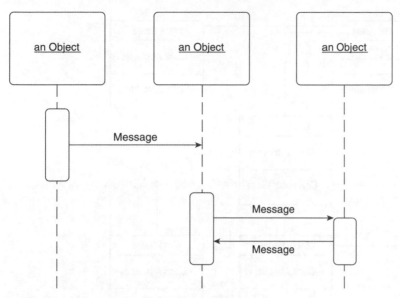

Figure 9.6: UML sequence diagram example

Source: Lucidchart

A *sequence diagram* is a type of interaction drawing that describes how and in what order the identified business objects interact through messages to implement the use case's purpose.

The main purpose of sequence diagrams is to model the interactions between objects that participate in the implementation of the digital product use cases. Note that each message received by an object is an operation performed by that object to contribute to the implementation of the use case's purpose.

Defining the Digital Product's Data Model

The bottom line in this task is to design the digital product's data model. Figure 9.7 provides an example of such a model.

A *class diagram* illustrates the relationships and dependencies among classes (business objects) in the digital product and service source code. In this context, a *class* defines the operations and attributes of a business object. It is the formal description of the business objects handled by the digital product to deliver the expected services and customer experience.

The class is composed of two fundamental elements including the attributes and the operations:

- An *attribute* represents a data definition for a business object. A business object can have any number of attributes or none at all.

- An *operation* is concretely a business object's function performed to implement a use case and by extension deliver the digital product's expected service.

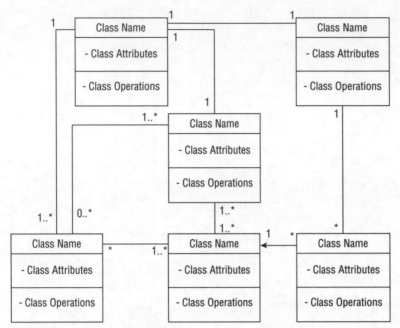

Figure 9.7: UML class diagram example

Source: Lucidchart

Designing the Innovative Digital Product Using a UML Package Diagram

The purpose of this activity is to design the N-Tier software architecture underpinning the digital product. The design phase follows AWS Modern Application principles and builds on the N-Tier architectural pattern.

The *N-Tier pattern* is a computing pattern in which presentation, application business logic, and data management functions are logically separated. The most common use of multitier architecture is three-tier architecture.

The marketing, sales, IT, cloud solutions architect, product designer, and software developers are part of the workshops underneath this activity.

The product development team will collaboratively carry out the following tasks:

- Design of the presentation layer
- Design of the microservices underneath the business logic layer
- Design of the data management layer

The following sections elaborate on these tasks.

Designing the Presentation Layer

The *presentation layer* refers to the user interface and communication layer of the application. It's where the user interacts with the application.

Running on a web browser, as a desktop application or a graphical user interface (GUI), its primary goal is to display information to and collect information from the user.

The focus in this task is on designing the user interface including the look and feel, interactions, and user experience elements to implement.

Designing the Microservices Underpinning the Business Logic

The *business logic layer* is the heart of the application. It's a set of UML packages where information collected in the presentation layer is processed using a specific set of business rules.

In this task, the classes of the digital product's data model are reorganized into consistent business packages. Depending on the company's policy, the business packages can be organized by organizational units, business segment, or business areas of concern.

Each package represents a microservice and provides an interface that gives access to its data and operations.

Designing the Data Management Layer

The *data management layer*, sometimes called *database layer*, is where the information processed by the application is stored and managed. The data management layer is implemented using either Amazon RDS, the Amazon's managed SQL database service, or Amazon DynamoDB.

Amazon RDS hosts database engines such as MySQL, Microsoft SQL Server, and Oracle. AWS NoSQL options allow the use of solutions such as DynamoDB, MongoDB, and Cassandra.

In this task, the digital product development team is mobilized not only to define the digital product's database structure but also to make data management architectural choices in terms of database type (SQL or No SQL) and database management solutions as well as system sizing and security.

Prototyping the Microservices Using AWS Amplify

Using AWS Amplify, the challenge is to implement API-driven services that simplify the use of AWS AI/ML, IoT, and big data.

The development team will make sure that the microservices are on-demand services that achieve scale horizontally across the company.

Developing and Deploying the Application Supporting the Innovative Digital Product

AWS Amplify imposes an object-oriented approach to software development, which is about structuring the application into simple, reusable pieces of code blueprints called *classes*. In Amplify, these reusable objects fall into two categories:

- *Back-end* objects support functions such as databases, file storage, and security. It relies on tools such as GraphQL.
- *Front-end* objects support user interface–related matters. They're created through frameworks such as React and Angular.

The following sections elaborate on the digital product and service development tasks.

Configuring the Back End

Building on the AWS Amplify backend frameworks, the developer starts by creating the back-end objects based on the framework represented in Figure 9.8.

Figure 9.8: AWS Amplify back-end creation framework

As shown in Figure 9.8, the developer can select, for instance, the data model option and be guided throughout the process, creating relational database tables by providing their names, primary keys, and field names, and then linking these tables based on adequate business rules.

Deploying the Back End

As illustrated in Figure 9.9, building on the AWS Amplify back-end framework, the developer would proceed to deploy the back end created, which is the data model in our example, to the target environment.

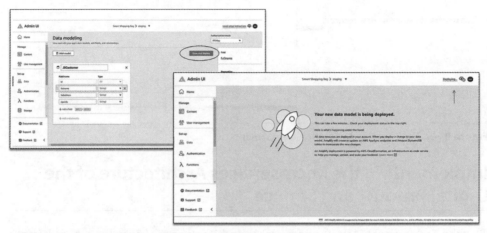

Figure 9.9: AWS Amplify back-end deployment framework

Even though the process is as easy as clicking the Save and deploy button, there are often tweaks needed to the generated code. Nonetheless, what you must bear in mind is the simplicity of the process and the substantial time savings.

Deploying and Connecting the Application to the Back End

Once the back end, the data model in our example, is created and deployed, the next step is to create the application that will take advantage of the data model. As illustrated in Figure 9.10, the developer relies on the framework provided by AWS Amplify.

The developer chooses a framework for the application's front-end elements and then clicks Deploy app to trigger the application deployment on the CICD pipeline.

As you can see from this simplified process, the development of the application intended to support digital product and service implementation is made simple by the automation and visual development tools provided by the AWS Amplify frameworks.

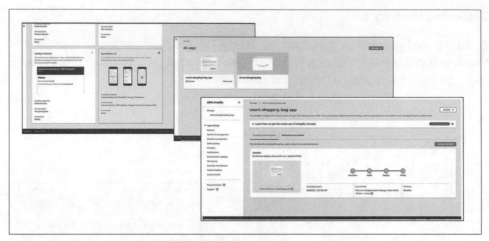

Figure 9.10: AWS Amplify application deployment

Implementing the Microservices Architecture of the Digital Product and Service

The challenge now is to set up a scalable architecture that enables rapid changes and deployment of the digital product. Experience shows that an N-Tier architecture, as shown in Figure 9.11, makes this objective possible.

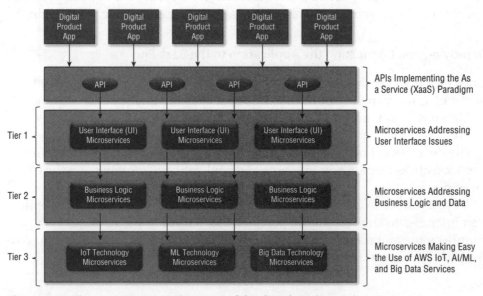

Figure 9.11: The microservices architecture of the digital product and services

The logic underlying the N-Tier architecture, as represented in Figure 9.11, is that to control the changes impacting the digital product, it is necessary to isolate the different microservices. This makes it possible to limit the impacts not only in terms of code quality but above all in terms of responsiveness and costs. Figure 9.11 also highlights three categories of microservices. Let's discuss them.

The User Interface Microservices

These are the microservices encapsulating the mechanisms managing user interfaces, both web-based and mobile. Product owners and the marketing department in general have a particular interest in this aspect, as the user interface is an essential element of the digital experience.

AWS Amplify, through front-end frameworks such as React, Angular, and Vue and while addressing platforms such as Android and iOS, allows companies to implement these types of microservice effectively.

React, Angular, and Vue are component-based frameworks that enable developers to rapidly build the microservices that form front-end applications.

React (also known as React.Js or ReactJS) is an open source front-end JavaScript (a scripting language for implementing complex features on web pages) library for building user interfaces or UI components. It's used as a base in the development of single-page or mobile applications.

Angular is a platform and framework used for building single-page client applications using HTML and TypeScript.

As for Vue (also known as Vue.js), it's an open source progressive JavaScript framework for building user interfaces (UIs) and single-page applications.

The Business Logic Microservices

These are the microservices that address the business logic of the digital products and services. They're the epicenter of each digital product.

The business logic microservices hold the business rules, data, and metadata handled by the digital products. They're under the business and functional responsibility of the product owner and the marketing department.

AWS Amplify, through back-end frameworks like GraphQL, allows companies to implement these types of microservices effectively to provide database access and file storage and address security issues.

The Technology Microservices

These microservices are intended to encapsulate the innovative technologies used by the company such as AI/ML, IoT, and big data. Their bottom line is to facilitate the use of these innovative technologies by abstracting their complexity.

The technology microservices are under the strategic responsibility of the chief technology officer (CTO) and the operational responsibility of the AWS Solutions Architect.

Through the AWS Amplify PubSub category (publish/subscribe messaging mechanisms), AWS provides connectivity with cloud-based message-oriented middleware that connects to the proper functions of the AI/ML, IoT, and big data applications on the host. PubSub is used to pass messages between app instances and an app's back end creating real-time interactive experiences. PubSub is available with AWS IoT and third-party providers of MQTT over WebSocket, a messaging solution that allows it to receive MQTT data directly into a web browser.

Key Takeaways

The development of innovative technology products and services within short deadlines is a complex process that should not be improvised. It requires proven design approaches and automated implementation procedures.

In this chapter, we discussed a methodology for developing microservices that can facilitate the use of artificial intelligence/machine learning, IoT, and big data technologies.

You familiarized yourself with the Unified Modeling Language software design process adapted for the AWS computing environment context.

You learned about the rules for translating a class diagram into a package representing the set of microservices intended to deliver innovation as a service mechanism to developers.

Finally, you learned about the power of AWS Amplify, which dramatically reduces the time, effort, and costs of developing digital products and services.

The following chapters will illustrate how J&S Food will use the methodology and the AWS Amplify framework to develop and deploy the smart shopping bag digital product.

References

1. Creately, "Class Diagram Relationships in UML Explained with Examples," *Creately* (December 1, 2020). `https://creately.com/blog/diagrams/class-diagram-relationships/`

2. Amazon Web Services, "AWS Amplify: Fastest, easiest, way to build mobile and web apps that scale" *Amazon Web Services* (2021). `https://aws.amazon.com/amplify/`

3. TutorialsPoint, "UML Tutorial," *Tutorialspoint* (2021). `https://www`
    `.tutorialspoint.com/uml/index.htm`

4. Serkan Ozal, "Building Serverless Application with AWS Amplify" *The New Stack* (October 1, 2020). `https://thenewstack.io/building-serverless-applications-with-aws-amplify/`

Part

III

Developing World-Class Digital Products and Services Using AWS

Once the business has been transformed, including the implementation of its digital products and services development platform, the next step is to develop the digital products and services that deliver the digital experience that customers expect.

In Part III, consisting of Chapters 10–16, the development of an innovative digital product using AWS, J&S Food's smart shopping bag, is methodically illustrated and explained from specification and design to implementation, deployment, and launch.

Chapter 10, "J&S Food's Smart Shopping Bag Digital Product Project," presents the J&S Food's smart shopping bag digital product development project including its objectives, scope, organization, opportunity statement, and the pilot project management approach.

Chapter 11, "Specifying J&S Food's Smart Shopping Bag Digital Product," and Chapter 12, "Designing J&S Food's Smart Shopping Bag Digital Product," describe the digital products and services technical specification and design processes. These chapters show, step-by-step, how the key features of the UML methodology are leveraged to bring out the smart shopping bag digital product's building blocks along with the data and functions needed to support its operations.

Chapter 13, "Prototyping J&S Food's Smart Shopping Bag Using Innovation as a Service," and Chapter 14, "Implementing J&S Food's Smart Shopping Bag Application," provide insights into the software prototyping approach supporting the architectural spikes of the Extreme Programming (XP) agile development approach. They show how the UML methodology combined with the use of AWS Amplify framework helps to rapidly develop, test, validate, and deploy microservices architectures.

Chapter 15, "Launching J&S Food's First Digital Food Product," describes the process and key methodologies and tools needed to develop successful go-to-market strategies. It explains how tools and methodologies, such as the strategy map, are leveraged to ensure a successful smart shopping bag go-to-market.

Chapter 16, "Maintaining and Supporting J&S Food's Digital Business on a Daily Basis," provides a snapshot of how the transformed J&S Food's digital business works on a daily basis to deliver a superior digital food experience and continuously create value.

J&S Food's Smart Shopping Bag Digital Product Project

It doesn't matter how beautiful your theory is, it doesn't matter how smart you are.
If it doesn't agree with experiment, it's wrong.

—Richard P. Feynman

J&S Food's digital transformation project is underway. Substantial progress has been made; the company equipped itself with an AWS IaaS cloud (Chapter 7, "Digitizing J&S Food's Business Model Using AWS—Implementing the VPC") that will host its ecommerce platform.

The company has also implemented a digital products and services development infrastructure in the form of an AWS DevOps platform (Chapter 8, "Implementing J&S Food's DevOps Platform Using AWS PaaS") that will support its digital products and services development projects.

Now is the go-to-market time—the time to deploy this operational model and infrastructure and make the company a leader in the digital food business.

Nevertheless, the chief executive officer (CEO) is cautious. And he is right to be so: "We have to make it gradually. We'll start with a pilot experiment project involving three regional stores."

The company's board of directors wants the smart shopping bag digital product development project to serve as the basis for evaluating the new digital business infrastructure.

This chapter provides a summary of the minutes of the board of directors meeting held a couple of days earlier.

Transformation Journey's Fourth Stage: Experimenting with the Digital Business Model

The fourth phase of J&S Food's digital transformation consists of experimenting with the company's digital business model in actual business conditions. The objective is to make sure that the digital business model delivers the expected benefits as well as to identify possible weaknesses and areas of improvement.

Figure 10.1 illustrates where the team stands in the company's digital transformation journey.

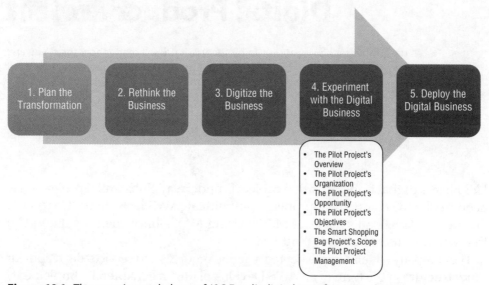

Figure 10.1: The experimental phase of J&S Food's digital transformation journey

As Figure 10.1 illustrates, the first step of the experimental phase is about deploying the digital operational model for the pilot project and sharing the smart shopping bag digital product project.

Let's examine what the board meeting minutes tell the pilot project team about the experimental phase and the new smart shopping bag digital product.

The Smart Shopping Bag Project Overview

The first lines of the minutes start with an overview of the pilot project. They present the smart shopping bag initiative as "The first step taken by the company as a digital business."

The project is described as an experimental step with a twofold objective: deploying the organizational and technological infrastructure and making sure, through the development of a digital product, that the digital business model delivers the expected benefits.

The project involves three regional stores, including J&S Food's grocery stores in Hoboken, New Jersey; Princeton, New Jersey; and Albany, New York. The target market for the pilot project is estimated at 700,000 people, and 300 J&S Food staff members are involved in the project in a variety of roles and areas ranging from product design and software development to sales, marketing, and customer service.

The Smart Shopping Bag Project's Organization

As to the project's organization, the board of directors suggests a clear division of roles between the stores located in Albany, Hoboken, and Princeton.

J&S Food's stores in Albany will lead the deployment of the digital business model and manage the changes across the stores located in Hoboken and Princeton, as well as in its own stores.

As to the J&S Food's store in Princeton, they will lead the development of the smart shopping bag digital product and will collaborate with Albany's and Hoboken's teams on facilitating the adoption of the organizational, operational, and technological changes.

The Smart Shopping Bag Project's Opportunity Statement

Regarding the smart shopping bag project's opportunity, the board meeting minutes remind the project team's members that the company has been left behind by its main competitors including Walmart Grocery Pickup, Fresh Direct, Instacart, and Amazon Fresh. What has been happening is that sales and market share have been gradually declining in recent years and sharply dropped due to the pandemic crisis to reach 72 percent now.

The board of directors is confident that aligning the company's staff, processes, practices, and technologies with the standards of the digital food business industry will help J&S Food survive. The development of the smart shopping bag will allow the company to rise to the level of its competitors.

The Smart Shopping Bag Project's Objectives

The board meeting minutes clarify the smart shopping bag project's three-month goals as follows:

- Move 70 percent of the Albany, Hoboken, and Princeton business to digital.
- Make 100 percent of Hoboken, Princeton, and Albany IT staff knowledgeable in AWS technologies.
- Ensure that 100 percent of Albany, Hoboken, and Princeton adopt the company's new digital operational model.
- Ensure that 175,000 consumers subscribe to the smart shopping bag service within the next three months.

The Smart Shopping Bag Project's Scope

Table 10.1 summarizes the project scope and related roles and responsibilities as defined by the board of directors.

Table 10.1: The Smart Shopping Bag Project's Scope

	ALBANY	PRINCETON	HOBOKEN
Introduction to J&S Food's digital food experience	Leader	Contributor	Contributor
Presentation of J&S Food's digital business operational model	Leader	Contributor	Contributor
Training on J&S Food's digital business operational model	Leader	Contributor	Contributor
Training on J&S Food's AWS infrastructure	Contributor	Leader with the support of the AWS Solutions Architect	Contributor
Training on J&S Food's digital product development platform	Contributor	Leader with the support of the AWS Solutions Architect	Contributor
Development of the smart shopping bag digital product	Contributor	Leader with the support of the AWS Solutions Architect	Contributor

The Pilot Project Management

To finish, the board meeting minutes recommend a pilot project management structured around a task force headed by a CEO's representative who will also act as an executive sponsor. The task force will consist of representatives from the digital business model deployment team (Albany), the smart shopping bag digital product development team (Princeton), and the business users (Hoboken).

Table 10.2 outlines the roles and responsibilities in the smart shopping bag project's task force.

Table 10.2: Roles and Responsibilities Within the Project's Task Force

TASK FORCE MEMBER	ROLES AND RESPONSIBILITIES
CEO representative	Arbitrates conflicts and priorities. Facilitates interactions. Reports overall progress, risks, and issues to the CEO.
Digital business model deployment team representative	Reports on deployment progress, risks, and problems. Recommends proactive action plan to mitigate risks and prevent problems on organizational deployment and training.
Smart shopping bag digital product development team representative	Reports on digital product development progress, risks, and problems. Recommends proactive action plan to mitigate risks and prevent problems on product development effort.
Business users' representatives	Plays the online customer role using the buy, customer service, and product usage processes. Reports and makes improvement recommendations on the previous processes.

Key Takeaways

J&S Food's board of directors understands the importance of involving executive management in the changes that are taking place in the company. Setting up a task force was the right thing to do.

A task force provides the resources required to implement the change. It is responsible for the digital transformation project and for building a commitment to the change, particularly at the senior management level across the company.

The next chapter will discuss the deployment of the digital business operational model in the IT organization and the kickoff of the smart shopping bag development project, including the product's functional and technical specification phase.

References

1. Neil Kokemuller, "Change Management (OD) Vs. Change Management (Operational)," *Chron* (February 21, 2018). `https://smallbusiness.chron.com/change-management-od-vs-change-management-operational-15706.html`

2. Christopher Smith, "Understanding Operational Change Management," *Change* (June 4, 2014). `https://change.walkme.com/understanding-operational-change-management/`

3. Ron Ashkenas and Nadim Matta, "How to Scale a Successful Pilot Project," *Harvard Business Review* (January 8, 2021). `https://hbr.org/2021/01/how-to-scale-a-successful-pilot-project`

4. Paul Leinwand and Mahadeva Matt Mani, "Digitizing Isn't the Same as Digital Transformation," *The New Stack* (March 26, 2021). `https://hbr.org/2021/03/digitizing-isnt-the-same-as-digital-transformation`

Specifying J&S Food's Smart Shopping Bag Digital Product

Systems Thinking is a mixed bag of holistic, balanced, and often abstract thinking to understand things profoundly and solve problems systematically.

—Pearl Zhu

This chapter illustrates how J&S Food's new digital product and service development team operates on a daily basis in terms of structure, team, roles, responsibilities, processes, practices, and tools. It shows how the principles of the digital business value chain and digital business operational model are implemented and applied to help the company deliver the promised superior digital food experience. Above all, it shows how systems thinking through an object-oriented approach improved J&S Food's digital product and service development process.

The information provided in this chapter will give you an accurate perspective of how digital product and service ideas and concepts gradually take shape, as well as providing the basic things that you need to know about Internet of Things (IoT) product implementation.

Transformation Journey's Fourth Stage: Specification of the Smart Shopping Bag Digital Product

The second step of the fourth phase of J&S Food's digital transformation is about specifying the features of the smart shopping bag digital product.

Figure 11.1 illustrates where the team stands in the company's digital transformation journey.

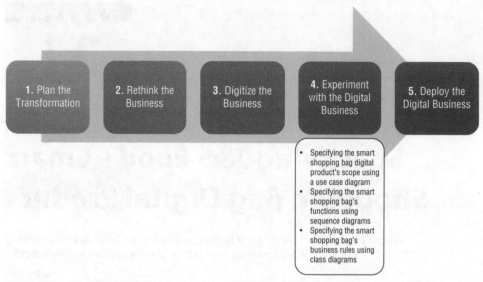

Figure 11.1: The digital product's specification phase of J&S Food's digital transformation journey

As Figure 11.1 illustrates, digital product and service specification is a three-step process including the specification of the digital product's scope using context and a use case diagram, functions using sequence diagrams, and business rules using class diagram.

Let's look at how the Princeton store's product development team specified the features of the smart shopping bag digital product.

Specifying the Smart Shopping Bag Digital Product's Scope

In most digital transformation projects, there is always an event that triggers the company's first steps into the digital business world. In the case of J&S Food, it's a Jira notification scheduled by the PMO manager that kicked off the company's digital food business. Jira is the agile project management tool underneath J&S Food's agile digital operational model.

This Jira notification invited the product owner, the Scrum master, developers, testers, and operations as well as the AWS Solutions Architect to a product backlog definition session whose purpose was to specify the smart shopping bag features.

The following sections illustrate how the company's digital product and service development processes have improved.

Using Context Diagrams to Improve the Specification Process

Unlike the old approach where the marketing and sales departments, in a silo mentality, developed the business requirements and submitted them to IT, by stressing collaboration, the new approach is viewed as simple, effective, and efficient by the new J&S Food's digital product development team. In fact, the adoption of the Unified Modeling Language (UML) as a means of facilitating communication between the business users and IT staff members likewise introduced in the company's practice of the use of system context diagrams to help stakeholders to agree on the digital product's scope.

Developing the Smart Shopping Bag's Context Diagram

The specification process starts with a presentation of the product's functional, technological, and technical scope. The goal is to make sure that all the team members are on the same page.

Figure 11.2 provides an overview of the smart shopping bag's scope, as it emerged from the workshop.

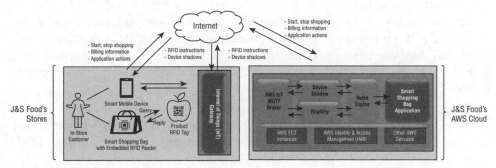

Figure 11.2: The smart shopping bag context diagram

The context diagram shows that the smart shopping bag's ecosystem is divided between J&S Food's stores and J&S Food's cloud infrastructure hosted by Amazon. Let's explore it now.

J&S Food's Stores IoT Infrastructure

The piece of the retail process that takes place in J&S Food's stores takes advantage of radio frequency identification (RFID) and IoT gateway technologies to remove the time that in-store customers waste in queuing up when ready to pay. It therefore improves the shopping experience and contributes to making the company's digital food experience superior.

An *RFID reader* is a network-connected device attached to the smart shopping bag. It's closely associated with the RFID tag attached to food items. The tag sends radio waves to an antenna where they're translated into data.

In-store customers use their smartphone to start and stop shopping sessions. The smartphone initiates an IoT connection with the smart shopping bag application hosted in the company's AWS cloud. The IoT gateway serves as a wireless access portal to give the RFID reader access to the Internet and J&S Food's AWS cloud.

Each item put in the bag is associated with an RFID tag, which allows the RFID reader embedded in the smart shopping bag to account for the items for billing and payment purposes.

J&S Food's AWS IoT Core Platform

As for the piece of the retail process that takes place in the cloud, it performs the *AWS IoT Core functions*. These managed service functions include connecting smart mobile devices and RFID readers to the cloud, facilitating interactions with the smart shopping bag applications hosted in J&S Food's AWS cloud, and processing and routing messages to AWS IoT endpoints. Each message issued by a smartphone is relayed by the IoT gateway to the smart shopping bag application via an IoT Message Queuing Telemetry Transport (MQTT) message broker. MQTT is a lightweight, standard messaging protocol for connecting devices within the IoT.

J&S Food's AWS IoT Core platform builds on a *registry* that stores information about the RFID readers embedded in the smart shopping bags and the certificates that they use to secure communication with AWS IoT. The information is stored as JavaScript Object Notation (JSON) data. Each entry in the registry is referred to as a *thing*, or a representation of a specific RFID reader.

The *device shadow* is another component involved in J&S Food's AWS IoT Core. It's a JSON document used to store and retrieve an RFID reader's current state information. The device shadow service acts as an intermediary, allowing RFID readers and applications to retrieve and update state information.

The last component of J&S Food's AWS IoT Core platform is the *rules engine*. The rules engine provides message processing and integration with other AWS services. The AWS IoT rules engine listens for incoming MQTT messages that match a rule. When a matching message is received, the rule takes specific actions according to the data in the MQTT message.

The actions vary from instructing the RFID to count the items in the bag to triggering the payment function of the smart shopping bag application.

Developing the Smart Shopping Bag Use Case Diagram

The digital product development process proceeds with capturing and understanding the product's functions to develop.

The deployment of the digital business value chain, particularly that of its agile operational model piece, has significantly improved J&S Food's digital product development team's approach. In fact, rather than focusing solely on the product and technology, the new approach emphasizes the product's eco-system; it uses the UML use case diagram to model the ecosystem and provide a much broader perspective of the product's users, thus delivering a much more accurate vision of the functionalities to develop as a result.

The purpose of the smart shopping bag's use cases development is to build on the information provided by the context diagram to identify the digital prod-uct's use cases, describe these use cases, identify the product's functions that will deliver the expected digital food experience, and develop its data model.

The workshop takes place in a meeting room specially designed with UML, Scrum, and AWS process posters displayed on the wall and a virtual whiteboard for brainstorming and ideation. The intent is to speed up the participants' famil-iarization with these processes and practices.

Consistent with the collaborative mindset recommended by the agile meth-odology, the product owner (product functional expert) and the Scrum master (PMO product development facilitator), respectively from the Princeton store's sales and IT department, as well as the developers, testers, and cloud operations, contribute at all stages of the process.

In this phase, the product owner, assisted by the Scrum master, leverages the UML use case diagram via the Lucidchart tool to capture the smart shopping bag use cases, uses sequence diagrams to describe the use cases, and employs the class diagram to highlight the digital product's key business rules.

The use case diagram in Figure 11.3 builds on the UML formalism to show the functional scope of the smart shopping bag as well as the actors involved in the delivery of its functions.

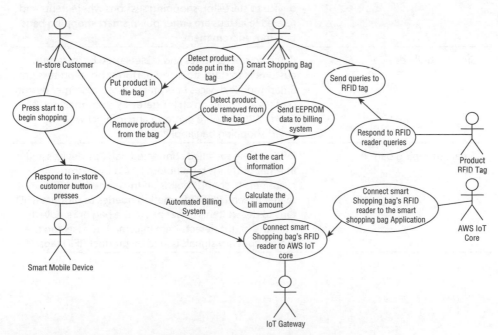

Figure 11.3: The smart shopping bag's use case diagram

As shown in the figure, the smart shopping bag ecosystem, as the participants defined it, is structured around a variety of actors including human, technology product, systems, and infrastructure.

Let's discuss the smart shopping bag ecosystem as participants.

Identifying the Smart Shopping Bag's Actors and Use Cases

In an atmosphere free from organizational barriers, dominated by a strong team spirit, business and IT experts discuss the human, operational, organizational, and technological aspects of the smart shopping bag's ecosystem. The following sections provide the ecosystem specification that resulted from this process, including the actors and the use cases.

Actors Identified

Seven actors are involved in the smart shopping bag's ecosystem including the in-store customer, smart mobile device, smart shopping bag, product RFID tag, automated billing system, IoT gateway, and AWS IoT core platform.

Table 11.1 outlines their role and characteristics.

Table 11.1: Actors of the Smart Shopping Bag Ecosystem

ACTORS	DESCRIPTION
In-store customer	Refers to a customer who subscribed to the smart shopping bag services. They use their smart mobile device to start/stop shopping sessions where items and related RFID tags are either put in smart shopping bags or removed from them.
Smart mobile device	Refers to smartphones and tablets used by in-store customers to start, stop, and perform shopping sessions. Smart mobile devices interpret in-store customer button presses and build on an IoT gateway to connect to J&S Food's AWS IoT Core platform and interact with the smart shopping bag application.
Smart shopping bag	Refers to the so-called connected bag (IoT devices in the Internet of Things terminology) used by in-store customers to shop. It builds on the embedded RFID reader to send RFID information queries to product RFID tags to detect items either put in the bag or removed from the bag. It detects item information based on the radio frequency signals issued by product RFID tags.

ACTORS	DESCRIPTION
Product RFID tag	Refers to a three-piece component supplied to each food item in the stores. These pieces include a microchip that stores and processes information, an antenna for receiving and transmitting radio frequency signals, and nonvolatile memory that stores the tag information.
Automated billing system	Refers to the billing system module of the smart shopping bag application hosted in J&S Food's AWS cloud. As messages are issued by smart mobile devices, it collects the shopping session's billing information and calculates the bill amount.
IoT gateway	Refers to the device hosted in each J&S Food's store. Its purpose is to connect the RFID readers embedded in each bag to J&S Food's AWS cloud and to the smart shopping bag application.
AWS IoT Core	Refers to the managed cloud service by which J&S Food outsources the management of its IoT infrastructure to Amazon. The AWS IoT core enables the smart shopping bag via its embedded RFID reader to interact securely with the smart shopping bag application.

Use Cases Identified and Described

Figure 11.2 also highlights the 13 use cases underneath the functions and services to be delivered by the smart shopping bag. These use cases are described in Table 11.2.

Table 11.2: The Smart Shopping Bag Use Cases Identified

USE CASES	DESCRIPTION
Press Start to Begin Shopping	This use case allows the in-store customer to initiate a shopping session using their smart mobile device. This use case also allows in-store customers to stop a shopping session.
Put Product in the Bag	This use case allows the in-store customer to put items and their associated RFID tags in the smart shopping bag. This causes the RFID reader to send RFID information queries to RFID tags.
Remove Product from the Bag	This use case allows the in-store customer to remove items and their related RFID tag from the smart shopping bag. This causes the RFID reader to send RFID information queries to RFID tags.

Continues

Table 11.2 (continued)

USE CASES	DESCRIPTION
Detect Product Code in the Bag	This use case allows the RFID reader associated with the smart shopping bag to send information queries to the RFID tag associated with the item put in the bag.
Detect Product Code Removed from the Bag	This use case allows the RFID reader associated with the smart shopping bag to send information queries to the RFID tag associated with the item removed from the bag.
Send EEPROM Data to the Billing System	This use case allows the RFID reader to collect the shopping information stored in its embedded electronically erasable programmable read-only memory (EEPROM) and send it to the smart shopping bag application's billing module via the IoT gateway and the AWS IoT core.
Send Queries to the Product RFID Tag	Triggered whenever an item and its related RFID tag is either put in the bag or removed from the bag, this use case allows the RFID reader of the smart shopping bag to send item information queries to the associated RFID tag.
Respond to Product RFID Queries	Triggered whenever the RFID reader of the bag issues information queries, this use case allows to the RFID tag to reply with radio frequency signals to convey the requested information.
Connect the Smart Shopping Bag's RFID Reader to the AWS IoT Core	This use case allows the IoT gateway hosted in each J&S Food's store to connect the smart shopping bag's RFID reader securely to the company's AWS IoT core.
Connect the Smart Shopping Bag's RFID Reader to the Smart Shopping Bag Application	This use case allows the smart shopping bag's RFID reader to interact with the smart shopping bag application in the cloud via the IoT gateway.
Get the Cart Information	This is triggered by the smart shopping bag application whenever the in-store customer has completed the shopping session. It sends an EEPROM data request to the RFID reader to collect the billing information.
Calculate the Bill Amount	The smart shopping bag application performs this use case as part of the in-store customer charging process. Based on the data collected from the RFID chip's memory, it calculates the bill amount.
Respond to In-Store Customer Button Presses	The purpose of this use case is to interpret the in-store customer interactions with the smart shopping bag application via smart mobile devices.

Specifying the Smart Shopping Bag's Functions Using Sequence Diagrams

The second step of the digital product's specification process is to identify the functions that will enable the delivery of the promised superior digital food experience.

Once again, the combination of agile principles and UML techniques has improved J&S Food's digital product's specification practices. Indeed, the UML sequence diagrams allow the product owner and the development teams jointly to identify the objects and related functions and speed up the process. This leads to a reduction of the digital product's specification time by half, increased quality, and a faster return on investments.

The following sections discuss the specifications of the functions identified as key by the workshop's participants.

Use Case Description: Press Start to Begin Shopping

Figure 11.4 illustrates the dynamic beneath the use case Press Start to Begin Shopping.

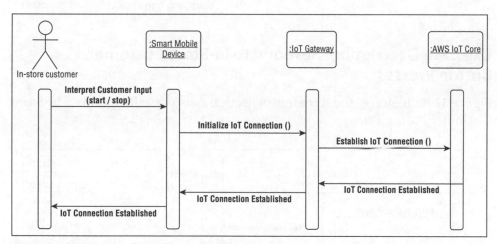

Figure 11.4: The sequence diagram specifying the use case Press Start to Begin Shopping

Table 11.3 sums up the objects and related operations identified as part of the smart shopping bag digital product.

Table 11.3: Objects Implementing the Use Case Press Start to Begin Shopping

OBJECT	OPERATIONS	DESCRIPTION
Smart mobile device	`Interpret Customer Input()`	This operation is delivered by the mobile part of the smart shopping bag application. It interprets in-store customer interactions with the smart mobile device and accordingly triggers the specific actions on the smart shopping bag applications in J&S Food's AWS cloud.
IoT gateway	`Initialize IoT Connection()`	This function, provided by the IoT gateway library and software development kit (SDK), initiates and handles the connections between the smart mobile device and the AWS IoT Core.
AWS IoT Core	`Establish IoT Connection()`	This function, provided by the AWS IoT Core library and SDK, initiates and handles the connections between the smart mobile device and the RFID reader on one side and the smart shopping bag application on the other.

Use Case Description: Respond to In-Store Customer Button Presses

Figure 11.5 illustrates the dynamic beneath the use case Respond to In-Store Customer Button Presses.

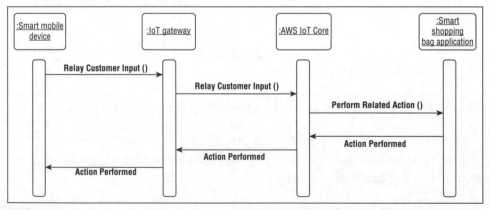

Figure 11.5: The sequence diagram specifying the use case Respond to In-Store Customer Button Presses

Table 11.4 sums up the objects and related operations identified as part of the smart shopping bag digital product.

Table 11.4: Objects Implementing the Use Case Respond to In-Store Customer Button Presses

OBJECT	OPERATIONS	DESCRIPTIONS
IoT gateway	`Relay Customer Input()`	The purpose of this function, provided by the IoT gateway library and SDK, is to relay information back and forth between the smart mobile device and the RFID reader on one side and the AWS IoT core on the other.
AWS IoT Core	`Relay Customer Input()`	The purpose of this function, provided by the IoT Core library and SDK, is to relay information back and forth between the smart mobile device and the RFID reader on one side and the smart shopping bag application on the other.
Smart shopping bag app	`Perform Related Action()`	The purpose of this function is to perform actions instructed by the mobile part of the smart shopping bag application. Examples of action codes include `add_item_to_cart`, `remove_item_from_cart`, `calculate_bill_amount`, and `trace_shopping_session`.
Smart mobile device	`Display Action Performed Status()`	This operation is delivered by the mobile part of the smart shopping bag application. It displays the information returned either by the IoT gateway or by the AWS IoT on the smart mobile device.

Use Case Description: Detect Product Code Put in the Bag

Figure 11.6 illustrates the dynamic beneath the use case Detect Product Code Put in the Bag.

Table 11.5 sums up the objects and related operations identified as part of the smart shopping bag digital product.

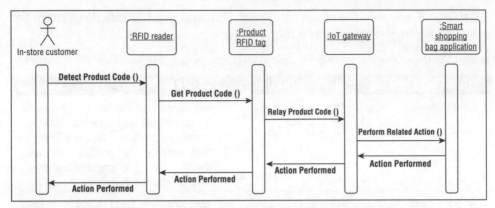

Figure 11.6: The sequence diagram specifying the use case Detect Product Code Put in the Bag

Table 11.5: Objects Implementing the Use Case Detect Product Code Put in the Bag

OBJECT	OPERATIONS	DESCRIPTIONS
RFID reader	`Detect Product Code()`	The purpose of this function, provided by the RFID reader's proprietary library and SDK, is to capture the signals issued by the RFID tags and extract the conveyed information and make it actionable.
Product RFID tag	`Get Product Code()`	The purpose of this function, provided by the RFID reader's proprietary library and SDK, is to issue RFID queries to RFID tags.
IoT gateway	`Relay Product Code()`	The purpose of this function, provided by the IoT gateway's proprietary library and SDK, is to relay RFID tag information to the AWS IoT Core platform via the IoT gateway.
Smart shopping bag application	`Perform Related Action()`	Defined in Table 11.4.
Smart mobile device	`Display Action Performed Status()`	Defined in Table 11.4.

Use Case Description: Send EEPROM Data to Billing System

Figure 11.7 illustrates the dynamic beneath the use case Send EEPROM Data to Billing System.

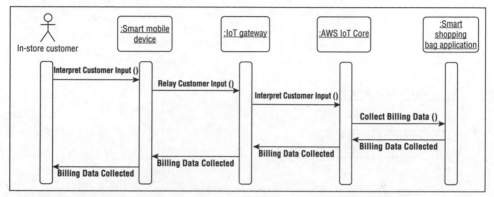

Figure 11.7: The sequence diagram specifying the use case Send EEPROM Data to Billing System

Table 11.6 sums up the objects and operations identified as part of the smart shopping bag digital product.

Table 11.6: Objects Implementing the Use Case Send EEPROM Data to Billing System

OBJECT	OPERATIONS	DESCRIPTION
Smart mobile device	`Interpret Customer Input()`	Defined in Table 11.3.
IoT gateway	`Relay Customer Input()`	Defined in Table 11.4.
AWS IoT Core	`Interpret Customer Input()`	Defined in Table 11.3.
Smart shopping bag application	`Collect Billing Data()`	The purpose of this function, provided by the cloud part of the smart shopping bag application, is to collect the shopping session information for charging and billing purposes.

Use Case Description: Respond to RFID Reader Queries

Figure 11.8 illustrates the dynamic beneath the use case Respond to RFID Reader Queries.

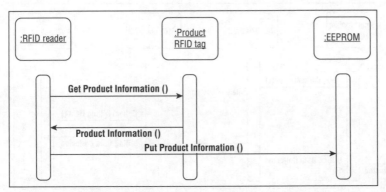

Figure 11.8: The sequence diagram specifying the use case Respond to RFID Reader Queries

Table 11.7 sums up the objects and related operations identified as part of the smart shopping bag digital product.

Table 11.7: Objects Implementing the Use Case Respond to RFID Reader Queries

OBJECT	OPERATIONS	DESCRIPTION
Product RFID tag	Get Product Information()	The purpose of this function, provided by the RFID reader's proprietary library and SDK, is to issue RFID queries to RFID tags and retrieve the related product information.
EEPROM	Put Product Information()	The purpose of this function, provided by the RFID reader's proprietary library and SDK, is to store the product RFID tags in the smart shopping bag to the RFID reader's memory prior to being relayed in the billing module of the smart shopping bag application.

Use Case Description: Calculate the Bill Amount

Figure 11.9 illustrates the dynamic beneath the use case Calculate the Bill amount.

Table 11.8 sums up the objects and related operations identified as part of the smart shopping bag digital product.

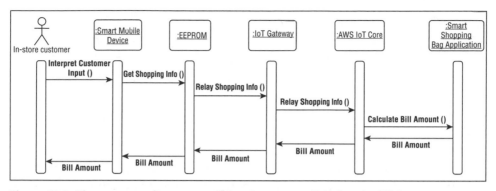

Figure 11.9: The sequence diagram specifying the use case Calculate the Bill Amount

Table 11.8: Objects Implementing the Use Case Calculate the Bill Amount

OBJECT	OPERATIONS	DESCRIPTION
Smart mobile device	`Interpret Customer Input()`	Defined in Table 11.3.
EEPROM	`Get Shopping Info()`	The purpose of this function, provided by the RFID reader's proprietary library and SDK, is to retrieve the product RFID tag information stored in the memory and relay it to the IoT gateway.
IoT gateway	`Relay Shopping Info()`	The purpose of this function, provided by the IoT gateway's proprietary library and SDK, is to relay the product RFID tag information to the AWS IoT Core.
AWS IoT Core	`Relay Shopping Info()`	The purpose of this function, provided by the AWS IoT Core's proprietary library and SDK, is to relay the shopping session information for charging and billing purposes to the billing module of the smart shopping bag information. This operation builds on the AWS IoT Core's via its MQTT message broker to transmit the information to the billing module.
Smart shopping bag application	`Calculate Bill Amount()`	The purpose of this operation is to calculate the bill amount and trigger the payment process.

Specifying the Smart Shopping Business Rules Using Class Diagram

The last step of the digital product specification process is about understanding the business rules underlying the smart shopping bag ecosystem. Unlike J&S Food's old practice where the focus was solely on the data model design, the new approach stresses the use of a UML class diagram because it fosters a systems thinking perspective.

The UML class diagram designed by the implementation team provided insights into the structure of the smart shopping bag. It helped the team to visualize, describe, and document different facets of the digital product including the domain entities represented as classes and their attributes, functions, and relationships. It provided the team with an overview of the smart shopping bag.

Figure 11.10 illustrates the class diagram that resulted from the discussions that involved the product owner, the Scrum master, and the implementation team.

The smart shopping bag's class diagram shows eight classes that enable J&S Food's new in-store shopping process. The following sections elaborate on their purpose in the shopping bag's ecosystem, as well as on the data that they handle and the functions that they provide.

The In-Store Customer

The in-store customer class represents any legal person or natural person including store employees who subscribed to J&S Food's smart shopping bag service. It handles the data and provides the functions needed for any processing related to the in-store customer entity.

The in-store customer class is composed of the shopping session and smart mobile device classes. This composition relationship highlights the mutual dependence of the three classes as well as these two fundamental business rules:

- A shopping session can be opened by one and only one in-store customer.
- A smart mobile device can be owned by one and only one in-store customer.

The composition relationship is a tightly coupled relationship that highlights the fact that the shopping session and smart mobile device classes are an integral part of the in-store customer.

The composition relationships are important for the AWS solutions architect and the software developers because they are based on this rule:

Classes linked by a tightly coupled relationship are inevitably intended to be grouped into categories and therefore into packages.

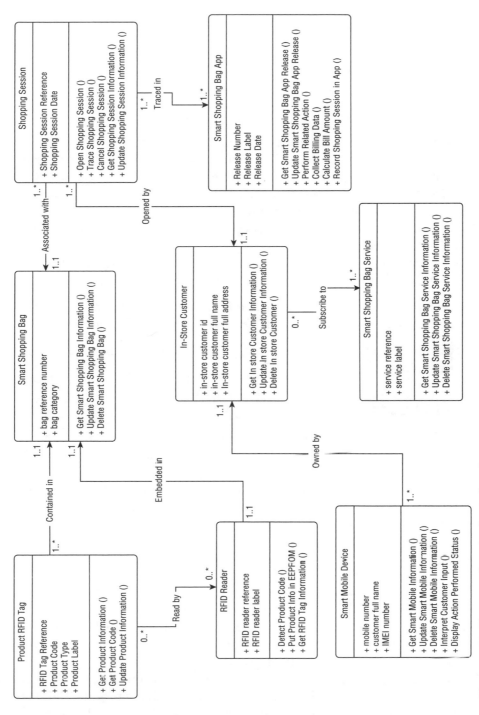

Figure 11.10: The smart shopping bag's class diagram

They are useful in identifying the UML packages that will be implemented as microservices.

The Smart Shopping Bag

The *smart shopping bag* is a class that represents the bag that the in-store customer uses in the shopping process. It therefore handles the data and provides the functions needed for any processing related to the shopping bag entity.

The smart shopping bag is connected with the RFID reader class by an aggregation link that highlights the fundamental business rule that an RFID reader can be embedded in one and only one online smart shopping bag. Both are linked by a tightly coupled relationship. Moreover, the smart shopping bag is linked to the shopping session and the product RFID tag classes by an association link that highlights the business rules that a product RFID tag can be read by one and only one RFID reader.

The second business rule is that the product RFID tag is contained in one and only one smart shopping bag.

The association relationships are important for the AWS Solutions Architect and the software developers because they are based on this rule:

Classes linked by a loosely coupled relationship can be potentially (as opposed to inevitably) grouped into categories and therefore into potential packages.

They are useful in identifying the UML packages that will be implemented as microservices.

The RFID Reader

The *RFID reader class* represents the network-connected device attached to the smart shopping bag. It handles the data and provides the functions needed for any processing related to the RFID reader entity.

The RFID reader is linked with the smart shopping bag by a tightly coupled relationship underpinning the business rule that an RFID reader is embedded in one and only smart shopping bag.

The second business rule is that an RFID reader can read one or more product RFID tags.

The Product RFID Tag

The *product RFID tag class* represents the microchip attached to the company's food items. It handles the data and provides the functions needed for any processing related to the store's food item entity.

The product RFID tag is linked with the smart shopping bag by a loosely coupled relationship underpinning the business rule that a product RFID tag is contained in one and only one smart shopping bag.

The second business rule is that a product RFID tag can be read by one and only one RFID reader.

The Smart Mobile Device

The *smart mobile device class* represents the in-store customer's smart mobile phones and tablets used to shop in J&S Food's store based on the smart shopping bag services. It handles the data and provides the functions needed for any processing related to the smart mobile device entity.

The smart mobile device is linked with the in-store customer by a loosely coupled relationship underpinning the business rule that a smart mobile device is owned by one and only one in-store customer.

The Shopping Session

The *shopping session class* represents the record of all the purchase and payment acts of the in-store customer. It handles the data and provides the functions needed for any processing related to the customer's purchase and payment entities.

The smart mobile device is linked with the in-store customer by a loosely coupled relationship underpinning the business rule that a shopping session is owned by one and only one in-store customer.

The second loosely coupled relationship is that a shopping session is associated with one and only one smart shopping bag, and the last business rule is that shopping sessions are traced across various smart shopping bag application releases.

The Smart Shopping Service

The *smart shopping service class* represents the business service to which in-store customers subscribe in order to use the smart shopping bag. It handles the data and provides the functions needed for any processing related to the smart shopping bag service entity.

The smart shopping service class is linked with the in-store customer class by a loosely coupled relationship underpinning the business rule that an in-store customer can subscribe to one and only one smart shopping bag service.

The Smart Shopping Bag Application

The *smart shopping bag application class* represents the infrastructure of the smart shopping bag ecosystem that manages the smart shopping bag business in the cloud.

The smart shopping bag application is linked with the shopping session by a loosely coupled relationship underpinning the business rule that shopping sessions are traced across various smart shopping bag applications.

Key Takeaways

Specifying a digital product and service is a difficult challenge due to the inevitable functional, technological, and technical complexity. Many businesses fail because of a lack of proven methods.

Until proven otherwise, systems thinking and its object-oriented approach that implements its principles and tools is the safest approach to develop digital products and services successfully.

This chapter took you on a journey across the systems thinking world through the object-oriented UML methodology. You familiarized yourself with the benefits that J&S Food's implementation team derived from the object-oriented approach.

The use of the context diagram as a means of clarifying a digital product's functional, technological, and technical scope was explained.

You learned how in a collaborative context fostered by the agile mindset a digital product development team takes advantage of the UML use case diagram to define the digital product's ecosystem. You also learned about how these teams leverage the UML sequence diagrams to identify the objects that make up the digital product and specify them in terms of attributes, data, and functions.

In the next chapter, you will discover how the object approach enables microservices design.

References

1. Zenbooth, "A Guide to Agile Workspaces: Why You Should Transform Your Office Now," *Zenbooth* (May 14, 2018). `https://zenbooth.net/blogs/zenbooth-blog/an-ode-to-agile-workspaces-why-you-should-transform-your-office-now`

2. Logan Derrick, "Five Advantages of Systems Thinking and How to Make Full Use of It," *Toggl Plan* (September 19, 2019). `https://toggl.com/blog/5-advantages-of-systems-thinking`

3. Alonso Del Arte, "Object-Oriented Thinking is Easy," *GitConnected* (January 08, 2021). `https://levelup.gitconnected.com/object-oriented-thinking-is-easy-93aa51162f72`

4. Harrison Wheeler, "Object-Oriented Design for Product Designer," *UX Collective* (May 29, 2020). `https://uxdesign.cc/object-oriented-design-for-product-designers-be93c6405139`

Designing J&S Food's Smart Shopping Bag Digital Product

Ultimately, the best operating model is one that is owned and accepted by the teams.
—**Thomas Blood**

The three-day digital products and services specification process (Chapter 11, "Specifying J&S Food's Smart Shopping Bag Digital Product") of J&S Food's agile operational model is now validated, followed by the smart shopping bag architecture design process, which ended three days later.

In a validation meeting, as the leader of the task force you once again have the responsibility to validate J&S Food's new agile operating model process: the digital products and services design.

Throughout this process, the stake was the application of agile principles in terms of work organization, people interactions, decision-making, and problem-solving, as well as that of the Unified Modeling Language (UML) of identifying packages likely to be implemented as microservices.

The leaders of the digital business model deployment (Albany) and of the smart shopping bag development (Princeton) teams are now going to co-present the feedback report.

Let's pay attention to the message the Albany and Princeton team leaders deliver to the task force.

Transformation Journey's Fourth Stage: Designing the Smart Shopping Bag Digital Product

Evaluation of J&S Food's new digital products and services design process in actual business conditions is the primary purpose of this phase. Figure 12.1 shows the highlights that will be discussed in the validation meeting.

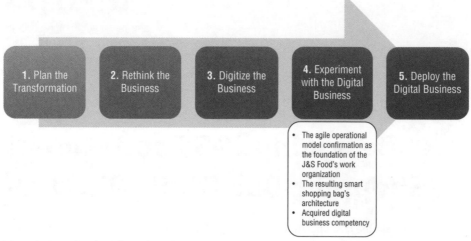

Figure 12.1: The digital product design phase in J&S Food's digital transformation journey

As illustrated in Figure 12.1, these highlights include the agile operational model's confirmation as the foundation of the company's work organization, the smart shopping bag's package architecture, and the set of competencies acquired by the company during this phase.

Let's take a look at the feedback report that the Princeton store's product development team issued to the task force.

The Agile Operational Model Confirmed as the Foundation of J&S Food's Work Organization

The first message of the report is clear: J&S Food's staff has definitely adopted the agile operational model as well as the underlying infrastructure and tools.

J&S Food's New Organization of Work

Albany's team leader starts by announcing the good news:

"Our teams have adopted the new work environment. In addition, the agile processes have significantly improved the team's productivity, the digital product design process responsiveness, and also product quality."

The Princeton's Digital Product Development Team Defined

Albany's team leader explained the following:

"Unlike the old monolithic organization that mixed IT application and digital service developments, today's digital product development department is a distinct entity, fully dedicated to J&S Food's digital products and services development activities."

Figure 12.2 illustrates J&S Food's digital products and services organization.

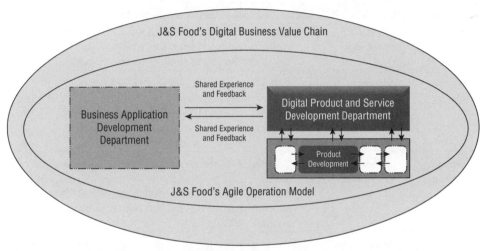

Figure 12.2: J&S Food's new digital products and services development organization

As illustrated in Figure 12.2, the new J&S Food's IT organization is structured around two distinct entities immersed in the company's agile operating model: the business applications development department and the digital products and services development department.

The Princeton's team leader justifies this division as follows:

"The reason for the split is that putting product developers together is more likely to keep the team's focus on the digital product development business, fostering information sharing, and therefore accelerating the learning curve."

In fact, the primary reason for this division is that applications and digital services target different populations: internal business users for applications and customers for the digital product development.

Digital products and services development has a direct impact on J&S Food's revenues—it requires additional methodologies, such as understanding customer insights, developing user experience, and business case development.

The Princeton's team declares the following:

"The new digital product development team is consistent with Scrum team principles. It puts together relevant sales, marketing, and IT contributors under the leadership of the product owner and Scrum master."

Table 12.1 outlines the roles and responsibilities of Princeton's team in the smart shopping bag design process.

Table 12.1: Roles and Responsibilities in the Smart Shopping Bag Design Process

ROLES	ORIGIN	RESPONSIBILITY
Product owner	Online marketing	Initiates digital products and services projects. Leads digital products and services specifications. Provides digital products and services testing scenarios.
Scrum master	Information technology (IT)	Acts as a project management office (PMO) representative. Facilitates communication between the business side and IT. Facilitates digital product development effort from specification and development to deployment.
Software developers	Information technology (IT)	Contributes to the digital products and services specification as well as to the architectural design effort. Develops the software enabling the digital products and services, tests it, and contributes to the CICD pipeline configuration.
Software testers	Information technology (IT)	Works with the software developers, IT operations, and business users on designing testing scenarios. Configures the build and acceptance testing stages of the CICD pipeline. Monitors automated build and acceptance testing processes.
IT operations	Information technology (IT)	Works with the product owner and Scrum master as well as with software development, software testing, and business users on the deployment strategy. Contributes to the acceptance test stage of the CICD pipeline. Configures the production stage of the CICD pipeline.
Business users	Marketing, sales, other business units	Contributes to the configuration of build and acceptance testing stages of the CICD pipeline. Monitors the acceptance tests in collaboration with the software developers and software testers.

In perfect sync with Princeton's team leader, Albany's project leader announces another piece of good news:

"Our digital products and services design process performs beyond expectations."

UML Package Diagram Facilitates the Microservices Architecture Design Process

Albany's team leader explains the digital products and services design process in J&S Food's agile operational model as follows:

"Digital products and services architecture design takes place in the early stages of the agile process in a planning meeting known as a 'planning game' through what we now refer to as 'architectural spike.'"

Princeton's team leader provides further details as follows:

"Architectural spikes are organized as workshops involving the product owner, Scrum master, developers, testers, and IT operations. The primary goal of an architectural spike is to eliminate technical risks by writing just enough code to explore the use of a technology or a technique with which the product development team is unfamiliar."

"Our architectural spikes stress one fundamental area; that is, the microservices that make the software underpinning digital product modular enough to ensure responsiveness and scalability."

Lucidchart Confirmed as the Best Architecture Tool

Albany team's leader informs the participants that Lucidchart Enterprise was chosen as the best UML tool, and then Princeton's team leader explains how this was determined:

"During the workshops, the UML formalism provided by Lucidchart Enterprise was used by both the business and IT side teams as a common and rich visual modeling language for architecting the complex smart shopping bag system both structurally (architectural components) and behaviorally (system reactions to events)."

Overall Feedback

As Table 12.2 shows, J&S Food's staff from both the business and IT sides praised the benefits of the company's new agile operational model.

As Figure 12.3 shows, a large majority of J&S Food staff is satisfied with the new working environment.

Eighty-eight percent of the staff involved in the smart shopping bag architectural design process are fully satisfied with the company's new agile operating model, 8 percent have mixed feelings about it, while only 4 percent are unsatisfied with it.

Table 12.2: J&S Food's Satisfaction with the Agile Operational Model

	PRODUCTIVITY	TIME-TO-MARKET	QUALITY
Business side	Team spirit and collaborative mindset increase the team's productivity.	The workshops involving staff from the business and IT sides accelerate the overall design process.	Team and collaborative mindsets as well as the architecture workshops involving staff from both the business and IT sides help to achieve quality design.
IT side	Architectural design patterns and tools increase the team's productivity.	The various visual tools used impact the overall time to market.	Same as above.

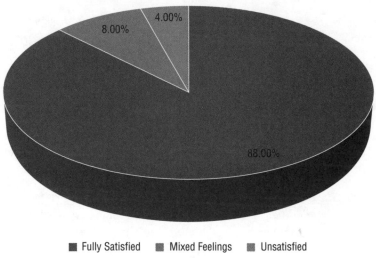

■ Fully Satisfied   ■ Mixed Feelings   ■ Unsatisfied

Figure 12.3: J&S Food's staff satisfaction with the new operational model

Overall, the involved staff prefer the agile digital business work environment because of the processes provided, best practices, methodologies, and tools that increased productivity, sped up processes, and guaranteed better deliverable quality.

The Resulting Smart Shopping Bag's Architecture

The implemented agile operational model, with all of its underlying methodologies and tools, has equipped J&S Food with the ideal digital products and services development platform. That's the message that Princeton's team leader, a passionate mind, is trying to convey to the audience.

The Smart Shopping Bag Blueprint

Princeton team's leader next explains the following:

"The blueprint (see Figure 12.4) represents our smart shopping bag's logical microservices architecture. It results from the strict application and use of our architectural spikes principles, processes, tools, and methodologies. In the old organization, we would have taken twice as much time to deliver such an architecture."

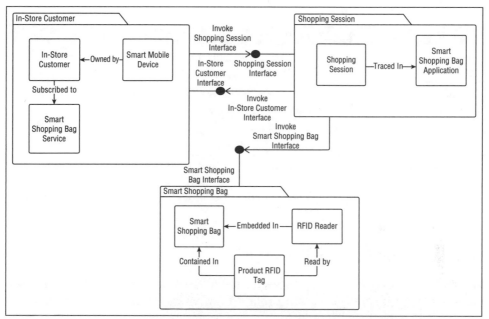

Figure 12.4: The smart shopping bag component diagram (designed with Lucidchart Enterprise)

The Princeton team leader now elaborates on the smart shopping bag component diagram as follows:

"The folders, packages in UML terminology, represent the AWS containers and Docker containers that encapsulate the microservices underpinning the smart shopping bag digital product."

The Princeton team leader then states the following:

"The UML component diagram makes the translation of the logical architecture into a concrete microservices architecture easy and fast. Packages are converted into containers, class operations are translated into AWS Lambda functions implementing the microservices, and package interfaces are the APIs giving access to the microservices."

The In-Store Customer Package

The in-store customer package represents the AWS container hosting the microservices that support all processing related to the in-store customer, smart shopping bag, and smart mobile device objects.

Table 12.3 outlines the in-store customer package constituents as well as their role in the overall architecture.

Table 12.3: Description of the In-Store Customer Package's Constituents

	DESCRIPTION
In-store customer	This class implements the microservices related to the business entity in-store customer.
Smart shopping bag service	Implements the microservices related the business entity smart shopping service.
Smart mobile device	Implements the microservices related to the business entity smart mobile device.
Interface	This interface class implements the API gateway and event-driven mechanisms that give access to the microservices implemented by the classes that form the in-store customer package.

The Shopping Session Package

The shopping session package represents the AWS container hosting the microservices that support all processing related to the shopping session and smart shopping bag application objects.

Table 12.4 outlines the shopping session package constituents as well as their role in the overall architecture.

Table 12.4: Description of the Shopping Session Package Constituents

	DESCRIPTION
Shopping session	Implements the microservices related the business entity smart shopping session
Smart shopping bag application	Implements the microservices related to the business entity smart shopping bag application
Interface	This interface class implements the API gateway and event-driven mechanisms that give access to the microservices implemented by the classes that form the shopping session package

The Smart Shopping Bag Package

The smart shopping bag package represents the AWS container hosting the microservices that support all processing related to the smart shopping bag application, the RFID reader, and product RFID tag objects.

Table 12.5 outlines the smart shopping bag package constituents as well as their role in the overall architecture.

Table 12.5: Description of the Smart Shopping Bag Package Constituents

	DESCRIPTION
Smart shopping bag	This class implements the microservices related to the business entity smart shopping bag.
RFID reader	Implements the microservices related the business entity RFID reader.
Product RFID tag	Implements the microservices related to the business entity product RFID tag.
Interface	This interface class implements the API gateway and event-driven mechanisms that give access to the microservices implemented by the classes that form the smart shopping bag package.

Acquired Digital Business Competency: Digital Products and Services Architecture Design

In this design phase of the smart shopping bag's architecture, J&S Food's staff acquired the following skills:

- Deployment of agile operating model for digital business including staff training and implementation of a digital products and services development department

- Design of microservices architecture based on UML and Lucidchart Enterprise design web-based platform

Key Takeaways

Designing digital products and services in an organizational change management context within a disruptive industry is not easy—it's challenging! It takes training the concerned staff in record time, enforcing the agile operational and organizational requirements, and identifying areas of improvements.

The example illustrated in this chapter confirms that setting up a task force to lead the change and assigning the operational responsibility of the change deployment to enthusiastic and motivated people is the right thing to do.

In this chapter, you learned about the benefits of productivity, responsiveness, and quality that an organization can derive from implementing an agile operating model. You also learned that setting up an organization dedicated to the development of digital products and services is an option likely to accelerate your staff's learning curve.

Finally, you learned how the object-oriented approach through UML as implemented by J&S Food allows them to design a microservices architecture quickly.

In the follow-up task force meeting described in the next chapter, you will learn how Amazon SageMaker is used to support J&S Food's digital food experience and how combining the prototyping approach and AWS Amplify platform helped the Princeton team develop the microservices and software underlying the smart shopping bag digital product in record time.

References

1. Christopher Smith, "Change Management vs. Digital Transformation — What's the Difference?," *Change* (December 23, 2018). `https://change .walkme.com/change-management-vs-digital-transformation/`

2. James Davidson, "Change Management: The Key to Successful Digital Transformations," *CMSWire* (July 30, 2018). `https://www.cmswire .com/digital-workplace/change-management-the-key-to- successful-digital-transformations/`

3. Muntazir Fadhel, "Why Object-Oriented Code Accelerates Microservices Adoption," *DZone* (March 21, 2019). `https://dzone.com/ articles/why-object-oriented-code-accelerates-microservices`

4. Holly Avila, "Digital Product Development vs Application Development," *Big Nerd Ranch* (September 15, 2020). `https:// bignerdranch.com/blog/digital-product-development- vs-app-development/`

CHAPTER

13

Prototyping J&S Food's Smart Shopping Bag Using Innovation as a Service

The design process is about designing and prototyping and making. When you separate those, I think the final result suffers.

—Jonathan Ive

The successful adoption of the smart shopping bag specification and design agile processes (Chapter 11, "Specifying J&S Food's Smart Shopping Bag Digital Product" and Chapter 12, "Designing J&S Food's Smart Shopping Bag Digital Product") has enabled J&S Food to equip itself with a solid digital product and service design capability.

J&S Food's digital products and services development staff is now able to organize itself into an agile team and take advantage of the Unified Modeling Language (UML) methodology to convert any product or service idea into an actionable digital product and service architecture.

As the task force leader, your satisfaction is evident. Nonetheless, you're thinking: *"I'll only be fully satisfied when I can see how the AWS innovation as a service tools (Chapter 1, "The Digital Economy's Challenges, Opportunities, and Relevance of AWS") help to deliver the tangible digital products and services that our customers expect."*

This is another goal of the digital products and services prototyping process. To make an informed validation decision about the new J&S Food's digital products and services prototyping process, you have decided to become part of it as an observer.

This chapter answers all of your questions about how to use the AWS IoT platform and how the prototyping process works using AWS Amplify and its impact on J&S Food's digital food experience in terms of time to market, team productivity, product and service quality, and customer satisfaction.

Transformation Journey's Fourth Stage: Prototyping the Smart Shopping Bag's Application

This third step of the smart shopping bag development process of the experiment with the digital business phase is part of J&S Food's digital products and services design approach; it's a key element of the architectural spike session. The goal is to identify and mitigate the technological and technical risks of the AWS innovation services like Internet of Things (IoT) and microservices architectures while developing the smart shopping bag prototype that will serve as the baseline for implementing the final product.

Figure 13.1 shows where the team currently stands in the company's digital transformation journey.

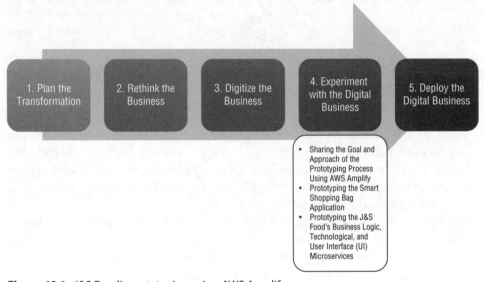

Figure 13.1: J&S Food's prototyping using AWS Amplify

As Figure 13.1 illustrates, the digital product and service prototyping process includes the following steps:

- Sharing the goal and approach of the prototyping process using AWS Amplify

- Prototyping the smart shopping bag application

- Prototyping J&S Food's business logic, technological, and user interface (UI) microservices

Let's pay attention to the key aspects of J&S Food's prototyping process, which helped to increase the team's productivity and accelerate the company's time to market while simplifying the use of AWS IoT and Radio Frequency Identification (RFID) technologies.

Sharing the Prototyping Process Goal and Approach

The first thing that will attract your attention is the pivotal role played by the AWS Amplify framework in the company's prototyping process; J&S Food's smart shopping bag development team takes full advantage of its features.

Prototyping Using AWS Amplify Defined

The Scrum master asks for the team's attention as follows:

> *"Before we get started, may I have your attention for five minutes? I would like to reiterate the rules, principles, and practices of our digital products and services prototyping process."*

The Prototyping Iterations Using AWS Amplify

The Scrum master draws the team's attention to the iterative prototyping process represented in Figure 13.2.

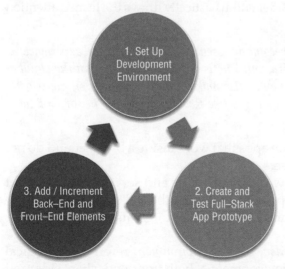

Figure 13.2: J&S Food's digital products and services prototyping process

J&S Food's digital products and services prototyping approach is a three-step iterative process including setting up the development environment, creating and testing full stack web application prototypes, and adding back-end and front-end elements.

Let's first pay attention to what the Scrum master has to say about the smart shopping bag development environment.

Defining the Smart Shopping Bag Development Environment

The Scrum master clicks to move to the presentation's next page, as represented in Figure 13.3.

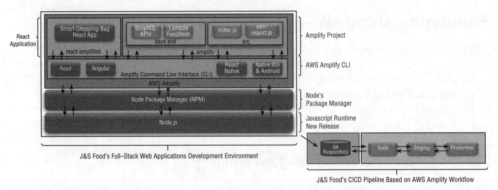

Figure 13.3: J&S Food's AWS Amplify development platform

Then the development team's leader enthusiastically draws the team's attention to an important point:

"Since smart mobile devices have become an essential part of the digital experience, full-stack serverless web apps with continuous deployment hosted in the cloud aren't only becoming the norm, they're also making the adoption of single-page application (SPA) JavaScript frameworks like React, Angular, Vue, or Gatsby indispensable."

Single-page applications (SPAs) are apps that work inside a browser and do not require page reloading during use.

As you can see, J&S Food's new digital products and services development platform is made up of two components including the full-stack web applications development environment and the continuous integration and continuous delivery (CICD) pipeline.

The *full-stack web applications development environment* refers to the logical four-layer platform used for the development of both front-end (client side) and back-end (server side) portions of web applications. Let's discuss these layers.

Node.js   The first layer is *Node.js* (also known as Node). It's an open source development platform for executing JavaScript code on the server side. It's useful for developing applications requiring persistent connections from the browser to the server. It's suited for applications such as chat, news feeds, and web push notifications.

Node is intended to run on dedicated HTTP servers and to employ a single thread with one process at a time. Node.js applications are event-based and run asynchronously.

Node Package Manager   The second layer is *Node Package Manager (npm)*. npm has two purposes: The first is to serve as an online repository for the publishing of open source Node.js projects. Examples of such projects include Angular, React, and jQuery. The second purpose is to act as a command-line utility for interacting with this repository, which aids in package installation, version management, and dependency management. npm is a package manager for the JavaScript programming language maintained by npm, Inc.

AWS Amplify Command Line Interface   The *AWS Amplify command-line interface (CLI)* is the third layer. It's a rich set of commands that are included in a unified toolchain used to create, integrate, and manage the AWS cloud services for applications.

Amplify CLI makes it easy to create and configure AWS cloud services as needed on applications directly from local environments. Amplify CLI uses AWS CloudFormation (AWS infrastructure as code capability) to allow developers to add or modify configurations locally before they push them for execution.

Amplify Project   The Amplify project organizes application resources into folders. Folders are the locations where utilities including Amplify CLI and NPM store application resources. React applications are stored in the `react-amplified` folder, while the application sources are stored in the `Amplify` folder, respectively, in the subfolders `src` and `backend`.

The back-end subfolder's purpose is to store the back-end component sources such as GraphQL APIs and Lambda function sources, while the `src` subfolder stores the front-end element sources.

The other key element of J&S Food's digital products and services development platform is the AWS Amplify deployment workflow. It's integrated to the company's Git repository.

Each time a new release of the back-end, front-end, and application elements is pushed to the Git repository, it automatically triggers the build and staging test processes and then deploys the recent version of the prototype.

The Scrum master next focuses the conversation on more strategic concerns that are closer to the CIO's interests:

"The benefits of AWS Amplify and its CICD workflow are that they make our processes and practices, as well as the underpinning infrastructure, consistent with DevOps principles and the AWS modern application development recommendations."

The Scrum master is right. What the organization gets is strongly modularized software that is easy to maintain, update, upgrade, and deploy. This has a strong impact on the team's productivity and, by extension, on the company's time to market.

Prototyping the Smart Shopping Bag

After two hours discussing their technical features, sharing tips and advice about AWS Amplify's framework, augmenting the generated code templates with smart shopping bag–specific code pieces, and performing unit tests, the microservices prototypes as well as the smart shopping bag application prototype are ready. The microservices and the smart shopping bag application will serve as the basis for validating whether the implemented architecture is suited for developing innovative digital products and services in record time.

Prototyping software based on the AWS Amplify framework allowed the Princeton team to cut in one-third the development time of similar applications.

Table 13.1 outlines the different iterations that resulted in the microservices and application prototypes.

Table 13.1: Iterations That Led to the Microservices and Application Prototypes

ITERATION #	ITERATION PURPOSE	CODE AND AMPLIFY CLI COMMAND EXAMPLES
1	Set up the development environment by installing Node.js and npm and Amplify CLI. Configure Amplify.	In order of precedence: 1. `sudo yum install -y nodejs` 2. `npm install -g @aws-amplify/cli` 3. `amplify configure`
2	Installed necessary libraries for using Amplify on the client side of the application.	`Npm install aws-amplify @ aws-amplify/ui-react`
3	Initialized Amplify and created a new Amplify project.	`amplify init`

ITERATION #	ITERATION PURPOSE	CODE AND AMPLIFY CLI COMMAND EXAMPLES
4	Made the smart shopping bag application aware of the AWS cloud resources by editing the file `App.js` whose purpose is to act as a basic HTTP web server to handle your web app startup, routing, and other functions.	Add the following lines in the `App.js` file: 1. Import Amplify from `'aws-amplify'` 2. Import config from `'./aws-exports'` 3. `Amplify.configure (config)`
5	Created the smart shopping bag application's GraphQL APIs, answered related questionnaire, and deployed the APIs.	In order of precedence until expected scalability and reusability objectives are achieved: 1. `amplify add api` (select GraphQL) 2. `amplify push`
6	Added Lambda functions (microservices) to the smart shopping bag back-end elements, answered the related questionnaire, and pushed the function to the AWS cloud and tested it.	In order of precedence until expected scalability and reusability objectives are achieved: 1. `amplify add function` 2. `amplify push -y` 3. `amplify console function`
7	Connected front-end elements to the API to enable interactions between the user interface and the API.	See references "Connect frontend to API."

The Scrum master elaborates on the pivotal role of AWS Amplify in the new prototyping process:

> *"By providing code generators for full-stack web applications, data model schema, GraphQL APIs, and Lambda function APIs, the AWS Amplify framework is definitely improving not only the team's productivity, but it's also accelerating our software delivery lifecycle."*

Approving the Smart Shopping Bag Prototype

In the validation meeting involving the development team including the Scrum master and the product owner, participants attend a demonstration of the smart shopping bag application development process using the microservices.

The development team then rates the microservices architecture based on the criteria defined in Table 13.2 inspired from Martin Fowler's principles. Martin Fowler is a noted authority on software techniques and an early proponent of microservices-based development.

Table 13.2: Microservices Architecture Validation Criteria

CRITERIA	DESCRIPTION	APPROVAL RATE
Componentization via services	The software is composed of small independent services that communicate over well-defined APIs. These small components are divided so that each of them does just one thing—and does it well—while cooperating to deliver a full-featured application.	100%
Organized around business capabilities	When architecture and capabilities are organized around atomic business functions, dependencies between components are loosely coupled. As long as there is a communication contract between services and teams, each team can run at its own speed.	100%
Products not projects	To stay healthy, simplify operations, and increase efficiency, your engineering organization should treat software components as products that can be iteratively improved and that are constantly evolving.	90%
Smart endpoints and dumb pipes	Use message brokers. Microservice architectures favor these tools because they enable a decentralized approach in which the endpoints that produce and consume messages are smart, but the pipe between the endpoints is dumb.	90%
Decentralized governance	*Decentralized governance* means that each team can use its expertise to choose the best tools to solve their specific problem. Forcing all teams to use the same tools isn't reasonable because the problems they're solving aren't uniform.	25%
Decentralized data management	Decentralized data management enhances application design by allowing the best data store for the job to be used. Since each service team owns its own data, its decision-making becomes more independent.	25%
Infrastructure automation	Microservices not only need disposable infrastructure as code, but they also need to be built, tested, and deployed automatically. Continuous integration and continuous delivery are indispensable for microservices. Each service needs its own pipeline, one that can accommodate the various and diverse technology choices made by the team.	100%

CRITERIA	DESCRIPTION	APPROVAL RATE
Design for failure	Similarly, as microservices interact with each other over the network more than they do locally and synchronously, connections need to be monitored and managed. Latency and timeouts should be assumed and gracefully handled. More generally, microservices need to apply the same error retries and exponential backoff principles as advised with applications running in a networked environment.	100%
Evolutionary design	As a result of the evolutionary design principle, a service team can build the minimum viable set of features needed to stand up the stack and roll it out to users. The development team doesn't need to cover edge cases to roll out features. Instead, the team can focus on the needed pieces and evolve the design as customer feedback comes in. At a later stage, the team can decide to refactor after they feel confident that they have enough feedback.	100%

The Prototyping Team

As to the prototyping team, remarkable changes occurred in the team's overall behavior. These changes included individual and collective enthusiasm, a constant search for consensus, a problem-solving spirit, and a collaboration mindset.

Table 13.3 outlines the prototyping team's structure, roles, and responsibilities.

Table 13.3: The Prototyping Team's Structure, Roles, and Responsibilities

ROLES	RESPONSIBILITIES
Product owner	Defined and refined the smart shopping bag's overall UI. Detailed business rules and approved the overall smart shopping bag prototype.
Scrum master	Facilitated the prototyping effort. Enforced the agile rules of the game. When needed, clarified misunderstandings.
AWS solutions architect	Provided AWS Amplify and Node.js expertise. Clarified AWS modern application development framework misunderstandings.
Development team's leader	Developed business logic, technological, and user interface microservices. Assembled the smart shopping bag application using microservices.

The Scrum master explains this success as follows:

"The strict application and constant reminder of agile values and more importantly the key role of the AWS Amplify framework, which automates the key processes and practices via Amplify CLI code generators and continuous integration and continuous delivery (CICD) automated pipeline, have significantly improved software quality and the company's time to market."

The Team's Feedback

The Princeton development team favorably rated (see Table 13.2) the new digital products and services prototyping process. Figure 13.4 confirms the general satisfaction.

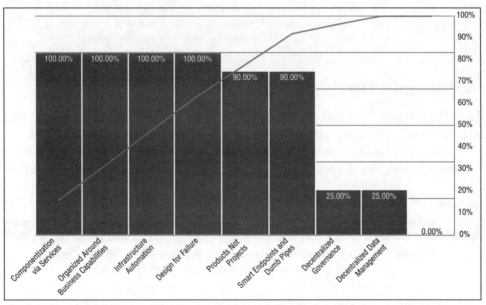

Figure 13.4: J&S Food's Princeton development team's satisfaction with the prototyping process

The majority of J&S Food's implementation team is satisfied with the prototyping process. The entire team (100 percent) thinks that the prototyping process's ability to meet the componentization, organization around business capabilities, infrastructure automation, and design for failure requirements is likely to allow the company to deliver repeatedly any digital product and service prototype in record time.

Ninety percent of the team (that's significant!) think that the new prototyping process is likely to help them tackle digital products and services development as business initiatives and not as IT development projects.

However, only 25 percent of the team think that the new prototyping process helps enough to decentralize the digital products and services development and management effort. The reason why is that the Princeton team is small, and it is dealing with a single digital product and service.

Let's discuss the application and related microservices that resulted from the prototyping session.

The Smart Shopping Bag Application Prototype

The use case and sequence diagrams defined in Chapter 11 and the package diagrams assembled in Chapter 12 were a solid foundation for identifying the functions and data that would support the smart shopping bag's operations.

The challenge in this prototyping session was to identify among these functions those that are suited to become microservices.

Table 13.4 illustrates the microservices discovery table along with the class functions identified as potential microservices.

The following sections detail the business logic, UI, and technological microservices identified by the development team.

Table 13.4: Microservices Discovery Table

USE CASE	FUNCTION	FUNCTION	FUNCTION	FUNCTION	FUNCTION
Start Shopping Session	Class: Smart Mobile Device Function: Interpret Customer Input()	Class: IoT Gateway Function: Initialize IoT() Connection ()	Class: AWS IoT Core Function: Establish IoT() Connection ()		
Respond to In-Store Customer Button Presses	Class: IoT Gateway Function: Relay Customer Input ()	Class: AWS IoT Core Function: Relay Customer Input ()	Class: Smart Shopping Bag App Function: Perform Related Action ()	Class: Smart Mobile Device Function: Display Action Performed Status ()	Class: Smart Shopping Bag App Function: Perform Related Action ()
Detect Product Code Put in Bag	Class: RFID Reader Function: Detect Product Code ()	Class: Product RFID Tag Function: Get Product Code ()	Class: IoT Gateway Function: Relay Product Code ()	Class: AWS IoT Core Function: Relay Product Code ()	
Send EEPROM Data to Billing System	Class: Smart Mobile Device Function: Interpret Customer Input ()	Class: IoT Gateway Function: Relay Customer Input ()	Class: AWS IoT Core Function: Interpret Customer Input ()	Class: Smart Shopping Bag App Function: Collect Billing Data ()	
Respond to RFID Reader Queries	Class: Product RFID Tag Function: Get Product Information ()	Class: EEPROM Function: Put Product Information ()			
Calculate the Bill Amount	Class: Smart Mobile Device Function: Interpret Customer Input ()	Class: EEPROM Function: Get Shopping Info ()	Class: IoT Gateway Function: Relay Shopping Info ()	Class: AWS IoT Core Function: Relay Shopping Info ()	Class: Smart Shopping Bag App Function: Calculate Bill Amount ()

The Business Logic, Technological, and UI Microservices Prototyped

Developing the application prototype as well as the related microservices prototypes in only two hours was made possible because the team had the wisdom to use the UML methodology to design the smart shopping bag digital product. The resultant use case, sequence, class, and package diagrams proved to be decisive.

The following sections define how the package diagram specified in Chapter 12 simplified the implementation of the application and related microservices.

The Microservices Development Process in the AWS Amplify Context

The AWS Solutions Architect warned the participants:

"Despite the many AWS services provided to develop them, microservices are complex to implement. That's why I recommended that you rely on AWS Amplify to make the development process easier and faster."

AWS Amplify provides an abstraction layer that simplifies the implementation of microservices. Figure 13.5 illustrates the AWS Amplify microservices development framework.

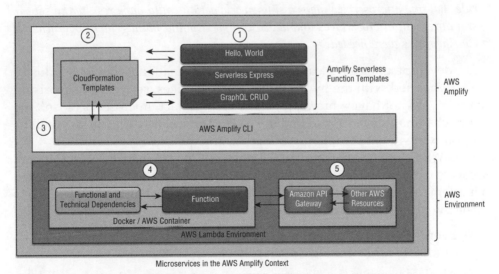

Microservices in the AWS Amplify Context

Figure 13.5: The microservices development process in the AWS Amplify Environment

The AWS Amplify microservices development framework is logically organized into two layers that facilitate their development. These layers include the AWS Lambda layer, and the AWS Amplify abstraction layer. Let's discuss them.

The Solutions Architect proceeds as follows:

"The key thing to understand is that AWS Amplify acts as an abstraction layer which makes the development of microservices easy and fast.

(1)   Using specific Amplify CLI directives, the developer chooses the suited serverless function templates.

(2)   The Amplify framework converts the chosen serverless function template into an AWS CloudFormation template which describes the Lambda function intended to implement the microservice as well as the related AWS services."

The Solutions Architect concludes the following:

"3, 4, and 5 are based on the CloudFormation template. The AWS Lambda platform automatically provisions the required resources including the Docker or AWS container and the function implementing the microservice, as well as the related API building on Amazon API gateway."

Defining the Microservices Granularity

As the development team's leader explains:

"One of the big questions we had was the granularity of the microservices. The rule that one microservice maps a single basic action could have resulted in several dozens of microservices and added complexity and management overhead. Clarifications were needed."

The development team's leader is right. The information technology industry is overwhelmed with the hype around microservices, so it is not surprising that many do not have a more pragmatic view. In fact, microservices isn't the point; what matters most is to find the level of granularity that ensures agility, reusability, ownership, rapid go-to-market, and quality.

The AWS Solutions Architect had the ingenious idea to share the microservices discovery table (see Table 13.4). It highlighted the class functions that were invoked to implement the main use cases of the smart shopping bag digital product.

The microservices discovery rules were as follows:

- Every class function implementing a business operation is a potential candidate for becoming a microservice.

- All class functions used across several use cases are potential candidates for becoming microservices.

- Potential microservices might be refined into smaller functions to meet the requirement that a microservice perform a single action and perform it well.

The Smart Shopping Bag Business Logic Microservices Implemented

In line with Martin Fowler's second recommendation, organized around business capabilities (see Table 13.2), J&S Food's microservices have been organized based on business line considerations. The business logic microservices have been organized into three categories including in-store customer, shopping session, and smart shopping bag.

Let's see how the business logic microservices work and how they are implemented.

The Smart Shopping Bag Business Logic Microservices Documented

Five functions were identified as business logic microservices including `Perform Related Action()`, `Collect Billing Data()`, `Calculate Billing Amount()`, `Interpret Customer Input()`, and `Put Product Information()`.

Table 13.5 sums up the information to know about the business logic microservices underpinning the smart shopping bag in terms of purpose (description), APIs (endpoints), functions on which they depend (dependencies), runbooks, and documentation (onboarding guide).

All of these microservices are Lambda functions, and as back-end services they are automatically provisioned, freeing developers from the process.

Table 13.5: The Smart Shopping Business Logic Microservices Documentation

	PERFORM RELATED ACTION	COLLECT BILLING DATA	CALCULATE BILLING AMOUNT
Description	This is the main function of the smart shopping bag application. It's implemented as an AWS Lambda function. Based on the action codes provided as input, this microservice accordingly invokes other microservices to perform related business actions.	This function is implemented as an AWS Lambda function to act as a microservice collecting the billing data of the in-store customer's current shopping session.	This function is implemented as an AWS Lambda function to act as a microservice, calculating the billing amount of the in-store customer's current shopping session.

Continues

Table 13.5 (continued)

	PERFORM RELATED ACTION	COLLECT BILLING DATA	CALCULATE BILLING AMOUNT
Endpoints	This microservice's API is structured as follows: URL: `https://jsfood.org/` Method: GET Header: user-agent Body: "business action"	This microservice's API is structured as follows: URL: `https://jsfood.org/billing/` Method: GET Header: user-agent Body: "billing data"	This microservice's API is structured as follows: URL: `https://jsfood.org/billing/` Method: GET Header: user-agent Body: "billing amount"
Dependencies	`Interpret Customer Input()`	`GraphQL Get Billing Data()`	`Collect Billing Data()`
Runbooks	Automatic and intelligent observability for AWS Lambda functions.	Automatic and intelligent observability for AWS Lambda functions.	Automatic and intelligent observability for AWS Lambda functions.
Onboarding guide	J&S Food's business microservices documentation.	J&S Food's business microservices documentation.	J&S Food's business microservices documentation.

Table 13.6 summarizes the information to know about two additional business logic microservices.

Table 13.6: Additional Smart Shopping Bag Business Logic Microservices Documentation

	INTERPRET CUSTOMER INPUT	PUT PRODUCT INFORMATION
Description	This function is implemented as an AWS Lambda function to act as a microservice reading and interpreting the action code delivered by the IoT gateway following an action initiated by the in-store customer from the smart mobile device.	This function is implemented as an AWS Lambda function to act as a microservice tracing the billing data of the in-store customer's current shopping session.

	INTERPRET CUSTOMER INPUT	PUT PRODUCT INFORMATION
Endpoints	This microservice's API is structured as follows: URL: `https://jsfood.org/` Method: GET Header: user-agent Body: "interpret action code"	This microservice's API is structured as follows: URL: `https://jsfood.org/billing/` Method: PUT Header: user-agent Body: "trace billing data"
Dependencies	*AWS IoT API Reference.*	*AWS IoT API Reference.* `GraphQL Put Billing Data().`
Runbooks	Automatic and intelligent observability for AWS Lambda functions.	Automatic and intelligent observability for AWS Lambda functions.
Onboarding guide	J&S Food's business microservices documentation.	J&S Food's business microservices documentation.

The Smart Shopping Bag Technological Innovation Microservices Implemented

Five categories of technological innovation microservices were identified. The purpose of these microservices is to simplify the use of the software development kit (SDK) functions of IoT, Elastic Map Reduce (EMR), and AI/ML AWS services. They were defined as part of the AWS innovation as a service in Chapter 1, "The Digital Economy's Challenges, Opportunities, and Relevance of AWS." Let's discuss them now.

IoT Gateway Microservices

Four functions were identified as technological microservices in the IoT gateway area including `Initialize IoT Connection()`, `Relay Customer Input()`, `Relay Product Code()`, and `Relay Shopping Information()`.

Table 13.7 summarizes the information to know about the IoT gateway microservices underpinning the smart shopping bag in terms of purpose (description), APIs (endpoints), functions on which they depend (dependencies), runbooks, and documentation (onboarding guide).

Table 13.7: The Smart Shopping Bag IoT Gateway Microservices Documentation

	INITIALIZE IOT CONNECTION	RELAY CUSTOMER INPUT
Description	This function is implemented as an AWS Lambda function to act as a microservice initiating the connection with J&S Food's AWS IoT Core platform.	This function is implemented as an AWS Lambda function to act as a microservice relaying the in-store customer's action from the smart mobile device to J&S Food's AWS IoT Core platform.
Endpoints	This microservice's API is structured as follows: URL: `https://jsfood.org/iot/` Method: POST Header: user-agent Body: "interpret action code"	This microservice's API is structured as follows: URL: `https://jsfood.org/iot/` Method: POST Header: user-agent Body: "trace billing data"
Dependencies	*AWS IoT Gateway API Reference.*	*AWS IoT Gateway API Reference.*
Runbooks	Automatic and intelligent observability for AWS Lambda functions.	Automatic and intelligent observability for AWS Lambda functions.
Onboarding guide	J&S Food's technological innovation microservices documentation.	J&S Food's technological innovation microservices documentation.

Table 13.8 summarizes the information to know about additional IoT Gateway microservices.

Table 13.8: The Smart Shopping Bag IoT Gateway Microservices Documentation

	RELAY PRODUCT CODE	RELAY SHOPPING INFORMATION
Description	This function is implemented as an AWS Lambda function to act as a microservice getting a product code from the RFID tag associated with a product put in the bag.	This function is implemented as an AWS Lambda function to act as a microservice getting the in-store customer's shopping information from the chip's memory and relaying them to J&S Food's AWS IoT Core.

	RELAY PRODUCT CODE	RELAY SHOPPING INFORMATION
Endpoints	This microservice's API is structured as follows: URL: `https://jsfood.org/iot/iot-gateway` Method: GET Header: user-agent Body: "relay product code"	This microservice's API is structured as follows: URL: `https://jsfood.org/iot/iot-gateway` Method: PUT Header: user-agent Body: "relay shopping information"
Dependencies	*AWS IoT Gateway API Reference.*	*AWS IoT Gateway API Reference.*
Runbooks	Automatic and intelligent observability for AWS Lambda functions.	Automatic and intelligent observability for AWS Lambda functions.
Onboarding guide	J&S Food's technological innovation microservices documentation.	J&S Food's technological innovation microservices documentation.

AWS IoT Core Microservices

Five functions were identified as technological microservices in the AWS IoT Core area including `Establish IoT Connection ()`, `Relay Customer Input()`, `Relay Product Code()`, `Interpret Customer Input()`, and `Relay Shopping Information()`.

Table 13.9 sums up the information to know about the AWS IoT Core microservices underpinning the smart shopping bag in terms of purpose (description), APIs (endpoints), functions on which they depend (dependencies), runbooks, and documentation (onboarding guide).

Table 13.9: The Smart Shopping Bag AWS IoT Core Microservices Documentation

	ESTABLISH IOT CONNECTION	RELAY CUSTOMER INPUT	RELAY PRODUCT CODE
Description	This function is implemented as an AWS Lambda function to act as a microservice establishing the connection with J&S Food's AWS IoT Core platform.	This function is implemented as an AWS Lambda function to act as a microservice interacting with the J&S Food's IoT gateway to relay the in-store customer's input to the J&S Food's AWS IoT Core platform.	This function is implemented as an AWS Lambda function to act as a microservice interacting with the J&S Food's IoT gateway to relay product code extracted from the RFID tag to J&S Food's AWS IoT Core platform.

Continues

Table 13.9 (continued)

	ESTABLISH IOT CONNECTION	RELAY CUSTOMER INPUT	RELAY PRODUCT CODE
Endpoints	This microservice's API is structured as follows: URL: `https://jsfood.org/iot/` Method: POST Header: user-agent Body: "establish IoT connection"	This microservice's API is structured as follows: URL: `https://jsfood.org/iot/` Method: POST Header: user-agent Body: "relay customer input"	This microservice's API is structured as follows: URL: `https://jsfood.org/iot/` Method: POST Header: user-agent Body: "relay customer input"
Dependencies	*AWS IoT Core API Reference*	*AWS IoT Core API Reference*	*AWS IoT Core API Reference*
Runbooks	Automatic and intelligent observability for AWS Lambda functions	Automatic and intelligent observability for AWS Lambda functions	Automatic and intelligent observability for AWS Lambda functions
Onboarding guide	J&S Food's technological innovation microservices documentation	J&S Food's technological innovation microservices documentation	J&S Food's technological innovation microservices documentation

Table 13.10 summarizes the information to know about additional AWS IoT Core microservices.

Table 13.10: Additional Information About AWS IoT Core Microservices Documentation

	INTERPRET CUSTOMER INPUT	RELAY SHOPPING INFORMATION
Description	This function is implemented as an AWS Lambda function to act as a microservice interpreting action codes relayed by the IoT gateway to the proper microservice to invoke.	This function is implemented as an AWS Lambda function to act as a microservice relaying the in-store customer's shopping information issued by the IoT gateway to the J&S Food's AWS IoT Core.

	INTERPRET CUSTOMER INPUT	RELAY SHOPPING INFORMATION
Endpoints	This microservice's API is structured as follows: URL: `https://jsfood.org/iot/` Method: GET Header: user-agent Body: "interpret customer input"	This microservice's API is structured as follows: URL: `https://jsfood.org/iot/iot-gateway` Method: POST Header: user-agent Body: "relay shopping information"
Dependencies	*AWS IoT Core API Reference. React Component Libraries.*	*AWS IoT Core API Reference.*
Runbooks	Automatic and intelligent observability for AWS Lambda functions.	Automatic and intelligent observability for AWS Lambda functions.
Onboarding guide	J&S Food's technological innovation microservices documentation.	J&S Food's technological innovation microservices documentation.

RFID Reader Microservices

Three functions were identified as technological microservices in the RFID Reader area including `Detect Product Code()`, `Put Product Information()`, and `Get Shopping Information()`.

Table 13.11 sums up the information to know about the RFID Reader microservices underpinning the smart shopping bag in terms of purpose (description), APIs (endpoints), functions on which they depend (dependencies), runbooks, and documentation (onboarding guide).

Table 13.11: The RFID Reader Microservices Documentation

	DETECT PRODUCT CODE	PUT PRODUCT INFORMATION	GET SHOPPING INFORMATION
Description	This function is implemented as an AWS Lambda function to act as a microservice detecting and extracting the product codes and information, as well as the shopping session information associated with the product RFID tags.	This function is implemented as an AWS Lambda function to act as a microservice recording in the RFID reader chip's memory, the product code and information extracted from the product RFID tags, as well as the shopping session information.	This function is implemented as an AWS Lambda function to act as a microservice getting shopping session information recorded in the RFID reader chip's memory.
Endpoints	This microservice's API is structured as follows: URL: `https:// jsfood.org/ rfid/` Method: GET Header: user-agent Body: "detect product code"	This microservice's API is structured as follows: URL: `https:// jsfood.org/ rfid/` Method: PUT Header: user-agent Body: "put product information"	This microservice's API is structured as follows: URL: `https:// jsfood.org/ rfid/` Method: GET Header: user-agent Body: "get shopping information"
Dependencies	*AWS RFID Reader API Reference.*	*AWS RFID Reader API Reference.* `Detect Product Code().` `Get Shopping Information().`	*AWS RFID Reader API Reference.* `Detect Product Code().`
Runbooks	Automatic and intelligent observability for AWS Lambda functions.	Automatic and intelligent observability for AWS Lambda functions.	Automatic and intelligent observability for AWS Lambda functions.
Onboarding guide	J&S Food's technological innovation microservices documentation.	J&S Food's technological innovation microservices documentation.	J&S Food's technological innovation microservices documentation.

RFID Tag Microservices

Two functions were identified as technological microservices in the RFID Tag area including `Get Product Code()` and `Get Product Information()`.

Table 13.12 sums up the information to know about the RFID Tag microservices underpinning the smart shopping bag in terms of purpose (description), APIs (endpoints), functions on which they depend (dependencies), runbooks, and documentation (onboarding guide).

Table 13.12: The Information About the RFID Tag Microservices Documentation

	GET PRODUCT CODE	GET PRODUCT INFORMATION
Description	This function is implemented as an AWS Lambda function to act as a microservice interpreting action codes relayed by the IoT gateway to the proper microservice to invoke.	This function is implemented as an AWS Lambda function to act as a microservice relaying the in-store customer's shopping information issued by the IoT gateway to the J&S Food's AWS IoT Core.
Endpoints	This microservice's API is structured as follows: URL: `https://jsfood.org/rfid/` Method: GET Header: user-agent Body: "interpret customer input"	This microservice's API is structured as follows: URL: `https://jsfood.org/iot/rfid` Method: POST Header: user-agent Body: "relay shopping information"
Dependencies	*AWS RFID Reader API Reference.*	*AWS RFID Reader API Reference.*
Runbooks	Automatic and intelligent observability for AWS Lambda functions.	Automatic and intelligent observability for AWS Lambda functions.
Onboarding guide	J&S Food's technological innovation microservices documentation.	J&S Food's technological innovation microservices documentation.

The Smart Shopping Bag UI Microservices Implemented

Two functions were identified as technological microservices in the user interface (UI) area including `Interpret Customer Input()` and `Display Action Performed Status()`.

Table 13.13 sums up the information to know about the UI microservices underpinning the smart shopping bag in terms of purpose (description), APIs (endpoints), functions on which they depend (dependencies), runbooks, and documentation (onboarding guide).

Table 13.13: The Information to Know About the UI Microservices Documentation

	INTERPRET CUSTOMER INPUT	DISPLAY ACTION PERFORMED STATUS
Description	This function is implemented as an AWS Lambda function to act as a microservice interpreting the information entered by in-store customers from their smart mobile device.	This function is implemented as an AWS Lambda function to act as a microservice displaying on the customer's smart mobile device, information returned from the smart shopping bag application.
Endpoints	This microservice's API is structured as follows: URL: `https://jsfood.org/amplify/` Method: GET Header: user-agent Body: "interpret customer input"	This microservice's API is structured as follows: URL: `https://jsfood.org/amplify/` Method: POST Header: user-agent Body: "display shopping session information"
Dependencies	*React Component Libraries.*	*React Component Libraries.*
Runbooks	Automatic and intelligent observability for AWS Lambda functions.	Automatic and intelligent observability for AWS Lambda functions.
Onboarding guide	J&S Food's technological innovation microservices documentation.	J&S Food's technological innovation microservices documentation.

Key Takeaways

Developing innovative digital products and services in a tense competitive environment requires controlled risk management, an ability to accelerate delivery, and a capability to guarantee the expected superior digital experience.

As illustrated by the smart shopping bag digital product prototyping process discussed in this chapter, the prototyping approach automated by the AWS Amplify CICD workflow was definitely one that makes it possible to control the risk, accelerate delivery, and meet quality requirements.

In this chapter, you learned that automating the digital products and services prototyping process using the AWS Amplify framework was likely to divide the prototyping effort and time in half.

You also learned about how certain AWS Amplify CLI utilities acted as code generators to simplify and accelerate not only the development of GraphQL and Lambda function APIs but also the implementation of data models. These features make the company's digital product and development practices consistent with AWS modern application development.

Finally, you learned about the importance of the AWS Amplify CICD workflow in automating the build, acceptance test, and deploy stages, which made J&S Food's digital products and services development platform consistent with DevOps principles and philosophy.

References

1. Amplify Docs, "Installation: Install the Amplify CLI," *Amplify Docs* (2021). `https://docs.amplify.aws/cli/start/install`

2. Nader Dabit and Rene Brandel, "How to Use Lambda Layers with the Amplify CLI" *AWS Blog* (July 07, 2020). `https://aws.amazon.com/blogs/mobile/how-to-use-lambda-layers-with-the-amplify-cli/`

3. Amplify Docs, "Set Up Fullstack Project," *Amplify Docs* (2021). `https://docs.amplify.aws/start/getting-started/setup/q/integration/react-native/`

4. Amplify Docs, "Connect frontend to API," *Amplify Docs* (2020). `https://docs.amplify.aws/start/getting-started/data-model/q/integration/react-native/#connect-frontend-to-api`

5. AWS, "Error Retries and Exponential Backoff in AWS," *AWS* (2020). `https://docs.aws.amazon.com/general/latest/gr/api-retries.html`

6. AWS, "Running Containerized Microservices on AWS," *AWS*. (2020). `https://docs.aws.amazon.com/whitepapers/latest/running-containerized-microservices/welcome.html`

14

Implementing J&S Food's Smart Shopping Bag Application

The agile movement in software is part of a larger movement towards more humane and dynamic workplaces in the 21st century.

—Rowan Bunning

The recent smart shopping bag project task force meeting (Chapter 13, "Prototyping J&S Food's Smart Shopping Bag Using Innovation as a Service") was a success; the experimentation of the prototyping process confirmed that the company implemented a state-of-the-art digital products and services development platform.

The promises of the AWS Solutions Architect are now a reality: the combined effect of the agile methodologies deployment and that of the AWS Amplify platform across J&S Food's digital business value chain has drastically increased the Princeton's team productivity and accelerated the software development lifecycle (SDLC).

After a 60-day development period, the first release of the smart shopping bag digital product has been deployed to production.

You are invited to attend the demonstration that will help to validate the industrial release of the smart shopping bag digital product and the efficiency of its overall ecosystem.

This chapter highlights the points you should emphasize so that you can make an informed go/no go-to-market decision.

Transformation Journey's Fourth Stage: Implementing the Smart Shopping Bag's Production Release

This last step of J&S Food's digital transformation journey is concerned with developing and deploying the final version of the smart shopping bag digital product to production. This final version is also known as the *production release*.

Figure 14.1 illustrates where the team stands in the company's digital transformation journey.

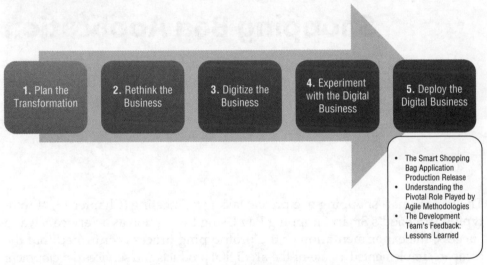

Figure 14.1: The implementing the Smart Shopping Bag's Production Release phase

Let's evaluate the smart shopping bag application and its overall digital products and services development ecosystem and assess the go-to-market decision.

The Smart Shopping Bag App: Production Release

After the usual introductions, the Princeton's team leader recalls the project's objectives:

> "Our bottom line was to deliver robust software that enables a smart shopping bag digital product. The software was designed to run on and take advantage of the AWS computing environment."

Blueprint of the Smart Shopping Bag in Production

The blueprint of the smart shopping bag's production release is shown in Figure 14.2.

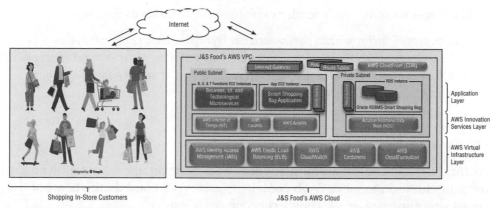

Figure 14.2: The blueprint of the production release of the smart shopping bag application

As illustrated, the production release is composed of three primary building blocks including the application layer, the AWS innovation services layer, and the AWS virtual infrastructure resource layer.

Understanding the Production Release Building Blocks

Now let's pay attention to what the Princeton team's leader has to say about the smart shopping bag application's building blocks.

Application Layer

Being more specific, the development team's leader adds the following:

"To achieve the robustness objective, the team complied with the AWS modern application development (MAD) recommendations. It leveraged the AWS MAD's five levers including architectural pattern, computing in modern application, data management, developer agility, and operational model."

Architectural Pattern

As to the architectural pattern dimension, the team engineered the smart shopping bag application so as to have the software and its constituents organized in separated AWS instances.

In addition to the App EC2 instance hosting the smart shopping application, these instances included the business (*B* for business logic functions in Figure 14.2) instance hosting the container running the business microservices, the UI instance (*U* for user interface functions in Figure 14.2) hosting the container running the UI microservices, and the technological instance (*T* for technological functions in Figure 14.2) hosting the container running the technological microservices.

The development team's leader explained the benefits as follows:

"In terms of security, you can secure each tier separately using different approaches. As for ease of management, each tier can be managed separately without effect on the others. Finally, as to scalability, additional resources can be added to each tier without affecting the others."

Computing in Modern Application

As for the computing in modern application dimension, the team followed the recommendation to make AWS containers and AWS Lambda the heart of the smart shopping bag application's runtime environment.

The development team's leader clarified this aspect of the smart shopping bag application as follows:

"Containers made it easier for IT Ops to deploy and update the smart shopping bag app and related microservices. Because of the containers' independent nature, IT Ops didn't have to concern themselves with the compatibility of each microservice."

Data Management

Regarding the need to rely on the proper datastore decoupled from the application principles, the team did not change the architectural option retained in the prototyping phase.

In the prototyping phase's architectural spike, the development team agreed upon an Oracle relational database management system (RDBMS) hosted in a separate AWS relational database service (RDS) instance. For security reasons, this was located within a private subnet.

Developer Agility

Developer agility is probably the area where the investment has been the most spectacular. Deploying the AWS Amplify framework increased the agility of the development processes.

The development team's leader argued the following:

"With only four AWS Amplify CLI commands, we are able to generate the template of a digital product as complex as the smart shopping bag."

The team took advantage of the AWS Amplify framework to generate full-stack web application templates built on AWS containers and AWS Lambda functions, which are serverless in nature. They helped to accelerate development.

In the old-world context, the development of such a complex digital product and service would have taken three times as long.

Operational Model

The various AWS services and tools made available to the Princeton team increased the developers' performance.

One of the developers in the room stated the following:

"The agility provided by the AWS Amplify framework and the microservices allowed us to code, test, and deploy three times faster than using old-world methods. In the old-world approach, we probably would have taken three to four months to develop an application like this."

The fact of the matter is that the deployment of tools such as AWS Amplify and AWS Lambda, combined with the extreme programming (XP), Scrum, and Unified Modeling Language (UML) methodologies, have increased efficiency, speed, and quality across J&S Food's digital business value chain.

AWS Innovation Layer

The Princeton team's leader proceeds as follows:

"Another building block of the smart shopping bag application's ecosystem to which you need to pay attention is what we have called in our jargon, the 'AWS innovation layer.'"

The *AWS innovation layer* refers to the library of microservices developed by the team around the AWS services and features needed to develop and deploy digital products and services rapidly involving Internet of Things (IoT), big data, and AI/ML technologies.

The primary purpose of these microservices is to simplify the use of the software development kit (SDK) functions of the AWS IoT, AWS Lambda, AWS Amplify, and Amazon Elastic MapReduce (EMR) in a way that abstracts much of their complexity and speeds software development.

Table 14.1 summarizes the relevant AWS services and the related technological microservices.

Table 14.1: J&S Food's AWS Innovation Microservices Library

AWS SERVICE/FEATURE	LIST OF MICROSERVICES
AWS IoT	Developed by the Princeton team. Note that () symbolizes software functions: `Initialize IoT Connection()`, `Relay Customer Input()`, `Relay Product Code()`, `Relay Shopping Information()`, `Establish IoT Connection()`, and `Interpret Customer Input()`.
AWS Amplify and AWS Lambda	Provided by AWS Amplify to create Lambda serverless functions acting as microservices: AWS Amplify command-line interface (CLI) command `amplify add function`.

AWS Virtual Infrastructure Layer

As to the last building block, the AWS virtual infrastructure resource layer, the Princeton team's leader informs the attendees of the following:

"In order to guarantee the expected superior digital food experience, the smart shopping bag application is deployed in a computing environment consistent with AWS Universal Architecture." (Chapter 1, "The Digital Economy's Challenges, Opportunities, and Relevance of AWS")

The recommended combination of AWS infrastructure resources is likely to guarantee a secure, reliable, and fast computing environment.

Table 14.2 summarizes the relevant AWS virtual infrastructure resources and their contribution to the computing environment's security and reliability.

Table 14.2: The AWS Virtual Infrastructure Resources Underpinning the Smart Shopping Bag Application's Production Environment

AWS VIRTUAL INFRASTRUCTURE RESOURCES	ROLE IN THE PRODUCTION ENVIRONMENT
AWS Identity and Access Management (IAM)	Provides user management as well as the authentication and authorization mechanisms that ensure secure access to J&S Food's AWS services and resources.
AWS Elastic Load Balancing (ELB)	Provides the mechanisms needed to monitor the smart shopping bag application's health and performance in real time with AWS CloudWatch metrics, logging, and request tracing.
Amazon CloudWatch	Provides monitoring and operational data about the smart shopping bag application and related AWS services and resources in the form of logs, metrics, and events.

AWS VIRTUAL INFRASTRUCTURE RESOURCES	ROLE IN THE PRODUCTION ENVIRONMENT
AWS Containers	Encapsulates the lambda serverless functions acting as microservices to make easy and fast their deployment, development, and maintenance.
AWS CloudFormation	Helps to develop the infrastructure as code templates helping the implementation of J&S Food's AWS computing environment. Supports the infrastructure as code template generated from AWS Amplify to create the Lambda serverless functions acting as microservices.

Understanding the Pivotal Role Played by Agile Methodologies

The agile methodologies (extreme programming and Scrum) underpinning J&S Food's digital operating model played a role as pivotal as that of the AWS Amplify platform.

In the following sections, the Princeton team's leader details the key role that Extreme Programming (XP) and Scrum played in the development effort.

The Architectural Spike and Prototyping Benefits

As to XP's architectural spike and prototyping process, the development team's leader explains the following:

"Making architectural spikes and software prototyping the starting points of the software development effort was a smart move."

The development team's leader further clarifies:

"The proactive identification of technological and technical obstacles (we could also call them 'risks') through developing a smart shopping bag prototype resulted in a software foundation that made the rest of the application development easier and faster."

The Importance of Scrum Sprints in the Incremental Development Effort

A *Scrum sprint* is a fixed period of time, not longer than four weeks, in which a defined set of activities are performed. These activities include sprint planning, daily Scrums, development work, sprint reviews, and a sprint retrospective. At the end of each sprint, a tangible and actionable product increment is delivered.

To underline the importance of the sprint concept in the Scrum methodology, the leader of the Princeton team explains the following:

"Scrum sprints are the basic element that allowed us to incrementally deliver the smart shopping bag application. The initial sprint backlog included four sprints:

1. *Implementation of the user interfaces, user interactions, and the associated UI microservices. (The Hoboken team's business users were involved in order to act as in-store customers.)*

2. *Development and invocations of the IoT microservices implementing the connectivity between the smart mobile devices and J&S Food's IoT platform in the AWS cloud.*

3. *Development and invocations of the business microservices implementing the application logic. (The Hoboken team's business users were involved in order to act as in-store customers.)*

4. *Execution of the operational acceptance tests (OAT) and the user acceptance tests (UAT) involving the Hoboken team's business users acting as in-store customers."*

Understanding the Vital Role of the Daily Scrums

As the Princeton team's leader explains, the daily Scrums have played a fundamental role in the performance of J&S Food's digital products and services development team.

The Princeton team's leader argues the following:

"The daily Scrum is a 15-minute meeting involving the development team's members and the Scrum master. The purpose is to inspect progress versus the sprint's expected product increment and adapt the sprint backlog as necessary, adjusting the upcoming planned work."

Daily Scrums were held in the morning. They helped to set the context for the coming day's work. These meetings were strictly time-boxed for 15–20 minutes. They made the discussions relevant and productive.

Tangible benefits observed by the Princeton's team include the following:

- Increased cross-functional collaboration throughout J&S Food's digital business value chain

- Improved software development progress visibility and exposure

- Increased and effective control of the software development effort

- Proactive identification and mitigation of technological and technical risks
- Accelerated time-to-market and higher customer satisfaction

The Development Team's Feedback: Lessons Learned

The go/no go-to-market decision was made involving the Princeton team's members and the Hoboken business users. The decision was based on two categories of criteria including a user acceptance test report and the application and its related ecosystem consistency with the AWS modern application recommendations.

Table 14.3 reports the feedback that would support the go/no go-to-market decision.

Table 14.3: Lessons Learned and Go/No Go-To-Market

CRITERIA	DESCRIPTION	APPROVAL RATE
User acceptance test (UAT)	Performed by the Hoboken team's business users to verify and accept the functional performance of the smart shopping bag digital product.	100%
Operational acceptance test (OAT)	Performed by J&S Food's IT operations and the AWS Solutions Architect to verify procedures including application performance, stress, security, backup, and disaster recovery.	100%
Architectural pattern	The smart shopping bag application builds on an architecture pattern that modularizes the software in a way that made coding, testing, deployment, and maintenance easy and fast.	100%
Computing in modern application	The smart shopping bag application builds on AWS containers and Lambda serverless functions to make the software strongly modular and easy and fast to deploy.	100%
Data management	The smart shopping bag application uses a proven data management solution hosted in a separate EC2 instance located in a private subnet to prevent direct access from the Internet.	100%
Developer agility	The digital products and services development team is provided with the operational and technological environment that increases their productivity.	100%
Operational model	The operational and technological assets underpinning J&S Food's digital products and services make the development team efficient.	100%

As illustrated by Table 14.3, the ability of the smart shopping bag application and its ecosystem to meet customer expectations and to deliver more releases in ever shorter deadlines is supported by all the participants in the pilot project, and the go-to-market decision is unanimously made.

Key Takeaways

Validating a digital product and service versus market and customer expectations and approving the ability of the digital product and service development department's ecosystem to provide the business with the competitive assets that it needs are not decisions to make from the so-called ivory tower.

Attending a demo whose purpose is to validate the reliability of the digital product and service, along with the operational and technological environment in which it is developed, is the right decision among many.

In this chapter, you learned that giving digital products and services development practitioners their say about the operational environment in terms of the relevance of deployed skills, staff, processes, methodologies, tools, and infrastructure is the safest way to make a go/no go-to-market decision.

The key lesson that you learned in this chapter is that evaluating the agile methodologies deployed across your organization's digital business value chain increases cross-functional collaboration, innovation, fast problem-solving, and decision-making, and it is a critical element of your go/no go-to-market decision.

The other key lesson that you learned is that assessing the microservices architecture's ability to guarantee productivity, agility, speedy delivery, and quality is an essential element of the go/no go-to-market decision.

In the next chapter, again in the IT executive role, you will be part of the development of the go-to-market strategy of J&S Food's smart shopping bag digital product.

References

1. Gennaro Cuofano, "Go / No-Go Decision Making and How to Use It in Business," *FourWeekMBA* (May 14, 2018). `https://fourweekmba.com/go-no-go-decision-making/`

2. Richard Li, "Microservices Essentials for Executives: The Key to High Velocity Software Development," *For Entrepreneurs* (September 19, 2016). `https://www.forentrepreneurs.com/microservices/`

3. Joe McKendrick, "What Business Leaders Can Learn from IT's Experience with Agile," *Forbes* (August 19, 2019). `https://www.forbes.com/sites/joemckendrick/2019/08/19/what-business-leaders-can-learn-from-its-experience-with-agile/?sh=1e9ddbe1602c`

Launching J&S Food's First Digital Food Product

Planning is bringing the future into the present so that you can do something about it now.

—Alan Lakein

The staff at all J&S Food stores have been trained on the new digital business model and underlying infrastructure and tools. The go-to-market decision was made. The next and final step is to send the smart shopping bag to the digital market.

Nevertheless, sending a digital product and service to market should never be improvised; go-to-market strategies are needed.

This chapter discusses the key steps and approach that resulted in the smart shopping bag go-to-market strategy.

Transformation Journey's Fourth Stage: Deploy J&S Food's Digital Business

This is the last step of J&S Food's digital transformation journey; it's about sending to market the smart shopping bag digital product.

Figure 15.1 illustrates where the team stands in the company's digital transformation journey.

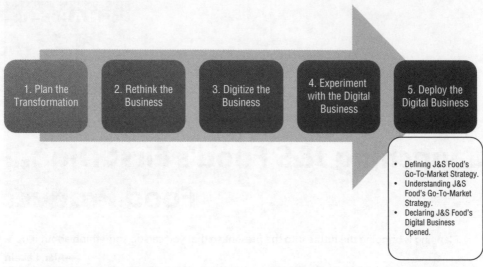

Figure 15.1: The deploy the Digital Business phase of J&S Food's digital transformation journey

As Figure 15.1 illustrates, digital business deployment is a three-step process including the following:

- Defining the go-to-market strategy in terms of target market, value proposition, and distribution and then making the go-to-market decision
- Understanding J&S Food's go-to-market strategy
- Declaring J&S Food's digital business open

Let's take J&S Food's smart shopping bag digital product to the market.

Defining J&S Food's Go-To-Market Strategy

The VP of Marketing starts the meeting with these congratulatory words:

"Kudos for this excellent work. Thanks to all of you, J&S Food is ready to take the digital road."

Nonetheless, the VP issues the following warning:

"We're not done yet! We need to enter the digital market successfully. As with the digital transformation of the business model and the migration of the IT infrastructure to AWS, improvisation and success aren't always good friends. Planning is necessary if we do not want to miss even a small detail that makes the difference. We need a go-to-market strategy."

The Go-To-Market Strategy Defined

The go-to-market strategy is primarily a marketing plan for making sure that your target digital market knows about your launch. The plan outlines key aspects of your target market, your value propositions, and your distribution plan.

A successful go-to-market strategy builds on various levers including customer personas, digital market understanding, and a solid grasp of the company's digital business strategy.

Articulating J&S Food's Go-To-Market Strategy

The VP of Marketing proceeds as follows:

"That's why it's critical to work collaboratively based on a proven strategy development framework: The Strategy Map."

Figure 15.2 illustrates the questionnaire underlying the go-to-market strategy development framework.

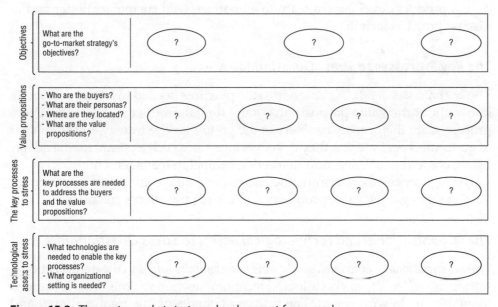

Figure 15.2: The go-to-market strategy development framework

The framework is based on a four-category questionnaire, each addressing a specific dimension of the go-to-market strategy including objectives, value propositions, the key processes to stress, and the technological and organizational assets to leverage.

The Objectives Questionnaire

The purpose of the *objectives questionnaire* is to capture and share with the workshop participants the objective of the go-to-market strategy. This questionnaire is important because it helps to get answers to critical questions, such as "What are we trying to achieve?" and "What tangible benefits are we seeking with the go-to-market strategy?"

The Value Propositions Questionnaire

The primary goal of the *value propositions questionnaire* is to determine the digital product and service target market as well as the related customer personas.

A *customer persona* is a semifictional depiction of the company's ideal buyer based on market research and actual data about its present customers. The concept of customer personas includes customer demographics, behavior patterns, motivations, and objectives. With customer personas, you can understand different sets or groups of customers.

Customer personas make it easier for the marketing department and the digital product development team to empathize with customers better and to discuss how to reach them.

The Key Processes to Stress Questionnaire

The *key processes questionnaire* refers to the practices needed to let the customers know about the value propositions of the digital product and service. These processes are the primary enablers of the go-to-market strategy. In the context of go-to-market strategies, they cover various areas such as social media advertising, content marketing, and marketing campaign management.

The key processes determine the success of a vital component of the go-to-market strategy: the value proposition to the organization's customers.

The Organizational and Technological Assets to Stress Questionnaire

The *organizational and technological assets questionnaire* refers to the organizational setting as well as the methodologies, technologies, and various tools leveraged to enable the key processes. The primary benefits of the organizational and technological assets are that they make the key processes efficient and effective.

Examples of organizational and technological assets include Twitter marketing tools like Social Pilot, Twitter Analytics, and Hootsuite Social Media tool.

J&S Food's Go-To-Market Strategy Defined

The VP of Marketing next projects the image shown in Figure 15.3.

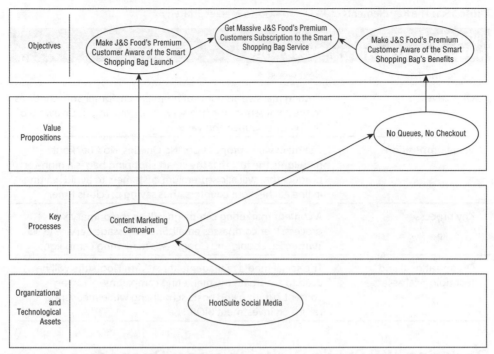

Figure 15.3: J&S Food's go-to-market strategy

As Figure 15.3 illustrates, J&S Food's go-to-market strategy targets the company's premium customers and uses a content marketing campaign to make customers aware of the smart shopping bag launch and its benefits.

Understanding J&S Food's Go-To-Market Strategy

Being more specific, the VP of Marketing clarifies the go-to-market strategy as follows:

"We'll build on our current customer base, focusing on our premium customers."

J&S Food's premium customers refers to luxury customers who spend big and derive satisfaction from purchasing exclusive, rare items, such as saffron, oysters, caviar, and exquisite vintage wines, and other high-quality products. As a statistical average, premium customers represent about 10,000 customers a week per store or a total of 3,750,000 customers at the company's 375 stores across the states of New York, New Jersey, and Connecticut.

Table 15.1 summarizes the key information the VP of Marketing provided about the go-to-market strategy.

Table 15.1: The Key Elements of J&S Food's Go-to-Market Strategy

GO-TO-MARKET STRATEGY ELEMENTS	DESCRIPTION
Go-to-market date	Next week.
Objectives	Getting massive amounts of premium customer subscriptions to the smart shopping bag services by making them aware of the product launch and values.
Value propositions	The main value proposition, "No Queues, No Checkout" highlights the fact that the smart shopping bag is a high-tech product that will allow premium customers to avoid waiting in line at checkout counters, thus saving precious time.
Key processes	A content marketing campaign will be the primary key process. It encompasses email, Short Message Service (SMS), Twitter, Facebook, and Google Ads marketing campaigns.
Organizational and technological assets	The social media management platform Hootsuite will be used to automate the marketing campaigns including content curating and posts scheduling while measuring return on investment (ROI).

Declaring J&S Food's Digital Business Opened

The VP of Marketing concludes as follows:

"As the IT systems underlying the smart shopping bag are already in production and that we've agreed on this go-to-market strategy, we may consider J&S Food's digital business officially opened."

Key Takeaways

Sending a product or a service to the digital market should never be improvised. This is a major best practice at J&S Food.

In this chapter, you learned that using the strategy map framework makes the go-to-market strategy development fast and easy. Above all, you learned that content marketing strategy is an essential element of successful go-to-market strategies.

The next and last chapter provides a snapshot of how J&S Food's digital business works on a daily basis.

References

1. Stefan Groschupf, "The Proven Process for Developing a Go-to-Market Strategy," *HubSpot* (April 28, 2021). `https://blog.hubspot.com/sales/gtm-strategy?toc-variant-b=`

2. Ramona Gligorea, "Why Use a Strategy Map," *The KPI Institute* (October 19, 2017). `https://www.performancemagazine.org/practical-use-strategy-map/`

3. Patty McCrystal, "Why Content Marketing Matters Now More than Ever," *MediaGroup Digital Marketing* (April 02, 2020). `https://www.performancemagazine.org/practical-use-strategy-map/`

Maintaining and Supporting J&S Food's Digital Business on a Daily Basis

We see our customers as invited guests to a party, and we are the hosts. It's our job every day to make every important aspect of the customer experience a little bit better.

—Jeff Bezos

Two months after the smart shopping bag digital product launch, 350,000 premium customers have subscribed to the service.

J&S Food's CEO tells the media, *"Success was predictable: We did the right things and we did them properly."*

J&S Food's business operations are now orchestrated around two activities: customer insights management driven by the marketing team and customer value increase management overseen by the customer service team. They both determine the rapid evolution of the smart shopping bag digital product.

This last chapter of the book provides a snapshot of how, on a daily basis, the company takes advantage of its digital business value chain and the underpinning AWS infrastructure as a service (IaaS) and platform as a service (PaaS) technologies to offer in-store customers the superior digital food experience that they expect.

The New J&S Food Day-to-Day Business

As expected, J&S Food's staff initially adapted to the company's digital business value chain practices and then ended up customizing it into what is now known as the *customer value creation virtuous circle*.

The customer value creation virtuous circle paces the new J&S Food's day-to-day business involving customer insights management, customer value increase management, and digital products and services development teams.

The following are some insights into how these three fundamental activities orchestrate the company's digital business on a daily basis.

J&S Food's Customer Value Creation Virtuous Circle

J&S Food's employees gradually adopted new processes, practices, AWS cloud infrastructure, and tools. As expected, most of the effort is focused on what J&S Food now calls the virtuous circle for creating customer value.

J&S Food's Virtuous Circle for Creating Customer Value

J&S Food's virtuous circle for creating customer value is the recurring set of events and related added-value activities that the staff mobilizes to improve the digital food experience continuously. Figure 16.1 provides a snapshot of how customer value is created on a daily basis at J&S Food.

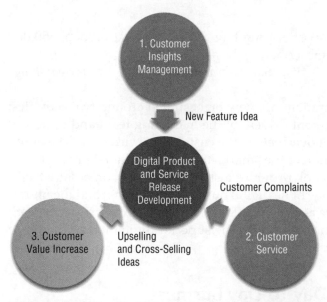

Figure 16.1: J&S Food's virtuous circle for creating customer value

Whenever an opportunity to add value to the customer arises, the digital product, service, or feature idea is analyzed by customer insights management, customer service, and customer value increase staff. They work together to evaluate the idea's value and determine the development of new smart shopping bag releases.

Let's see how AWS big data and AWS AI/ML solutions help to enable J&S Food's virtuous circle for creating customer value.

Customer Insights Management on a Daily Basis

Customer insights management at J&S Food refers to data science activities. *Data science* is the digital business area focused on obtaining insights and information, anything of value, out of data.

The primary purpose of data science at J&S Food is to spot new trends in the customer personas and derive from them potential new features for the smart shopping bag digital product.

J&S Food's AWS EMR Infrastructure

J&S Food's customer insights management activity is based on a three-component data infrastructure that takes advantage of Amazon Elastic Map Reduce (EMR) to keep data stored in accessible locations—cleaned up and regularly updated. Figure 16.2 illustrates J&S Food's data infrastructure.

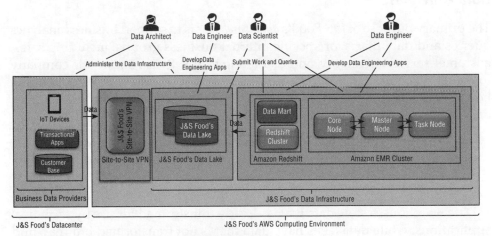

Figure 16.2: J&S Food's data science infrastructure

Four components make up J&S Food's data science infrastructure including business data providers, data lake, data warehouse, and data mart. Let's discuss them now.

Business Data Providers

The primary purpose of business data providers is to feed the data lakes with data. J&S Food's business data providers are the set of sources that feed its data lake with data. These sources include both relational and nonrelational data from IoT devices, social media, mobile apps, and corporate applications.

Data Lake

A *data lake* is usually a single store of data including raw copies of source system data, IoT devices data, social media data, and transformed data used for tasks such as reporting, visualization, advanced analytics, and machine learning.

The purpose of J&S Food's data lake is to provide vast and rich volumes of data that data scientists can use to give meaning to the data and extract value likely to improve the smart shopping bag features and functions.

J&S Food's data lake is primarily used by data scientists, data engineers, and data architects because it takes a level of skill to be able to sort through the large body of uncurated data and readily extract meaning from it.

Data Warehouse

The primary purpose of J&S Food's *data warehouse* is to support business analytics queries and data marts for specific internal business groups, including sales, customer service, inventory, and marketing teams. It also allows the company to handle structured data and have predetermined schemas for the data that it houses. The main predetermined schemas are focused on the smart shopping bag's business aspects including the following:

- The top food items for which the smart shopping bag is used
- The overall revenue generated by the smart shopping bag
- The revenue generated per food item

Data warehouses store data that is already transformed for use by analytical applications, while data lakes have data that is not transformed but may find future uses.

The key thing to know is that J&S Food's data warehouse is based on AWS Redshift. It stores curated data extracted from various online transaction processing applications.

Data Mart

A *data mart* is a structure or an access pattern specific to the data warehouse environment. They are used to retrieve client-facing data. The data mart is a subset of the data warehouse, and it is usually oriented to a specific business line or team.

J&S Food's data marts make specific data available to a defined group of business users, which allows them to access critical insights quickly without wasting time searching through an entire data warehouse.

The Big Data Analytics Activity in the Customer Insights Management Team

The primary mission of the big data analytics activity in the customer insights management team is to analyze data to identify patterns of changes in customer personas and in their consumption. These change patterns are likely to generate ideas for new digital products and services or new features for existing products and services.

Table 16.1 summarizes the activity's purpose as well as the roles and responsibilities.

Table 16.1: The Big Data Analytics Activity at J&S Food

ACTIVITY	DESCRIPTION
Big data analytics	Big data analytics at J&S Food encompasses data warehousing and data lake activities. The primary goal is to identify change patterns likely to result in new digital products and services, or new features for existing digital products and services.
Roles	**Responsibilities**
Data architect	The data architect's responsibilities encompass adopting big data technologies that J&S Food can leverage, supporting data scientists and data engineers, and interacting with the AWS technical support team to address issues as varied as installing and managing master, task, and core nodes.
Data scientist	The data scientist's primary responsibility is to explore data by running on AWS EMR nodes, the applications and queries developed by the data engineer designed to spot change patterns in customer personas and consumption likely to result in new digital product and service ideas, or new features for existing digital products and services.
Data engineer	Under the leadership of the data scientist. The data engineer develops applications and queries likely to reveal change patterns likely to result in new digital product and service ideas, or new features for existing digital products and services.

Customer Value Increase Management's Day-to-Day Operations

Customer value increase management at J&S Food refers to cross-selling and upselling activities aiming at increasing the money spent by the customer with the company. This activity is enabled by an AI/ML development environment.

Let's discuss J&S Food's AI/ML development environment including the determinant role of the Amazon SageMaker platform as well as the organization of the AI/ML activities.

J&S Food's AI/ML Development Environment

The primary purpose of the AI/ML development environment is to help the customer value increase management team to identify cross-selling and upselling opportunities instantly. Figure 16.3 illustrates J&S Food's AI/ML development environment.

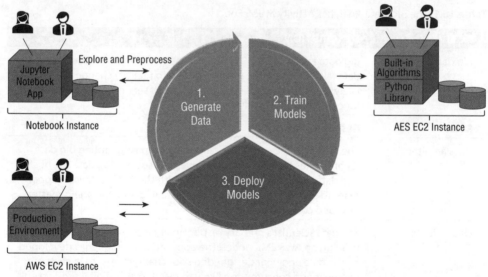

Figure 16.3: J&S Food's AI/ML development environment

Figure 16.3 shows that the identification of cross-selling and upselling opportunities involves the use of machine learning algorithms and models, and it goes through a three-step circular development cycle including generate data, train models, and deploy models. Let's discuss each of them.

Generate Data

In this step, the data scientist and the data engineer explore and preprocess the data that will be used to train the cross-selling and upselling inference models. *Inference* is concerned with the calculation of posterior probabilities based on one or more data observations.

This data primarily includes the customer's consumption trends, digital food market's consumption trends, and the customer's existing smart shopping bag service's features and options.

The data scientist and data engineer use a Jupyter Notebook app in their notebook instance to explore and preprocess data. The Jupyter Notebook is a web-based interactive computational environment for creating Jupyter Notebook documents.

Jupyter Notebook documents are those written in Markdown syntax, which helps to document workflows and to share data processing, analysis, and visualization outputs. They can also be used to create documents that combine code in programming languages, output, and text.

Train Models

Once the data is preprocessed and ready, the next step is to train the cross-selling and upselling models.

J&S Food's machine learning models are documents that have been trained to recognize certain types of cross-selling and upselling patterns.

To train the cross-selling and upselling models, the data scientist and the data engineer create a training job. The training job includes the following information:

- The URL of the Amazon S3 bucket where the preprocessed data are stored

- The notebook instance to use for the cross-selling and upselling models training

- The URL of the S3 bucket where the output of the job, that is, the predictions, will be stored

To train the cross-selling and upselling models, the data scientist and data engineer use an algorithm. They usually choose to use one of the algorithms that SageMaker provides.

A machine learning algorithm is the method by which the SageMaker engine conducts its task, generally predicting output values from given input including customer consumption trends, digital food market trends, and customer personas data.

After the training job creation, SageMaker launches the ML compute instances and uses the training code and the training dataset to train the models. It saves the resulting model artifacts and other output in the S3 bucket that you specified for that purpose.

Deploy Models

After the cross-selling and upselling models have been trained, the data engineer and the data scientist deploy them into a production environment using SageMaker hosting services. SageMaker then provides an HTTPS endpoint where the cross-selling and upselling models are available to provide inferences.

The Customer Increase Value Management Team's Activity

The primary mission of the customer increase value management team is to leverage AI/ML technologies, particularly Amazon SageMaker machine learning solutions, to identify cross-selling and upselling opportunities and increase in-store customer value.

Table 16.2 summarizes the AI/ML activity at J&S Food.

Table 16.2: The AI/ML Activity at J&S Food

ACTIVITY	DESCRIPTION
AI/ML	AI/ML activity at J&S Food is focused on identifying, from the various customer interactions with the company's customer service, opportunities for increasing the money spent by the customer with the company.
Roles	**Responsibilities**
Data architect	The data architect's responsibilities encompass planning the implementation of AI solutions, choosing the right technologies and tools, and evaluating the evolution of the AI/ML platform architecture as J&S Food's needs change.
Data scientist	The data scientist at J&S Food works by sourcing, cleaning, and processing customer personas, customer consumption, and digital food market consumption trends data for analytical purposes in order to extract meaning out of it.
Data engineer	The data engineer at J&S Food acts as a machine learning engineer and sits at the intersection between the smart shopping developers and data scientists. The data engineer leverages J&S Food's AWS EMR platform and AWS Amplify frameworks to ensure that the raw data gathered from the business data providers are redefined as scalable cross-selling and upselling models.

Digital Product and Service Releases Development

J&S Food's digital product development team mobilizes itself following three events: initiation of a new digital product and service, evolution of an existing digital product and service, and digital product and service dysfunction.

Figure 16.4 illustrates how the digital product and service development team works.

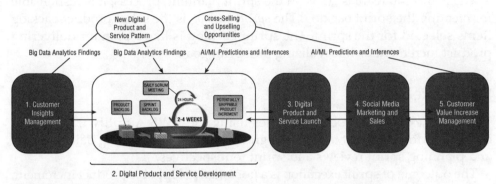

Figure 16.4: Dynamic of J&S Food's digital product development activity

The three events trigger the digital products and services development cycle, which includes the product backlog definition, sprint planning, sprint execution, sprint review, and sprint retrospective.

Let's see how the overall process works on a daily basis.

Defining Product Backlog

The defining product backlog step is triggered whenever a new digital product and service idea, or changes to the smart shopping bag, is identified following the customer insights management team's big data analytics activity or the customer value increase management team's AI/ML activity.

The marketing department's product owner, using Jira, the company's agile project management tool, calls a product backlog meeting involving the Scrum master and the development team to discuss the change patterns identified and most importantly the impacts either on the smart shopping bag or on J&S Food's digital products and services portfolio.

The meeting results in a *product backlog*, which is a prioritized list of deliverables (such as new features) to implement as part of the smart shopping bag digital product development.

Sprint Planning

The same day, or a couple of days later depending on the size of the product backlog, the Scrum master uses Jira to call a sprint planning meeting involving the marketing department's product owner and primarily Princeton's digital product and service development team.

Most of the *sprint planning* effort is devoted to structuring the development of new smart shopping bag releases into product increments (deployable modules).

The Princeton team is active in the sprint planning process; it is responsible for creating the sprint backlog. The *sprint backlog* is the set of product backlog items selected for the sprint. The sprint backlog is like a plan for delivering product increments while realizing the sprint goal.

Sprint Execution

The *sprint execution* process includes using the AWS Amplify framework, coding, performing unit testing, integrating software, attending daily Scrums, and planning sprint reviews and sprint retrospectives.

The outcome of sprint execution is a potentially shippable product increment, based on the selected product backlog.

The Princeton team completes the sprint execution by performing two inspect-and-adapt activities. In the first, called the *sprint review*, the digital product and service development team, including developers, testers, and business-side representatives, inspect through user acceptance tests (UAT) and operational acceptance tests (OAT) practices the smart shopping bag release being built.

In the second step, called the *sprint retrospective*, the digital products and services development team inspects, for continuous improvement purposes, the Scrum process being used to create the product.

Key Takeaways

The new digital working environment and the underlying methodologies and tools made available to J&S Food's staff have reinvigorated the company's competitiveness. Motivation, enthusiasm, productivity, collaboration, rapid time-to-market, and innovation are the words that best characterize the atmosphere all over the company. This is in contrast with the gloomy climate that took the company to the verge of bankruptcy a couple of months ago.

The migration of part of the company's IT to the AWS cloud was instrumental in the successful digital transformation of J&S Food. Nevertheless, technology was not the only determinant of this success. J&S Food was also successful because the company's leadership was wise enough to trust the enterprise architect who claimed this:

"The digital transformation of the company is primarily about automating its digital business model."

Throughout the 16 chapters of this book, you learned about five recommendations for successful digital business transformations with AWS:

Recommendation 1: Assess the Impact of Industry Disruptions   Spot your industry's primary disruptors and evaluate the organizational, operational, and technological impacts on your company's current business model.

Recommendation 2: Rely on Digital Business Value Chain Frameworks   Never improvise organizational, operational, and technological transformations. Always rely on proven digital business value chain frameworks to reengineer your business model to digital.

Recommendation 3: Build on the AWS Universal Architecture Framework   Build on AWS migration frameworks that offer the enterprise cloud architecture perspective. They make the migration effort easy and fast and guarantee security, scalability, and high performance.

Recommendation 4: Make DevOps Principles and Values the Foundation of Your Digital Products and Services Development Platform   Build on DevOps principles, values, and the related AWS services to implement your organization's digital products and services development platform.

Recommendation 5: Start a Pilot Project   Never go to market without experimenting with new digital business models. Train a panel of your organization's key function staff on the new digital business model, and go through a pilot project involving the trained staff.

References

1. Michal Rejman, "10 Examples of Successful Post-COVID Digital Transformation," *Ideamotive* (October 15, 2020). https://www.ideamotive.co/blog/examples-of-successful-post-covid-19-digital-transformation

2. Carla Rudder, "10 Ways DevOps Helps Digital Transformation," *The Enterprisers Project* (August 13, 2019). `https://enterprisersproject.com/article/2019/8/devops-role-digital-transformation`

3. Amazon Web Services, "Use Amazon SageMaker Built-in Algorithms," *Amazon Web Services* (2021). `https://docs.aws.amazon.com/sagemaker/latest/dg/algos.html`

Index